GOD'S ETERNAL DESIGN

GOD'S ETERNAL DESIGN

BY PERCY E. FARROW

HERALD PUBLISHING HOUSE
Independence, Missouri

Library of Congress Cataloging in Publication Data

Farrow, Percy E.   1902-
  God's eternal design.

  Includes bibliographical references.
    1. Eschatology. 2. Prophecy. 3. Kingdom of God. 4. Reorganized Church of Jesus Christ of Latter Day Saints—Doctrinal and controversial works.
  I. Title.
BT821.2.F3   236   79-26277
ISBN 0-8309-0272-4

Printed in the United States of America

To My Wife Clara

CONTENTS

Section III

The New Dispensation of Hope

Bibliography

ACKNOWLEDGMENTS

I hereby express my appreciation of the late Apostle Arthur A. Oakman who made the first suggestion to me that I should do more writing including book authorship. President F. Henry Edwards has given me invaluable help and encouragement, arising out of his many years as a ministerial administrator, teacher, and as an author of several books. Herald House Editor Paul A. Wellington has, with unusual patience, given many helpful suggestions and continued encouragement. Members of his staff deserve credit for encouragement given and help in typing. Studies in the atonement and in eschatology under Dr. Morris Ashcraft, professor of Systematic Theology at Midwestern Baptist Theological Seminary, opened a number of helpful insights.

Among those who have given sacrificially of time in typing and retyping are Mrs. Mable Andes, Mrs. Joyce Little, Mrs. Hazel Smith, and Mrs. Laura O'Neil Herdman. Mrs. Herdman has typed and retyped the greater part of the total manuscript. My appreciation also goes to Mrs. Elsie Townsend for correction in rhetoric.

Percy E. Farrow

INTRODUCTION

Apostle Paul M. Hanson often said, "Brethren, it is a marvelous thing to have been projected into the age in which we live." In this age, perhaps more than any other, the discerning person may look backward and recognize the many times that God has projected himself into the affairs of men and of nations to maintain his cause so that righteousness should not perish from the earth. In spite of wickedness, confusion, and human frustrations, and sometimes because of these, this present age delineates perhaps more than any other "signs of the times" elucidated by the prophets, Jesus, and the apostles which point in the direction of divine judgment and fulfillment.

Evaluation of Scripture and history in this light may give us confidence that God will never forsake his intent, but will continue his self-disclosure in the consummation of his purpose in creation, both for time and eternity. He does not "walk in crooked paths," neither can "his works and designs come to naught." Therefore, we are enabled to develop hope, both for here and hereafter, leading to a quality of living which eventually, by the grace of God, will overcome all evil as his kingdom becomes triumphant.

One of our most greatly feared enemies is death, both physical and spiritual. Consequently, to deal only with this present world is inadequate.

This book has been written with all of the above factors clearly in mind. Throughout all time God has been moving mightily by various media to keep the flame of truth glowing. Following the earlier centuries of the Christian era the reformation helped to pave the way for a renewed understanding of the gospel of divine grace. Scholarship, in spite of its conservative and liberal diversities, has made a number of essential, affirmative contributions. In the Restoration movement, commencing with the inspired ministry of Joseph Smith, we believe that God released a significant intellectual and spiritual force for the benefit of all mankind, and that his Spirit is moving through all of the powers which he has at work in the world. I have endeavored to bring fair and helpful recognition of these factors into proper perspective. I trust that this effort may be received in that light.

Percy E. Farrow

SCRIPTURAL ABBREVIATIONS

R.S.V.   Revised Standard Version
I.V.   Inspired Version
K.J.V.   King James Version
N.E.B.   New English Bible

Where none of these appear the reference is to the King James Version.

SECTION

**THE
SPIRIT
OF
PROPHECY**

A NEW LOOK 1 AT LAST THINGS

The Age in Which We Live

We are living in an age of scientific and technological advancement hitherto unexperienced. Since this advancement is accompanied by the use of power also hitherto unknown, there has been created the potential for the eventual self-destruction of humanity. Hence, we are confronted with a dilemma. Can science give us answers to the questions all human beings are impelled to ask: Who really are we? What is life's real purpose? Has it any design? What is our real destiny and how is it achieved? Are we creatures of happenstance cast into the universe by the same chemical forces that "rust iron or ripen corn"?

Perhaps the following are about the two most important questions for our times: (1) Is humanity on the road to total destruction? (2) Are we, rather, approaching a new age which shall lead to perpetual peace, security, and happiness such as mankind, as a whole, has never yet known? Isaiah (11:10) envisioned such a new age when he wrote, "They shall not hurt nor destroy in all my holy mountain; for the earth shall be full of the knowledge of the Lord, as the waters cover the sea." It most certainly will require such "knowledge of the Lord" and total compliance therewith to extricate us from our dilemma.

The current threat of the unwarranted and rapid use as well as the waste of our natural resources has become increasingly serious. This we are told is due, in part, to overpopulation, advanced scientific changes, especially in travel and in weapons of war, plus humanity's determination to live on a constantly accelerating standard. With lust for power, self-indulgences, and the methods of advancing technology, crime has increased and war has become more and more devastating. Concerning these problems warning and counsel have been given.

These are portentous times. The lives of many are being sacrificed unnecessarily to the gods of war, greed, and avarice. The land is being desecrated by the thoughtless waste of vital resources. You must obey my commandments and be in the forefront of those who would mediate this needless destruction while there is yet day.[1]

A hopeful challenge was given to the church at a slightly earlier date, yet with a similar element of warning.

The hopes of my people and the goals of my church, while not yet fully realized, and at times and to many seemingly distant, are closer to realization than many recognize. It is yet day when all can work. The night will come when for many of my people opportunity to assist will have passed.[2]

The above described situation is typical of human life throughout the ages. Yet with advanced technology, if something doesn't happen to change these threatening trends, we will be pushed closer and closer to total disaster and possible annihilation. Therefore, life's meaning must be seen in relationship to the divine purpose in us as it is associated with that which has been, that which now is, and that which is yet to be. God's purpose is based upon and also derived from his love for us—his justice, mercy, and compassion for those involved in both good and evil. Out of this vision of life stems what Emil Brunner in the title of his book has called *Eternal Hope*[3] and what Jurgen Moltmann has termed *Theology of Hope.*[4]

The Point of Beginning

Contemporary religious experience with its sacred literature, together with the biblical writings, provides a vast reservoir from which to draw in helping to find solutions to our problems. We must raise our sights beyond conjecture. We cannot afford to resort to speculative indulgences which give us ready-made answers. It is my hope to establish a realistic faith-inspiring point of view in relation to the ultimate purpose as portrayed in revelation and history and in relation to things hoped for, though not, as yet, fully envisioned. The hopes thus engendered in the broader view of *God's Eternal Design* should provide for us the wholesome perspective needed in our world of uncertainties.

The question now arises, where do we begin? The term *eschatology* came into doctrinal and theological usage during the nineteenth century. It is derived from two Greek words, *eschatos* and *logos*, meaning a discourse of last things. Thinking in terms of the ultimate entices many to explore fields of prophetic and apocalyptic literature. Sometimes persons resort to speculative writings of questionable authenticity. Generally, eschatology relates to three areas of God's design for human destiny. The first area is the individual or personal one. The second is that of the chosen people and the kingdom of God. The third is the historical area, including the world as a whole, plus the destiny of mankind and the cosmos.

Some recent scholars, such as Rudolf Bultmann, have advocated that biblical eschatology is inconsistent with modern, advanced thought, and seek to relegate much of the Jewish and Christian hope therein expressed to the realm of mythology.[5] Others are taking a new look at the doctrine and are expanding its concepts to include not only what happens at death and beyond but to what may be the total scope of divine action and purpose, past, present and future. In this, it would appear, lies the true and only hope for humanity. This expanded view gives greater meaning as well as greater challenge to our experience. In fact, all else has failed except that in which we relate our lives to God. Since the prophets of all ages have spoken forth the word of God as it has been revealed to them, naturally our beginning should be found within their teachings as these relate to history and to the future.

Jesus Christ is central to creation, prophecy, history, and salvation. This focus on Jesus, therefore, must be our point of beginning, a point from which we can view, with the utmost clarity, the exhibition of the pure love of God. Paul wrote:

But when the time had fully come, God sent forth his Son, born of woman, born under the law, to redeem those who were

under the law, so that we might receive the adoption of sons. And because you are sons, God hath sent the Spirit of his Son into our hearts, crying, "Abba Father!" So through God you are no longer a slave but a son, and if a son then an heir.—Gal. 4:4-8 R.S.V.

The principle herein expressed by Paul will be dealt with in a later chapter. We shall now turn our attention to the above designated focus of prophecy and history.

1. Doctrine and Covenants, Reorganized Church of Jesus Christ of Latter Day Saints, Herald Publishing House, Independence, Missouri, 1970, 150:7.
2. *Ibid.*, 142:5.
3. Emil Brunner, *Eternal Hope*, Westminster Press, Philadelphia.
4. Jurgen Moltmann, *Theology of Hope*, Harper and Row, New York and Evanston.
5. Rudolf Bultmann, *Jesus Christ and Mythology*, Charles Scribner's Sons, New York.

THE TESTIMONY 2 OF JESUS

The Living Testimony

The Revelator wrote: "The testimony of Jesus is the spirit of prophecy" (Rev. 19:10). This testimony is inherent in the Christian gospel. It joins the Old Testament predictive prophecy with the vitalizing forces of the New Testament witness.

The testimony of Jesus is indispensable to the processes of conversion and redemption. It is the motivational challenge in the life of the convert to Christ. The converted Christian meets the person who is seeking to know the Lord with the assurance of the testimony that Jesus is the living Christ. A person's conversion to Christ is prerequisite to the work of the Lord's redemptive grace. Redemption through the grace of Christ is the means by which the eternal destiny of life is both attained and experienced.

Testimony must be based upon the reality of experience, which leads to heavenly as well as earthly joy, in the achievement of the salvation of souls (see Luke 15:7). Both God's purpose and pleasure converge in bringing to pass mankind's immortality and eternal life. Eternal life denotes not only the immortality of the soul, which is eternal living guaranteed through the resurrection of

Jesus, but also constitutes a quality of living. It is, in short, living the life of God. Jesus called this the more abundant life (John 10:10).

The procedures in achieving eternal life require both divine action and human cooperation. Since "the glory of God is intelligence," this is an intellectual as well as a spiritual process.[1] The prophetic testimony of God's eternal design is clearly stated in the words: "This is my work and my glory, to bring to pass the immortality and eternal life of man."[2]

The testimony of Jesus is built upon the available truth pertaining to God and Christ. This truth relates to our own existence here and hereafter. By the media of prayer, study, and inspiration, we may acquire understanding of our Creator and his purposes in creation. We also may experience unending joys through that understanding. This perception is portrayed in the following concise yet all-encompassing statement: "The elements are eternal; and spirit and element, inseparably connected, receiveth a fullness of joy."[3] In his prayer at Gethsemane, Jesus said: "And this is life eternal, that they might know thee the only true God, and Jesus Christ, whom thou hast sent" (John 17:3). Jesus presupposes that knowing God, and himself as Lord and Savior, has a direct relationship both to the requirements for, and to the enjoyment of eternal life. Therefore, our comprehension of the doctrine of eternal life will rely upon our personal testimony that Jesus is the Christ, the only begotten Son of the living God. This personal testimony is experienced finally by the inner presence of the Holy Spirit. The apostles and many other Christians have experienced this testimony.

In his extensive examination of the efforts of certain theologians (from Reimarius to Wrede) to establish the foundation of Christianity by historic examination, apart from Christological faith, Dr. Albert Schweitzer reached this conclusion: "Jesus means something to our world, because a mighty spiritual force streams forth from him and flows through our time also. This fact can neither be shaken or confirmed by our historical discovery. It is the solid foundation of Christianity."[4] In truth it is the solid foundation of the Christian experience. Historical or any other investigative approaches to the foundation of Christianity are void of meaning without the accompanying testimony of the living presence of Jesus in the experience of those who believe in him and who seek to follow him. This always has been and always will remain true.

The spirit of prophecy and the testimony of Jesus are so interrelated as to make it impossible, significantly, to separate them. Messianic predictions preceded Christ's coming into the world. All that follows after his first advent either gives affirmative witness of him or foretells his future coming in triumphant glory. We shall learn more of this prophetic principle as we proceed, but to those who seek to follow him today, it is still "the Spirit that beareth witness, because the Spirit is true" (see I John 5:6 and Romans 8:16).

Incarnation, Atonement, Resurrection

In order to experience this living testimony of Jesus, we must believe in and accept his incarnation, his atonement, and his resurrection. At whatever cost in all that this involves we must be willing to take up our cross, as designated for us, and follow him. Immortality and eternal life rest upon these three basic Christian precepts.

The incarnation, or how God could and did become embodied in flesh in the person of his Son Jesus the Christ, is both mysterious and miraculous. But for our sakes it had to happen. We must realize, however, that this divine condescension in no way impedes the infinitude of God. Dwelling in the flesh did not ultimately circumscribe God within the boundaries of our finiteness. One of the most important things connected with incarnation is that it makes possible the personal revelation of God, at the level of human experience. Thus, to us who are finite, incarnation may make possible, through the Spirit, experiences enabling us to perceive truth which is infinite in nature. "The Word was God. . .and the Word became flesh and dwelt among us, full of grace and truth; we have beheld his glory, glory as of the only Son from the Father" (John 1:1, 14 R.S.V.). The presence of God, in the flesh, in the person of his Son, Jesus, becomes the focus and ultimate medium of all revelatory experience. Incarnation and divine-human communication are inseparable.

Since we are sinners by nature, we are in rebellion against the will of God. We need repentance, forgiveness, and redemption. In this regard we are no different now than our predecessors. This fact is made clear in the following words: "Every man walketh in his own way, and after the image of his own God, whose image is in the likeness of the world, and whose substance is

22

that of an idol, which waxeth old and shall perish in Babylon, even Babylon the great, which shall fall." In the same reference the cause of this frightening dilemma is described: "For they have strayed from mine ordinances, and have broken mine everlasting covenant; they seek not the Lord to establish his righteousness."[5]

As we are incapable of knowing God without the word being revealed in terms of human comprehension, so we are incapable of both the ingenuity and the power to save ourselves from the consequences of our rebellion. Who would claim the power to forgive his/her own sins? Or who would claim the power to bring to pass his/her resurrection from the dead? Hence, the atonement for us must become an experience as well as a theological proclamation.

First, the atonement gives assurance of forgiveness; second, it guarantees victory over death. In order to be forgiven we must sense the movement of God in the remission of our sins. This is exemplified in the reception, by the father, upon the return of his prodigal son. We are all prodigal sons and daughters of our heavenly Father. But since Christ died for our sins and arose again from the dead, assurance is available to all that God, through Christ, is thoroughly competent to deal with death, which is our greatest and final enemy. Paul wrote: "Death is swallowed up in victory. O death, where is thy sting? O grave, where is thy victory?" (I Cor. 15:54-55). In the atonement, for sin which brings death, the powers of immortality resident in Jesus Christ triumphed over sin and death. First Christ dealt with the cause—sin. Second, he dealt with the effect—death. We are the beneficiaries of his triumph.

23

Neither incarnation nor atonement can be separated from the resurrection of Jesus. No one of these precepts can stand alone, nor be completely effective by itself. The greatest messages ever communicated were these: first, the tidings of the birth of Jesus Christ; second, the fact of his resurrection, after the crucifixion. In these events the atonement was everlastingly established; and it becomes efficacious to all who believe, repent, and keep his commandments.

Angels, proclaiming a divine triumph, attended both the birth of Jesus and his resurrection. At his birth the heavenly host burst forth with "Glory to God in the highest; and on earth, peace; goodwill to men" (Luke 2:14). On the resurrection morning the angels, at the tomb, said to the women who came to anoint the body of Jesus, "Why seek ye the living among the dead? He is not here but is risen" (Luke 24:4-5). The resurrection of Jesus guarantees to us, as nothing else can, the ultimate indwelling of the presence and power of his Spirit, by which we are, upon repentance, cleansed of our sins and by which the miracle of our resurrection shall take place. The principle of the resurrection is also effective in giving to us the prior experience of everlasting life now, as we become new creatures in Christ Jesus. Here and now we may experience that newness of life, as well as recognize the final claim he has upon our souls in bringing to pass our resurrection. Because he lives, by his Spirit he will dwell in us, and we are thereby assured that God's work and his glory is to "bring to pass the immortality and eternal life of man."

Furthermore, we not only actually may know that He is but we may come to know who He is. As

Dr. Schweitzer has written, no historical research can either substantiate or refute these facts. Dr. Schweitzer also concludes his extensive investigation of the efforts of scholars to establish the historicity of Jesus thus: "He comes to us as one unknown as of old, by the lakeside, he came to those men who knew him not." But he does not obscure himself totally as an "ineffable mystery." In fellowship with him, as we take up our crosses to follow him, and in the experience of the toil, conflicts, and sufferings we may pass through, we learn "who he is."[6] We have already learned from John 17:3 that to know God and Christ is life eternal. Every true Christian must be imbued with the conviction of this truth; upon this conviction our testimony, which is the living testimony of Jesus, is founded.

Testimony and Evangelism

The testimony of Jesus is fundamental in our efforts of evangelistic outreach. The coming of Jesus Christ into our world is predicated upon the supreme value God places upon the souls of men and his consequent love for mankind. Jesus' voluntary suffering and sacrifice upon our behalf is inseparable from his loving evaluation of our souls. "God so loved the world that he gave his only begotten Son, that whosoever believeth on him should not perish but have everlasting life" (John 3:16). God reserves nothing from us that relates to our salvation.

The spiritually energizing and life-preserving elements are retained within the earthly corporate body of Christ, his church. They are expressed through evangelistic efforts leading to soul-awakening and reclamation. Each convert to Jesus Christ must be motivated by a divinely inspired love for an urge to win others to Him. This is necessary for the convert himself in order to remain spiritually alive. It is exemplified in the New Testament experiences of His disciples. What must it have meant to Peter to be able to proclaim (Matt. 16:17), "Thou art the Christ"!

Salvation is the immediate objective and ultimate goal of evangelism. The immediate objective involves a sacred experiential commitment to Jesus Christ and, through him, to the divine purpose. The ultimate goal involves the process of maturation, both in procuring "light and truth" pertaining to God and Christ and in fully taking into one's own life the nature of the divine life. Jesus said, "You therefore must be perfect as your heavenly Father is perfect" (Matt. 5:48 R.S.V.). Perfection is the outcome of a more extended process than immediate commitment. Important as instantaneous commitment is, one must have the opportunity after his conversion to "grow in grace and in the knowledge of our Lord and Savior Jesus Christ" (II Peter 3:18).

Happily God made us with the potential for this growth. Nothing can replace time-rewarding experience interpreted in the light of our spiritual growth patterns. Hope is paramount in the experience of salvation. There is no greater instrument of evangelism than that of generating in another the hope of eternal life. This is both the hope of the more abundant life here and everlasting life succeeding death. The aim of evangelism is to establish this hope in the heart of the needy by bringing them in touch with God. Nothing can be more meaningful in the transforming process of salvation than that of the hope of immortality and eternal life, validated in the teachings of Christ and experienced within the life of his disciples. All believers, faithful followers, and colaborers with Jesus are his disciples.

Testimony and Mission

God places inestimable worth upon the human soul. No one soul is of more worth to him than another. The total scope of the mission of Jesus Christ is contained in the salvation of souls, and by this means eventually to bring about the redemption of the world. Each saint has the commission to use his or her testimony of Jesus in the work of saving souls. The following excerpt expresses this mission:

Remember the worth of souls is great in the sight of God, for, behold, the Lord your redeemer suffered death in the flesh; wherefore he suffered the pain of all men that all men might repent and come unto him. And he hath risen again from the dead that he might bring all men unto him on conditions of repentance. And how great is his joy in the soul that repenteth. Wherefore you are called to cry repentance unto this people. And if it so be that you should labor all your days, in crying repentance unto this people, and bring save it be one soul unto me, how great shall be your joy with him in the kingdom of my Father! And now, if your joy would be great with one soul that you have brought unto me into the kingdom of my Father, how great will be your joy, if you should bring many souls unto me! Behold, you have my gospel before you, and my Rock, and my salvation.[7]

27

This statement of the church's mission is in accord with that in which Jesus said: "For what shall it profit a man if he shall gain the whole world and lose his own soul? Or what shall a man give in exchange for his soul?" (Mark 8:39). Each believer is drawn to the Lord, by his love, through the inviting and enlightening influence of his Spirit, which by its prophetic persuasion engenders within the believer the testimony that Jesus is Christ. Our response to that testimony must be exhibited in evangelistic witness. Thus the way is provided by which the redeemed may give evidence of their recognition of Jesus' mission to the world, in which his love has motivated them to join. Jesus demonstrated that all mankind should come to fully comprehend not only the nature of his personhood—who he is—but also the nature of his mission to the world. Both the first calling and the final commission given to his disciples made his mission their mission also. This is true of us today.

The qualities of Jesus' mission to the world, in which we are invited to participate, are clearly stated in his sermon at the Nazareth synagogue which was based upon Isaiah 61:1-2. Here he defines his mission to reach out to the blind, the captive, the poor, the bereaved, the downtrodden, and the unfortunate. Jesus always carried deep concern that his disciples should become fully committed to this compassionate ministry. However, as is confirmed in his meeting with his disciples at Caesarea Philippi, they first had to be certain as to who he was. His quick response to Peter's confession, "Thou art the Christ, the Son of the living God," was "upon this rock I will build my church, and the gates of hell [powers of death, R.S.V.] shall not prevail against it"

(Matt. 16:17-19). This indicates that the church was to be built upon the "rock" of the revealed testimony that Jesus is the Christ. The fact that the church was built to become involved in a worldwide mission is further portrayed in what is often termed the last commission. (See Matthew 28:17-20; Mark 16:15-20; Luke 24:45-49.)

Christ's church was instituted by him to become involved in mission. His ministry consistently shows the concern which he demonstrated, at all times, that all people, particularly his disciples, should come to understand the nature of his mission and his Messiahship. At no time was Jesus' anxiety for his disciples more profoundly exhibited than when his crucifixion was approaching. Careful study of the fourth gospel (John, chapters 12-17), elucidates the growing intensity of his concern as it increased his anxiety and deepened his ministry to meet the uncertainties and lack of understanding on the part of his disciples, and also to meet the prejudices and craftiness of his enemies. His first concern was to prepare the disciples for the shock of his execution, and to have them understand that there could be no evasion of the cross inasmuch as this great event is inseparable from the divine purpose.

Second, he fortified his disciples with the promise that they would not be left comfortless. He promised to send them "another Comforter...even the Spirit of truth" (John 14:16-18). His apprehension for the future ministry of the apostles is succinctly expressed in his prayer at Gethsemane (John 17). He prayed to the Father, saying: "Glorify thy Son that thy Son also may glorify thee." Later in this prayer, he exhibited the importance of that which had not yet been achieved fully. The disciples must be drawn into complete union with him and the Father. Oneness in Christ and Christ in God is at the heart of the Christian message and mission.

Jesus continued his ministry of deepening the insights of His disciples pertaining to their worldwide mission after his resurrection. His confrontation with Peter in regard to Peter's love for him was for the purpose of impressing upon Peter and all of the disciples that their ministry must be based upon their love for God through him (John 21:15-17). This irrevocable aspect of the testimony of Jesus also must be implanted in our hearts by the Holy Spirit, enabling us to declare, with an enrichment of understanding, that Jesus is Christ. Such testimony will be productive and it is central to the church's mission.

Prophecy and Testimony

There are two elements in prophecy. The first is that of forthtelling. This relates generally to historical influences, good or bad, and current situations at the time. The preaching of the gospel of repentance and salvation should be prophetic in nature. This is the proclamation of the prophetic message of redemption. The second is foretelling, which discloses the predictive element of prophecy. In this, prophecy relates to the future. The prophets speak according to revealed foreknowledge. This is miraculous.

Arising out of these dual principles of prophecy, the Old Testament is foundational in its relationship to the New Testament. The New Testament produces an enrichment of prophecy as it fulfills Old Testament pre-dictions. The New Testament is a fulfillment of the hopes and expectations portrayed in the ministry of the prophets. The Old Testament exhibits a profound theology of hope.

The hope of the coming of the Messiah is at the heart of Old Testament predictions. The expectation of the establishment of his everlasting kingdom presents a progressive predictive component of Old Testament theology. This was affirmed by Jesus when he said: "Abraham rejoiced to see my day and he saw it and was glad" (John 8:56). By prophetic insight Abraham saw far beyond his day and envisioned the coming of the Messianic kingdom. Jesus affirmed his own preexistence when he said, "Before Abraham was, I am" (John 8:58). Jesus is "the Alpha and the Omega, the beginning and the ending, the Lord, who is, and who was, and who is to come, the almighty" (Rev. 1:8 I.V.). Prophetic expectancy of the Messianic kingdom will be discussed in more detail in Chapter Twelve of this book.

The world is always in need of deep prophetic insight. Though there have been long periods of prophetic silence, God in his own time and with foreknowledge, in fulfillment of his promises, has broken that silence to make bare his arm of power and his heart of love. Thus, Joseph in Egypt declared to his brethren who had sold him into slavery: "God sent me before you to preserve you a posterity in the earth, and to save your lives by a great deliverance. So it was not you who sent me hither but God" (Genesis 46:7-8). Moses bore testimony at the mountain of the Lord (see Exodus, Chapter 3). Isaiah had an experience at the Jerusalem temple (Isaiah,

Chapter 6). Amos, herdsman from Tekoa, really began a new age of prophecy in North Israel. That nation had reached its zenith of prosperity during the reign of Jeroboam II, 782-753 B.C. But with this prosperity there came dishonesty, oppression of the poor, deliberate leisureliness, debauchery, idol worship, and almost every evil imaginable. The people were oblivious to the rising Assyrian threat, not only to their national security but to national subsistence. Amos proclaimed most vehemently against these evils and forewarned Israel that there were no alternatives, even though Jeroboam II had issued orders for him to cease to prophesy. Israel must repent and trust in God or be destroyed. Hosea endured the unfaithfulness of his wife, Gomer, and continued to love her, thus demonstrating the love of God for his people Israel.[8] John the Baptist declared "the voice of one crying in the wilderness, Prepare ye the way of the Lord, make his paths straight" (Mark 1:3). Finally we have the contemporary message of prophetic testimony of which the following is typical:

Hearken, O ye people of my church, saith the voice of him who dwells on high, and whose eyes are upon all men; yea, verily I say, Hearken ye people from afar, and ye that are upon the islands of the sea, listen together; for verily the voice of the Lord is unto all men, and there is none to escape, and there is no eye that shall not see, neither ear that shall not hear, neither heart that shall not be penetrated; and the rebellious shall be pierced with much sorrow, for their iniquity shall be spoken upon the housetops, and their secret acts shall be revealed; and the voice of warning shall be unto all people, by the mouths of my disciples, whom I have chosen in these last days, and they shall go forth and none shall stay them, for I the Lord have commanded them.... Wherefore the voice of the

Lord is unto the ends of the earth, that all that will hear may hear; prepare ye, prepare ye for that which is to come, for the Lord is nigh; and the anger of the Lord is kindled, and his sword is bathed in heaven, and it shall fall upon the inhabitants of the earth; and the arm of the Lord shall be revealed; and the day cometh that they who will not hear the voice of the Lord, neither the voice of his servants, neither give heed to the words of the prophets and apostles, shall be cut off from among the people; for they have strayed from mine ordinances, and have broken mine everlasting covenant; they seek not the Lord to establish his righteousness, but every man walketh in his own way, and after the image of his own god, whose image is in the likeness of the world, and whose substance is that of an idol, which waxeth old and shall perish in Babylon, even Babylon the great, which shall fall.[9]

Experiential Testimony

Jesus made this conditional promise: "If any man will do his will he shall know of the doctrine, whether it be of God, or whether I speak of myself" (John 7:17). Jesus is willing that his word shall be put to the test. Taking him at his word we have the guarantee of cognitive experience. He never fails to verify his promises.

Religious experience is real. It is essential to testimony. There are two levels of testimony. First "To some it is given by the Holy Ghost to know that Jesus Christ is the Son of God." Second, "To others it is given to believe on their words, that they also might have eternal life."[10] There is a parallel representation of this in the statement Jesus made to Thomas: "Thomas, because thou hast seen me thou hast believed; blessed are they that have not seen, and yet have believed" (John

20:29). Assurance comes to many by faith as is stated in Hebrews 11:1 I.V.: "Now faith is the assurance of things hoped for, the evidence of things not seen." Peter stated that sure knowledge came to him by way of his experiences. "We have not followed cunningly devised fables, when we made known unto you the power and coming of our Lord Jesus Christ, but were eyewitnesses of his majesty" (II Peter 1:16-21). When John the Baptist baptized Jesus he received the audible testimony, "This is my beloved Son, hear ye him." Joseph Smith and Sidney Rigdon had such an experience and wrote:

And, now, after the many testimonies which have been given of him, this is the testimony, last of all, which we give of him, that he lives; for we saw him, even on the right hand of God; and we heard the voice bearing record that he is the Only Begotten of the Father; that by him, and through him, and of him, the worlds are and were created; and the inhabitants thereof are begotten sons and daughters unto God.[11]

There is no substitute for the knowledge which comes through the Holy Spirit, in witness of the Lord Jesus. Because of this fact, Jesus commanded his disciples to remain at Jerusalem until they had been endued with the Holy Spirit on the day of Pentecost. Then they went forth witnessing repentance and remission of sins not only at Jerusalem and in Judea but throughout the whole world. We are likewise commissioned today. Nothing can replace the power of testimony. Finally we need to take serious recognition of the fact that those who are not valiant in the testimony of Jesus, after having received it, deny themselves the fullness of glory otherwise available to them.[12]

1. Doctrine and Covenants 90:6.
2. *Ibid.*, 22:23b.
3. *Ibid.*, 90:5.
4. Dr. Albert Schweitzer, *The Quest of the Historical Jesus*, The Macmillan Company, New York, p. 399.
5. Doctrine and Covenants 1:3e.
6. *The Quest of the Historical Jesus*, p. 403.
7. Doctrine and Covenants 16:3c-4a.
8. Abraham J. Heschel, *The Prophets*, Harper and Row, New York and Evanston, p. 52f.
9. Doctrine and Covenants 1:1, 3.
10. *Ibid.*, 46:5d-e.
11. *Ibid.*, 76:3g-h.
12. *Ibid.*, 76:6.

THE SACRED 3 LITERATURE

Enlightenment Through the Scriptures

I have already indicated that in order to obtain the best possible insight into God's design for humanity, we must explore that which has been as well as endeavor to take a look at that which is yet to be. This must be done with honest, open-minded appreciation and assessment of all available sources. In spite of all the critical analyses, doctrinal disagreements, and divergent interpretations, the latter two covering centuries of time, our greatest means of enlightenment on both things past and future requires not only a growing understanding of history but also an authentic knowledge of the scriptures. Competent knowledge of the word of God is obtained only by experience and prayerful study under the guidance of the Holy Spirit (II Peter 1:16-21). Enlightenment comes in proportion to our faith in God and in his word as we study to show ourselves approved unto him. The field is immense and the task is great but the reward for such efforts is beyond description. We shall deal here only with Judaic and Christian literature.

On the one hand the work of sincere scholars has produced great benefits by clarifying many mysteries and misunderstandings in regard to biblical writings. For instance, by cross references among Hebrew, Assyrian, Ptolmaic, and Babylonian records, it is now possible to establish fairly accurate, if not absolute, dates for some previously uncertain historical events. This is especially true in regard to the regnal periods of the kings of Israel and of Judah, for which no dates are given in the Bible.[1] On the other hand the varying analyses of historical and textual criticism, together with erroneous and often speculative interpretations, have in no way diminished the authority of God's word, nor its value to us as a guide in daily living.

The Purpose of Scripture

Holy Scripture is primary in the sacred literature. The written word affirms that Jesus is Christ and this witness of him is paramount in our lives in obtaining eternal life. The viewpoint of Latter Day Saints is that contemporary and additionally revealed scripture provides further confirmation that Jesus is Christ to a world distraught with doubt and confusion. The following is a very good example of such confirmation:

which is to show unto the remnant of the house of Israel what great things the Lord hath done for their fathers: and that they may know the covenants of the Lord, that they are not cast off for ever; and also to the convincing of the Jew and Gentile that Jesus is the Christ, the Eternal God, manifesting himself unto all nations. And now if there are faults, they are the mistakes of men; wherefore, condemn not the things of God, that ye may be found spotless at the judgment seat of Christ.[2]

That which enhances the testimony of Christ is not to

be condemned nor rejected. Such should be prayerfully and sincerely investigated for its values.

Jesus said to those Jews who were persecuting him and seeking to find grounds upon which to put him to death: "You search the scriptures: because you think that in them you have eternal life; and it is they that bear witness to me" (John 5:39 R.S.V.). The Jews to whom Jesus was speaking utterly failed to see in him the fulfillment of their own scriptures. However, truth always will remain self-vindicating for those who search diligently and discerningly under the guidance of the Holy Spirit. His message, his wisdom, his works, and the undefiled integrity of his ethics stand as irrefutable evidence to the believer that in Jesus is embodied, "the way, the truth, and the life" (John 14:6). Christ's qualities of living and of ministering, plus his confrontation with death and his victorious resurrection, offer to all who follow him the hope of living eternally with him. This is in harmony with Lehi's statement: "Men are that they might have [this] joy."[3]

The Authority of the Scriptures

Our faith presupposes that the scriptures contain the word of God. We, however, need to distinguish between the revealed word of God and the written word. Revelation is experience with God. The written word is contained in the scriptures. Scripture, therefore, becomes the record of the experience and not essentially the revelation itself. The first, as stated, is the experience of revelation. The second is the recording of the experience.

38

This is not to say that the written word is not revelatory in substance and in its nature. If we sincerely and prayerfully study the written word the Spirit will bear witness to us of its divinity. This is pervasive revelation to which all sincere seekers are entitled by promise.

The word of God is authoritative for our lives and for our times. Christ is the personal Word, which in this context is the Word made flesh, whom the apostle John equates with God (John 1:1, 13). Historical discrepancies, or even the use of mythological allegories, should not affect our faith in the overall authority of the word of God. Times and cultures have had their influence upon the manner in which his word appears. The fact that some myths may have been used allegorically is not evidence that the writer believed the myth. Recognition of this fact should help in our understanding of, and faith in, the holy word.

We also must remember that in the process of revelation humanity is involved with divinity. God may speak to us either directly or through his chosen servants by whatever medium he may choose. As prophets have been inspired, so they have spoken and written. This is attested to in the following language: "Behold I am God, and have spoken it; these commandments are of me, and were given to my servants in their weakness, after the manner of their language, that they might come to understanding."[4] Jesus Christ, the greatest of all authorities, spoke and manifested the revelation of God which was resident in him. Testimony of his revelation was given often by his disciples.

The whole panorama of creation speaks the word of God, in evidence of his being and his creative power.

Paul wrote: "All scripture given by inspiration of God, is profitable for doctrine, for reproof, for correction, for instruction in righteousness that the man of God may be perfect, thoroughly furnished unto all good works" (I Tim. 3:16-17 I.V.). All scripture basically has been given by divine authority in definitive measures of inspiration. God uses various media through which to speak. Therefore, he is the giver, the prophet receives and interprets, and man is the recipient and beneficiary of his revealments.

Interpretation of Scriptures

The foregoing indicates that there is a further imperative. Revelation must be interpreted in terms of divine purpose and human needs. "No prophecy of the scripture is given of any private will of man, for prophecy came not in old time by the will of man, but holy men of God spake as they were moved by the Holy Ghost" (II Peter 1:20-21 I.V.). Paul instructed Timothy, the young evangelist, to "study to show thyself approved unto God, a workman that needeth not to be ashamed, rightly dividing the word of truth" (II Tim. 2:15).

In order to rightly divide the word of truth, the whole revelatory process must come under honest, studious scrutiny. Attention has already been given to the fact that in the process of revelation both the divine and human personalities interact, leading to that which is finally communicated. In this interaction God chooses the human instrument as well as the means by which he communicates. He must be free to act as he wills. He, likewise, by the principle of agency, leaves us free to respond as we may choose, deem wise or desirable. Therefore, the human instrument, the prophet, whom God uses, must prayerfully and with unrestrained integrity seek the divine will while being fully attentive to the conditions of the times and to the needs of God's people as the Holy Spirit inspires him in relation thereto. The statement, "Thou shalt not take the name of the Lord thy God in vain," applies to revelation as well as to profanity. However, this precautionary necessity should not repress the prophetic responsibility.

The nature and need of human attentiveness is illustrated in the following: "I was in the Spirit on the Lord's day, and heard behind me a great voice, as of a trumpet, Saying, I am Alpha and Omega, the first and the last, and, What thou seest, write in a book, and send it unto the seven churches which are in Asia" (Rev. 1:10-11). This same attentiveness is as essential in interpreting the word revealed as it is in the experience accompanying its reception. If interpretation does not lead to action it must surely lead to frustration and futility.

The Media of Revelation

Sacred literature contains a systematic structure of the media God has chosen in order to make the disclosure of who he is and what he wills. The author of the epistle to the Hebrews has described appropriately the divine prophetic action: "God, who at sundry times and in divers manners spake in time past unto the fathers by the prophets, has, in these last days spoken unto us by his Son, whom he hath appointed heir of all things, by whom also he made the worlds" (Hebrews 1:1-2).

Space will not permit us to cover all of the media through which God has spoken or yet may speak. I shall, therefore, confine our listing to a few helpful principles.

(1) There is the physical and natural medium. A great deal of nature theophany is to be found in the Old Testament, such as, "The voice of the Lord is upon the waters" (Psalm 29:2). Then again Elijah did not hear the voice of the Lord in the thunder and in other mighty forces of nature, but after the tempest, earthquake, and fire had passed, God spoke to Elijah in a still small voice. God may very well have used these natural forces to impress Elijah so as to enhance his expectancy and to gain his more alert attention (see I Kings 19:11-14). In the Book of Mormon the brother of Jared indicates that such nature theophany was present during the confusion of languages at the building of the biblical tower of Babel. As the Jaredites, desirous of retaining the original language, were preparing ships under divine guidance to come to the promised land of America, the Lord said to the brother of Jared:

What will ye that I should do that ye may have light in your vessels? For behold, ye can not have windows, for they will be dashed in pieces; neither should ye take fire with you, for ye shall not go by the light of fire; for behold, ye shall be as a whale in the midst of the sea; for the mountain waves shall dash upon you. Nevertheless, I will bring you up again out of the depths of the sea; for the winds have gone forth out of my mouth, and also the rains and the floods have I sent forth. And behold, I prepare you against these things; for howbeit, ye can

42

not cross this great deep, save I prepare you against the waves of the sea, and the winds which have gone forth, and the floods which shall come.[5]

As we continue to read this account we are made aware that God has control over nature. He provided for the Jaredites to have air and light in their vessels. These ships, under God's instruction, were built to endure the buffeting of the wind and waves of the sea, even though at times they were buried under the water. However, God is not limited by the forces of nature as pagan gods were believed to be—for example, the Caananite fertility god, Baal.[6]

(2) Angels are a medium of proclaiming God's message. Angels usually appear in human form as did the three men who visited Abraham (Gen. 18). Angels appear, disappear, and may reappear as in the case of Manoah. They do not always give their names as was true of Manoah and of John the Revelator (see Judges 13 and Revelation 19:10). Angels are messengers of God. Prophets are also messengers of God and sometimes are directed by angelic visitation. We have many examples of this in the sacred literature, especially in the apocalyptic writings.

(3) At times God has made his will known to his prophets and to his people through the prophets by means of divination. The Urim and Thummim has been one means of this type of revelation (see Exodus 28:30 and Leviticus 22:25).

Joseph Smith testified that he found the Urim and Thummim, along with Laban's sword and breastplate, in the box in which were contained the plates from which the Book of Mormon was produced. He was told by the angel who visited him three times (on the night of September 21, 1823) that the Urim and Thummim were contained in this box. He was told also that "the possession and use of these [the Urim and Thummim] was what constituted seers in ancient or former times, and that God had prepared them for the purpose of translating the book"—that is, the Book of Mormon. He also testified that he translated by means of the Urim and Thummim.[7] The Urim and Thummim thus connected with the work of the modern seer corresponds with that which is recorded in the Bible concerning the seer and divination. Another means of divination was the sacred lot which was used with faith that God would reveal the answer to the existing problem as lots were cast following prayer (see Acts 1:23-26). It is interesting to note that the Hebrew word for casting lots is Yarah which is similar to the word Torah, meaning law.

Hebrew use of divination is not to be equated with Egyptian and Babylonian mystical and magical efforts to obtain the will of the gods and knowledge of the future. Diviners were common among the Babylonians. This is indicated in the fact that Balak, king of the Moabites, sent for Baalam of Pethor, in Northern Mesopotamia, to place a curse upon the children of Israel (see Numbers, chapters 22-24).

Dreams and dream incubation in the sense of meditating thereupon to determine their meaning may also be classified as divination. God manifested himself to the pharaoh of Egypt in Joseph's time in a dream and to the king of Babylon in the time of Daniel. However, the fact that it took the men of God to interpret the dreams which these rulers had experienced cannot be overes-

44

timated. In each case, Joseph and Daniel were highly honored for their divinely inspired skill in interpreting dreams. By no means, however, are all dreams inspired of God. Misinterpretation of dreams can be very confusing and even personally devastating

(4) Accounts of signs and wonders as a medium of the exhibition of divine power are prevalent throughout scripture. These often were manifested to give confirmation to believers and nonbelievers alike that God was in the midst of his people, and that he is in control of nature and of history. Examples of signs and wonders as a means of God's revelatory activity are almost inexhaustible. The signs and wonders, including the ten plagues, wrought by Moses and Aaron in the presence of Pharaoh to induce him to let the children of Israel go are tangible evidences of the constructive use of God's universal design and control. Signs and wonders were manifested through Jesus and his apostles in New Testament times. Believers relied heavily upon these as vital supports to Jesus' Messiahship. "Many signs and wonders were done by the apostles" (Acts 2:43). We are reminded, however, that Jesus condemned abuses by wicked sign seekers. Power which may save us can destroy us if misused.

When we give consideration to any of the media used in obtaining the divine will we are confronted with the question, "Were they of ancient times any less intelligent than we are today?" We need to use the "plumb line" on our thinking. Our thinking must be straight, our faith must be on a sure foundation, and our hearts and minds must be kept open to receive the ministry of the Holy Spirit. We also need to be sufficiently percep-

45

tive to discern between that which is true and that which is counterfeit. We are told in the writings of Paul that the things of man are discerned by the spirit of man and the things of God are understood only by the Spirit of God.

(5) There is the personal medium of divine revelation. The prophet himself is a medium of divine revealment. In I Samuel 9:9 it is stated that "The prophet was formerly called a seer." The seer is one who sees. He discerns or apprehends and speaks forth the divine word relating to that which he sees. He must be aware of the historical situation regardless of the range of time involved, imminent or far-reaching. With inspirational understanding he becomes the instrument between God and the people, to forewarn, to call them to repentance, and to offer guidance as the Holy Spirit may direct. In this regard there is little if any difference between the functions of the seer and those of the prophet.[8] Prophets are called of God for their special ministries. Prophecy may be understood to relate to the immediate historical situation. Also, under some circumstances, as God purposes, it may be far-reaching when the predictive element becomes recognizable.

(6) From the foregoing it should be clear that the correct interpretation of God's mighty acts in history is revelation. It is important that we keep in mind this broader view of revelation. Faith is strengthened as we see the panorama of that which God has done. Hope is enlarged into challenge as we look forward to that which he will yet do. . . . It has been stated prophetically: "My word shall not fail, neither will my promises, for the foundation of the Lord standeth sure."[9]

(7) Finally there is the motivational component of inspiration in the processes of revelation. The prophet may speak as the Holy Spirit inspires him, but inspiration is not confined to the prophet alone. There is the pervasive principle in the revelatory process. God may inspire anyone as he wills. He even may give confirmation to others of that which he reveals through his chosen prophet. There is protection against error as well as affirmation of truth in this aspect of inspiration. The practice observed by Reorganized Latter Day Saints requires that that which is presented by the prophet in documentary form, with the intention that it should become law, is to be approved by common consent. This means that it is examined carefully, and accepted or rejected by the councils of the church and by the people of the conference to whom the revelation is made available. Purported contemporary revelation must not be in conflict with that which has been revealed in the past.

However, local leaders and even individuals presently need the more direct personal guidance of the Holy Spirit according to their responsibilities and needs. This fact is confirmed in the word already revealed as well as in personal experience. The famous words of John Robinson aptly apply and succinctly express what I am endeavoring to convey: "If God should reveal anything to you by any other instrument of his, be as ready to receive it as you were to receive any truth by my ministry; for I am very persuaded—I am very confident—that the Lord has more truth to break forth out of his word."[10] Doctor Frederick Madison Smith, one of the late prophets and president of the Reorganized Church of Jesus Christ of Latter Day Saints (1914-

1946), made the following observation:

At a certain time of my life it has become necessary for me, especially since I was asked to accept a position that is unique among all the organizations of the world, to give considerable thought to this question of how God shall reveal himself to his people. There was a disposition at one time on my part to limit God as to how he should reveal his will. But I have passed this point and have been able to say, If thou, O God, art desirous of revealing thy will to us, or to me, be it far from me to say how. If it be that thou desirest to write across the arch of thy heaven those words that thou shalt see fit to transmit to thy people, then give me the wisdom to read. Or if thou dost choose to manifest thy power in the thunderous tones that thou art capable of giving, so that they will ring through all the arch of heaven, let my ears be open. Or if, in the still, small voice that comes from within, thou shalt choose to reveal thy will to me, then let thy Spirit attune my spiritual ear to the reception of thy word. Or if thou dost choose to utilize those powers with which thou hast by nature endowed me, quickened by thine own processes of development, to transmit through them the message that thou hast to give to thy people, then my pen shall be ready. Or if thou dost choose to bathe my soul in thy Spirit until my spiritual vision shall behold what thou dost desire thy people to accomplish, even then shall I endeavor as thy instrument to transmit the message to thy people.

Strange to say, at times the very last of the ones that I would have believed probable, in trying to express his will through me to his people is the one he has chosen to use; for I have felt that quickening of spiritual vision until my spiritual eyes were enabled to see almost as a panoramic vision extending over the years to come, not in detail, but in one grand, general ensemble, the work to be accomplished by this people. And when I have thus seen the work yet to be done spread out before me, I have been at times suddenly turned from contemplation of these splendid things, and with my own natural eyes and powers have looked upon the work already done, I could not but exclaim, "How long, O Lord, how long."

President Smith went on from this point to discuss the tendency of some persons to claim revelation concerning that which they consider to be wrong and likewise that which they advocate to be right. He points out that God has safeguarded to his people not only the right but the duty to weigh that which shall come, and God will reveal himself in the way that pleases him best. But this will always be in harmony and consistent with his revealments in the past, however the revelation may come.[11]

Classifications of the Sacred Literature

In a comprehensive theological study of the sacred literature it is necessary for us to be aware of, and reasonably familiar with, the classifications of this literature. Quality and characteristics also should be carefully analyzed in order to understand and properly interpret the written word. Protestants generally have accepted the Hebrew canon of the Old Testament as it was recommended by the Council of Jamnia held ca. A.D 100.[12] According to the Hebrew canon of the Old Testament there are three main categories—the law, the prophets, and the writings. These categories were and still are given precedence by the Jews in the order in which they are listed. They were recognized as such by Jesus, the apostles, and other writers of the New Testament. Jesus gave recognition to two of these categories when he said: "Think not that I have come to destroy the law, or the prophets; I am not come to destroy, but to fulfill" (Matt. 5:17). These three main classifications of the Old Testament (Hebrew canon) were carried over into today and still are being used by Christians.

The law is comprised of the first five books of our Bible. They are called the books of the law because they contain in addition to the creation, the flood, and the patriarchal annals, the commandments of God given to Israel through Moses. The Jews called these first five books of the Bible the Torah, which means law. They also have been spoken of as the Pentateuch (Greek), meaning the five books of Moses. The Jewish rabbis believed that Moses wrote the first five books of the Old Testament, except for his own obituary found in the last chapter of Deuteronomy. This, they believed, was written by Joshua. It is interesting to note that in the Inspired Version of the Holy Scriptures, Joseph Smith attributed the writing of the Genesis account of creation to Moses. It seems logical to assume that since Moses personally entered into the books of the law, with the beginning of the book of Exodus, authorship which applies to the first part of Genesis in the Inspired Version would continue throughout the book of Genesis. It will not serve our purposes here to discuss modern historical criticism pertaining to the authorship of these first five books of the Bible. However, the assumption that Moses originally did write the Jewish Torah does not exclude later redactions and transcriptions. Nor would this necessarily exclude the development over the centuries that followed of the various sources which Old Testament scholars now claim were used in the final writing of these books. These sources are the Yahwehist, derived from the Jewish word for God; the Eloist, meaning Lord; the Deuteronomist, who is purported to have writ-

50

ten the law as contained in Deuteronomy; and finally the priestly source. These are symbolized by J.E.D.P.

The books of the prophets are divided into two main groups, the former and the latter prophets. The books of the former prophets include Joshua, Judges, Samuel, and Kings. The books of the latter prophets are comprised of the major prophets Isaiah, Jeremiah, Ezekiel, and the twelve minor prophets which include all other herein unnamed prophetic books of the Old Testament. The works of these minor prophets were shorter than those of the major prophets so that they were all included, in the original Jewish writings, on one scroll.[13] They are not necessarily inferior to the works of the former and major prophets who because of the length of their writings were accorded one scroll each. The Book of Judges was included with the former prophets because the Judges were essentially charismatic in their approach to fulfilling their responsibilities. However, the role of the Judges required them to be military leaders in times of attack or invasion. The two books of Kings as they appear in our Christian Bibles were included as one in the Jewish Bible. Likewise, the Jewish scripture combined our two books of Samuel into one. The Book of Kings was included with the prophets, in the Jewish canon, because it contains the accounts of the works of the prophets in relationship to the kings of Israel and of Judah. Prophets participated in calling and anointing kings (see I Samuel 10:1; 16:13).

Writings are comprised of the following classifications and books: (1) The poetic books include Psalms and Proverbs. (2) The five rolls include the Song of Solomon, Ruth, Lamentations, Ecclesiastes, and Esther.

(3) The historical books include Daniel, Ezra-Nehemiah, and the two books of Chronicles. The Book of Daniel was placed within the historical books rather than the prophets because whether it was written by the great Daniel of Babylon, claimed in the book itself, or by a later writer probably around 200 B.C. it is believed by Jews and Christian scholars alike that it related to an important historical period in Jewish affairs. Daniel is written in a particular style known as apocalypticism. This we will discuss later in the chapter. Much of the writings is called wisdom literature by theologians and biblical scholars.

Wisdom literature was not confined to the Hebrews. A similar type of literature is definitely known to have existed in other parts of the ancient Near East. Some of these were even earlier writings than those of the Hebrews. The Egyptians, Babylonians, Moabites, Persians, and others produced somewhat similar literature. This fact in no way discredits the inspiration of the "writings" found in the Old Testament. The adoption of a characterization of writing from another culture does not imply that those who did so believed either the mythological or pagan ideas and notions of that culture. The following previously quoted statement tends to support this assumption: "These commandments are of me, and were given unto my servants in their weakness, after the manner of their language."[14]

Two main qualities predominate the Hebrew wisdom literature: (1) Most of the Psalms were used in worship, and today they still inspire worship. (2) The spiritual and ethical qualities of the good life are set forth in the books of Job, Proverbs, and Ecclesiastes.

In addition to these three divisions of Old Testament literature there was a great deal of extra canonical material, some of which no longer exists. A number of books are mentioned in the Old Testament which have been lost.[15] Approximately fourteen books of the Apocrypha were not included in the Jewish canon later than ca. A.D. 100, although they still remain in Greek manuscripts which were translated from the Hebrew. They were in the septuagint or Alexandrian translation from Hebrew into Greek about 200 B.C. The Latin Vulgate (Roman Catholic) translation was made from the Greek and therefore contains the books of the Apocrypha. In spite of the fact that the Apocrypha was used by the apostles and the early Christian church fathers, the reformers rejected it as did the Jews.[16]

Beyond the above mentioned materials there are in both Jewish and early Christian literature many other writings. Most of these are considered to be spurious. Consequently, writings such as the Book of Enoch (see Jude, verse 14), the Epistle of Barnabas, St. Clement, and many others do not appear in Christian Bibles.[17]

It is important to understand the relationship between two terms which are often used in connection with revelation and scripture: (1) *Propheticism* relates to the works of most of the prophets. This we have discussed to some extent, pointing out that prophecy arises out of immediate historical situations but also contains predictive elements relating to the consequences of human action either imminent or remote, and portrays God's future works and designs on our behalf. It is quite evident that the prophets frequently were inspired to see far beyond their day, and gave hope to the people of their time. They projected their prophetic messages into the distant future. (2) *Apocalypticism* is a derivitive of the Greek word meaning revelation. However, apocalypticism has in it a more mystical element than prophecy and often endeavors to set forth a long-range sweep of future and final things such as resurrection and judgment, the final destiny of the wicked and of the righteous. It uses symbols and allegories. Symbols are often comprised of numbers relating to time such as the term 1,260 days or times, time, and half a time (see Revelation 12:6, 14 and Daniel 7:25). It also lays claim to angelic visitation and ministries. These characteristics are prevalent in the book of Daniel in the Old Testament and Revelation in the New Testament. This style of writing should not be interpreted so as to depreciate the inspiration of its messages.[18]

The New Testament is comprised of the four synoptic accounts of the gospel, which are the first four books of the Christian scriptures. It also contains the epistles which may be divided into two classifications: (1) Paul's epistles to congregations and his pastoral letters to Titus and Timothy and (2) the general epistles of James, Peter, John, and Jude. The third division of the New Testament is that of the book of Revelation which seems an appropriate conclusion to the biblical literature.

Latter Day Saints believe in contemporary revelation. We believe that the Book of Mormon and the Doctrine and Covenants are witnesses of the Lord Jesus. Specifically, the Book of Mormon is an account of God's dealings with peoples of ancient America. It is not claimed that these should replace or take precedence over the Bible. To us the three standard books of scripture are the Bible, the Book of Mormon, and the Doctrine and Covenants. The believer or inquirer is left free to investigate or study and use these as he/she may be guided by the Holy Spirit.

1. See Edwin R. Theils, *The Mysterious Numbers of the Hebrew Kings*, William B. Erdmans Publishing Company, Grand Rapids, Michigan.
2. Joseph Smith, Jr., Book of Mormon, Herald Publishing House, Independence, Missouri, 1957, p. iii.
3. *Ibid.*, II Nephi 1:115.
4. Doctrine and Covenants 1:5.
5. Book of Mormon, Ether 1:55-58.
6. George A. Buttrick (ed.), *Interpreter's Dictionary of the Bible*, Abingdon Press, New York and Nashville, Vol. 1, p. 328.
7. Joseph Smith III, Heman C. Smith, F. Henry Edwards, *The History of the Reorganized Church of Jesus Christ of Latter Day Saints*, Herald Publishing House, Independence, Missouri, Vol. 1, pp. 13, 18.
8. *Interpreter's Dictionary of the Bible*, Vol. 3, p. 897.
9. Doctrine and Covenants 140:5d.
10. Elias B. Sanford, *Cyclopedia of Religious Knowledge*, The S. S. Scranton Company, 1910, p. 818.
11. Church History, Vol. 7, p. 303 f.
12. Walter Harrelson, *Interpreting the Old Testament*, Holt, Rinehart and Winston, pp. 14-15.
13. Bernard W. Anderson, *Understanding the Old Testament*, Prentice Hall, Inc., Englewood Cliffs, N.J., p. 257.
14. Doctrine and Covenants 1:5.
15. For further study see *Interpreter's Dictionary of the Bible*, Vol. 1, p. 257.
16. *Ibid.*, Vol. 1, pp. 161-168.
17. *Ibid.*, Vol. 3, pp. 960-964 (Pseudepigrapha).
18. *Ibid.*, Vol. 1, pp. 159-161.

HISTORY, PROPHECY, 4 AND ETERNAL DESTINY

Eschatology—Last Things

Quite a number of years ago in company with three other then young appointee ministers, I listened to a sermon preached in the Saints church Auditorium in Independence, Missouri, by Apostle John W. Rushton. In his characteristic terminology Apostle Rushton used a phrase something like this: "in the eschatological hope." After the service, in conversation, our attention was focused upon that phrase. Only one in the group had any idea as to what he meant. Beginning with the rudimentary explanation which he gave I have been trying to pursue the meaning and significance of eschatology plus the hope it portrays ever since. Dr. Ray C. Petre of Duke University Divinity School has written: "Eschatology is a term virtually unknown."[1] Since its introduction by theologians in the nineteenth century, the term has come into gradual use, but the doctrine which eschatology really signifies extends throughout all scripture. In other words, theologians borrowed a Greek word with which to designate the doctrine of last things and used it to distinguish this doctrine from other areas of systematic theology.

Many persons have only a vague idea of the meaning

and significance of eschatology. This should not disturb us. The doctrine is very important in the Judaic and Christian religions and dominates both. In this chapter I wish to equate eschatology with God's design for our ultimate destiny. In spite of the thought of some scholars that some of the Judaic and Christian eschatology had its parallels in Persian and Greek mythology, it holds an inseparable relation not only to our religious concepts but to our very lives as persons created by God.[2] Efforts to associate these parallels with the origins of eschatology have not proved to be successful. God's eternal destiny for us must never be permitted to deteriorate in Christian thought nor vanish into obscurity. Indeed though concepts may change from time to time it is most unlikely that such shall ever completely vanish since persons always have been and still are disposed to probe every avenue which may offer security and hope. Hence, our eternal destiny very well may be described as the family of God living the life of God here and hereafter.

Briefly defined, eschatology is that branch of systematic theology which deals with final or last things. One who seeks to produce a work in this field is confronted with questions and problems which are produced by historical and textual criticism of the scriptures, wide variations in scriptural interpretations, divergent interpretative viewpoints of history, speculative ideas, and conjectural prophetic calculations and date predictions. These represent, at least in part, the problems with which one is likely to be confronted. Therefore, at the beginning it is important to the development of a sound and comprehensive treatment of the subject that the course we pursue be well understood and charted. One must have some insights in advance about where to begin and what deductions may be constructively sound and feasible.

Hope and Destiny

The title of Jurgen Moltmann's book *Theology of Hope* portrays the essence of that which we desire to pursue in this field. Certainly if ever theology has any contribution of hope to make in our world of conflicting ideologies, that contribution is needed now. When properly interpreted and expounded God's eternal design must become central to our deliverance from the present dilemma and to our future spiritual welfare. This interpretation deals not only with that which is yet to be but encompasses that which has been and that which now is.

This view assumes that God has been, still is, and always will remain in history. He is directing history toward the ultimate consummation of his purposes. There is no means by which God may be excluded from the affairs of men, for in the phraseology of Paul Tillich, "our ground of being" is in Him. God created us with potential, dominion, and agency. We are his. He loves us with infinite zeal and compassion. It is through us that he will achieve his purposes, ultimately bringing forth his kingdom upon this earth. It is to this end that we have being and existence. God will not fail; truth must eventually conquer all error with its consequent evils.

Pursuant to this affirmation of the divine movement and purpose, the following expresses the basic principle of a constructive view of both design and destiny:

> The works, and the designs, and the purposes of God, can not be frustrated, neither can they come to naught, for God doth not walk in crooked paths; neither doth he turn to the right hand nor to the left; neither doth he vary from that which he hath said; therefore his paths are straight and his course is one eternal round. Remember, remember, that it is not the work of God that is frustrated, but the work of men; for although a man may have many revelations, and have power to do many mighty works, yet, if he boast in his own strength, and sets at naught the counsels of God, and follows after the dictates of his own will and carnal desires, he must fall and incur the vengeance of a just God upon him.[3]

Persons alone cannot determine nor shape their own destiny any more than they can become the authors of their own beings or existence. The Lord's Prayer expounds in few words the ultimate hope which finds its centrality in God and in the triumph of his coming kingdom: "Thy kingdom come. Thy will be done on earth, as it is done in heaven" (Matt. 6:10).

God's Eternal Design in History

I have affirmed that God is directing history toward its final consummation; that is, toward the triumph of his kingdom, which is steadily maturing from its initial status into its complete dominion and fulfillment. Not all share this faith-inspiring hope. William Barclay presents three divergent views which historians have held and to which proponents, according to their philosophical outlooks, in varied measures still adhere.

(1) History is cyclic and repetitive. It is an eternal round of successively similar events in which God takes no more than a passive interest and an inert control. Things happen over and over again in the same way. This is the way it is, has been, and always will be. Dr. Barclay points out that this is basically the Stoic view. He cites the Greek philosopher Chrysippus, one of the chief leaders of Stoicism, as he is quoted by C. K. Barrett.[4] Chrysippus maintained that the planets at certain fixed periods of time return to their original relative positions. This results in the destruction of everything which exists: "Then the cosmos is restored anew in a precisely similar arrangement as before." Everything is repeated; even the individual man would live again with the same friends and fellow citizens. This process of restoration goes on unendingly. "Indeed to all eternity without end." Chrysippus adds that there will never be any new thing other than that which has been before. Dr. Barclay concludes, "On this view history is an iron determination from which there is no escape, world without end."

(2) History is a matter of haphazard chance succession. It has no order, plan, nor goal. There is no purpose nor end in it. Things occur and reoccur haphazardly. It is as a road that never ends and leads nowhere. History is one emergency following upon another. Nothing can explain, still less justify, the utter irrationality of history. "There is nothing which can make present suffering worthwhile because it is for the sake of something greater."[5]

(3) History is emergent. It is moving toward the con-

summation of a purpose and a goal. We may retard and even deflect the consummation of history's purposeful end. We may alter its course but we can never defeat its purpose because God is in it. He had a plan and a purpose to be executed even before the creation of things as they are and we can never ultimately defeat that purpose.

This first view of history leaves us without hope as does that school of thinking which holds to the philosophy that our origin as well as that of the universe is solely and finally a matter of chance. Without the governing force and intervention of a directing Intelligence, there never was and, from our point of view, there never can be any ground of being.

The second view it seems offers no more hope than the first. It lacks any challenge for existence and provides no incentive for living. The elements of faith, courage, and fortitude cannot exist in such a philosophical climate. The second view of history coincides with the philosophy of Jean Paul Sartre, the French atheistic existentialist. Quoting Dostoevski's (Russian author, 1821-1881) statement, "If God didn't exist, everything would be possible," Sartre states: "That is the very starting point of existentialism. Indeed everything is permissible if God does not exist and as a result man is forlorn because neither within him nor without does he find anything to cling to. He can't start making excuses for himself." Earlier in the book Sartre wrote:

Atheistic existentialism which I represent . . . states that if God does not exist there is at least one being in whom existence precedes essence, a being who exists before he can be defined by any concept. . . . What is meant here by saying that existence precedes essence? It means that, first of all, man exists, turns up, appears on the scene, and, only afterwards defines himself.... Thus there is no human nature since there is no God to conceive it. Not only is man what he conceives himself to be but he is also only what he wills himself to be after this thrust toward existence.[6]

It is not my purpose to question the integrity of honest thinkers no matter how extremely atheistic they may become. I recognize also that we must discriminate between atheistic and other schools of existential philosophy. The two points of concern here are that earth's inhabitants are left forlorn and that God has not the ability, even if he does exist, to change anything from what it is to what he wills or purposes, even though persons to a large degree have this ability. Another advocate of this hopelessly abysmal philosophy states,

... It is still quite impossible for us to regard man as the child of God for whom the earth was created as a temporary habitation. Rather must we regard him as little more than a chance deposit on the surface of the world, carelessly thrown up between two ice ages by the same forces that rust iron and ripen corn.... Man is but a foundling in the cosmos abandoned by the forces that created him. Unparented, unassisted and undirected by omniscient or benevolent authority, he must fend for himself and with the aid of his own limited intelligence find his way about in an indifferent universe.[7]

In view of these expressed concepts, it is more than reasonable—it seems mandatory—that we should not only "clarify our theology" but also have a clear perception of our sense of destiny.

The third view is the way history is regarded in the Holy Scriptures. Actually the scriptures, as seen in their proper perspective, point up the manner in which God has and will handle human actions and events pertaining both to the individual and to the whole of mankind, from the beginning to the end. Our hope for the future lies in the fact that God will not deviate from his plan or his purpose. The crises of history both past and present bind purpose to mission. The recognition of our mission should remove the undesirable speculative aspects of the final destiny to which many have hopefully held. Faith must be projected from our knowledge of foundational principles and not from fantasy.

A question should be dealt with here: Can we adequately consider the final consummation of the divine purpose in persons without giving retrospective as well as prospective attention to the total range of divine action? This means that we must understand the nature of God's past activities. Also, we must build the foundation of our faith upon his past and present activity. And we must look hopefully to the future, in which there shall come to pass, eventually, the complete accomplishment of his divine will in and through his creation—in and through us in our relationship to him and to his creation, "as good stewards of the manifold grace of God." This is the interpretation of history which the new look at God's eternal design seeks to establish.

The Lord represented himself to John the Revelator thus: "I am Alpha and Omega, the beginning and the ending, the Lord who is, and who was, and who is to come; the Almighty" (Rev. 1:8). If we endeavor to satisfy ourselves by taking a look only at that which is yet to be in the divine purpose, we see just half of the picture and then we do not see it in its relationship to our contemporary needs with their challenges. The ret-

63

rospective view, like the look toward the future, must be one of faith because faith is required for us to see the evidence of God's movement in the past as well as achieving "the assurance of things hoped for" (Heb. 11:1).

Theology vs. Revelation

God's eternal design is based on the fundamental premise that he is an eternally self-disclosing Being. Both creation and history are affiliated with his self-disclosure. He is always the "I am" to every generation (Exodus 3:14-15). As creation is eternally emergent, history is likewise continuously emergent throughout all time. The self-disclosure of God, which is to be seen both in creation and history, is imperative to our appreciation of the principle of divine revelation.

In all revelatory experiences both God and persons must be involved. How could an infinitely intelligent Being give revelation if there were no other existing intelligence than his own to be acted upon by the revelation? But "holy men of God spake as they were moved by the Holy Ghost" (II Peter 1:21). Without faith in the principle, in the experience, and in the Giver, revelation is meaningless. In the revelatory experience the human element becomes the vehicle of divine communication. While we are treating this as a theological enterprise, we must remember that systematic theology is not essentially revelatory. Theology is the effort to discover God or to state what we may think and believe in regard to God within a systematic framework.

Revelation is God's self-disclosure in an experience in which, by whatever media he may choose, he illuminates the soul of a person. In such divine self-disclosure the intelligence is enabled to perceive things which may be beyond the realm of human rationalization. Acceptance of the affirmation of those who have this kind of experience with God whether in the past, in the present, or in the future requires that we have faith in God and also in the testimony of him who has had or may have such experience. All of us place our trust in the Almighty when we have been the recipient of an experience in which God, by whatever media and to whatever extent he chooses, reveals himself to us, and we accept that as divine. Thus we become beneficiaries of his grace.

President W. Wallace Smith of the Saints Church made this illuminating statement:

Let me remind you that while theology is a field of inquiry of legitimate concern to all Christian people, and certainly to Christian ministers, there is a vast difference between theology in the sense of thinking about religion and Christian experience itself. If we keep this in mind we shall understand more readily the plight of the "God is dead" school of theologians (although that designation hardly seems sound to those who proclaim the death of God). These theologians it seems to me are trying to rationalize their own lack of experience with God. They seem to start from the viewpoint that everything which happens to a man or which is apprehended by a man has its rise in man. They think of revelation as man's discovery rather than as our heavenly Father's self-disclosure. Having ascribed to human origins every glimmering of insight, it is not long until they read God out of the picture entirely. For such people we who have had experience of revelation and have enjoyed the ministry of the Holy Spirit have something of vital importance to

say. It is that we have found God in our own experience and in the experience of the Restoration movement.[8]

This statement is self-explanatory in its support of the principle of divine revelation versus theology which I have endeavored to set forth. The principle for which I have been contending in the relationship of theology to revelation is that theology is our effort to state what we think and believe in regard to God and that revelation is God's self-disclosure through our experience with him, which is so splendidly elucidated in President Smith's statement. This will apply to any area of theology, in its relationship to revelation, where controversy exists. We must be able to make the distinction between revealed purpose or destiny and theological concepts, ideas, and personal impressions or speculations relating thereto.

Specific Characteristics and Importance of Sound Doctrine

Eschatology is that branch of systematic theology which deals with final and last things. While serving as an introduction to the subject, this falls quite short of expressing all which is ultimately involved pertaining to this world and to the hereafter. Eschatology must be thought of as embracing or subsisting within a dualistic framework. This involves people as they exist between the two opposing forces of good and evil, in which they have the freedom to choose one of the two. There is no neutral existence in this situation. This dualism is realistically as well as allegorically portrayed to us in the Garden of Eden's story of the forbidden fruit. The purpose of the subjection of Adam to the temptations of evil and the relationship of the atonement thereto is defined in these words:

Wherefore, the ends of the law which the Holy One hath given, unto the inflicting of the punishment which is affixed, which punishment that is affixed is in opposition to that of the happiness which is affixed, to answer the ends of the atonement; for it must needs be that there is an opposition in all things. If not so. . . . righteousness could not be brought to pass; neither wickedness; neither holiness nor misery; neither good nor bad. . . . And to bring about his eternal purposes in the end of man after he had created our first parents, and the beasts of the field and the fowls of the air, and in fine all things which are created, it must needs be that there was an opposition: even the forbidden fruit in opposition to the tree of life; the one being sweet and the other bitter; wherefore the Lord God gave unto man that he should act for himself. Therefore, man could not act for himself save it should be that he was enticed by the one or the other.[9]

Eschatology then on the one hand involves the powers of evil with their concomitants of sin, death, judgment, and punishment, including Hades or hell with its duration and purpose. To these may be added the "lake of fire" as the symbolic end of Hades and of the eternally wicked (Rev. 20:12-15). On the other hand, the instruments for good involve all the progressive processes of righteousness, including the principles and powers of reclamation and salvation. This accounts for our insistence that a sound doctrine of immortality and eternal life includes the retrospective as well as the forward look. Therefore, the justice of the law, the ministry of the prophets, the incarnation, the ministry of Jesus and his divine atonement, repentance and forgiveness, the kingdom of God, the resurrection and eternal life, the second coming of Christ, the end of this world and the new heaven and new earth emerge. Christ will triumphantly and totally fulfill his mission when he finally delivers the kingdom to God the Father after overthrowing every opposing rule, authority, and power. "For he must reign until he has put all enemies under his feet. The last enemy to be destroyed is death" (I Cor. 15:24-26). Although the scriptures give glimpses, perceivable to the finite mind, of that glory yet to be enjoyed by those who have been made worthy through the grace of God and by their obedience to the gospel of Jesus Christ, much is known only by a maturing experience. We must be careful not to speculate nor to be carried away by unsound theories, teachings, calculations, or misleading predictions.

Dangers of irrational thought and action always exist. Even though this has been evident in regard to the doctrine of ultimate reality, the importance of this doctrine of last things must not be minimized. The inseparable relationship which exists between the Infinite and his eternal design for his creation must never be overlooked. Evidently for these and other reasons there has been a detrimental trend in the direction of discounting and even discarding any hope germinated through God's ultimate victory over the powers of evil, in the achievement of his everlasting purposes. Misinterpretations, miscalculations, false teachings, and false predictions can never justify minimizing or discarding anything as important as that which "sound doctrine" has to offer to the human race.

The doctrine of "immortality and eternal life"

recognizes Jesus as at the center of all things. In evidence of this note two references in the book of Revelation: (1) "I am he that liveth, and was dead; and, behold, I am alive forevermore, Amen; and have the keys of hell and of death. Write the things which thou hast seen, and the things which are, and the things which shall be hereafter" (Rev. 1:18-19). (2) "I am thy fellow servant, and of thy brethren that have the testimony of Jesus: worship God; for the testimony of Jesus is the spirit of prophecy" (Rev. 19:10). As we minimize its values or permit the doctrine of eternal design and purpose to fade into obscurity, we are robbed of the hope that this testimony of Jesus brings to us.

It is encouraging to become aware that a number of prominent theologians have recognized, and others are coming to recognize, that the doctrine of the eternal design from its beginning to its fulfillment should be given its rightful place in Christian theology. Some of these works have been referred to already.

1. Ray C. Petry, *Christian Eschatology and Social Thought*, Abingdon Press, p. 13.
2. Doctrine and Covenants 22:23.
3. *Ibid.*, 2:1.
4. C. K. Barrett, *The New Testament Background Selected Documents* (New York: Harper and Row), pp. 63-64.
5. William Barclay, ed., *The Bible and History*, Abingdon Press, pp. 11-16.
6. Jean Paul Sartre, *Existentialism and Human Emotions* (New York: Philosophical Library), pp. 15, 22.
7. Carl L. Becker, *The Heavenly City of the Eighteenth Century Philosophers* (New Haven and London: Yale University Press), pp. 14-15.
8. W. Wallace Smith sermon, *Of Hope and Salvation*, World Conference Bulletin, RLDS Church, April 18, 1966.
9. Book of Mormon, II Nephi 1:80-82, 97-100. See also pp. 97-100.

THE FULLNESS 5 OF THE TIME

The Fullness of the Time

The title of this chapter is taken from Galatians 4:4 which states, "But when the *fullness of the time* was come, God sent forth his Son."

A new look at last things implies that it is necessary to see that which God already has been doing as well as look to the future expectantly. The purpose of this chapter is to emphasize God's action in history especially as it culminated in the Christ event.

Some two hundred years before the time of Julius Caesar's Gallic Wars, a considerable segment of Gaul, from what is now France, set out to capture the whole Greek peninsula. They failed but were granted a large section of central Asia Minor in which to dwell. Under Roman rule this territory became the province of Galatia. Consequently, the name Galatian is derived from its inhabitants, the Gauls. During his first journey through Asia Minor, Paul had succeeded in establishing churches at Durbe, Lystra, Iconium, and Antioch of Pisidia (not to be confused with Antioch of Syria). There is little doubt that it was to these churches that the Galatian Epistle was addressed.

On his first visit to Galatia, Paul received a joyful

response from numbers of Gentiles and from Jews also. He had presented the gospel of Christ in its fullness and evidently was surprised, and chagrined, to find that in a short time misunderstandings, false concepts, and even apostasy were in evidence. The epistle indicates that Judaizers among the Saints were teaching and insisting that the Gentile Christians must live as Jews. Judaizers is the term applied to Jews who insisted that Gentile Christians must be circumcised and observe all the legal formalities of Jewish law. These troublemakers (Galatians 1:7) had made the accusation, no doubt, that Paul was not an apostle since he was not one of the original twelve chosen by Jesus.

Paul defended his apostleship throughout the entire epistle, but his main thrust was to straighten out the more serious problem. He asserted, "All who rely on the works of the law are under a curse" (Gal. 3:10). In short, he told them to cease relying on the works of the law for salvation and to trust in the saving grace of God manifested in Jesus Christ. In order to make his point valid Paul proclaimed the message of the text from which the title of this chapter has been taken and proceeded to say "to redeem them that were under the law, that we might receive the adoption of sons." His purpose was to enable the Galatian Christians to see clearly that "the just shall live by faith" in Jesus Christ and not by the law of Moses. The text has true apostolic authorship and its setting is one of the most significant of the New Testament epistles.

Additional light is thrown on the subject in the epistle to the Ephesians: "For he has made known to us in all wisdom and insight the majesty of his will, according to

71

his purpose which he set forth in Christ as a plan for the fulness of time, *to unite all things in him*, things in heaven and things on earth" (Eph. 1:9-10, R.S.V.). Simply stated, God has a plan and a designated time for carrying out his purpose. God's plan enters into his self-disclosure in the person of his only begotten Son, Jesus Christ.

Jesus introduced the principle of fulfillment as relating to himself. As he came into Galilee preaching the gospel, Jesus proclaimed, "The time is fulfilled, and the kingdom of God is at hand; repent, and believe the gospel" (Mark 1:14). Jesus also said, "Think not that I am come to destroy the law, or the prophets; I am not come to destroy, but to fulfill" (Matt. 5:17; I.V. 5:19). By this we may understand Paul's reference to the fullness of the time as a time of fulfillment.

Divine Supremacy and Human Action

Paul's words, "The fullness of time," expresses the whole Israelite philosophy of God's activity on their behalf. God is the creator of the universe and he directs the destinies of men and of nations. This philosophy carries the implication that God ultimately is supreme in human affairs. Paul's sermon on Mar's Hill brilliantly describes the Hebrew conception of God's mighty acts: "He made from one every nation of men to live on all the face of the earth, having determined the allotted periods and the boundaries of their habitation,...for 'In him we live and move and have our being'" (Acts 17:26, 28 R.S.V.). Paul ended that sermon with his vibrant testimony of Christ's resurrection. He placed the Hebrew idea of God's supremacy in the universe, including history, within the Christian framework. He saw the miracle of redemption through Jesus Christ as the climax to and at the center of all God's works of salvation. Thus, the Hebrew conception of God's design became that of the Christians also—that is, as far as his supremacy may be concerned. The difference between the Jewish and Christian concepts centers in the acceptance or rejection of Jesus Christ as the revelation of God in the flesh. Dr. George A. Buttrick stated: "The Bible is therefore from our human side faith history, the story of man's response to God's acts. . . . Bible history is history focused in the redemption given in Christ and his cross."[1]

The combined Hebraic and Christian philosophy of God's design and supremacy in history has been shared by many, even reaching down to modern times. Merle D'Aubigne wrote:

This history acknowledges the supremacy and grandeur of the simple, profound principle, God in history. . . . It is necessary that history breathe the air congenial to its real existence and the life of history is from God, God is to be acknowledged, God ought to be declared in the pages of history: for in truth the history of the world must ever be regarded as the open annals of the government of the King of Kings.[2]

"The fullness of the time" does not make any distinction between sacred and secular history. This tends to imply that God is supreme in both. Both deal with the world of mankind of which God is in control, and in which he acts when and as he deems wise.

God is not an opportunist who takes advantage of certain events to fulfill his purpose. He is director of the complete range of history, past, present, and future. However, the fact that God directs and exercises control of history does not mean that he is responsible for all of the acts of men out of which history has arisen, or yet may arise. It does mean that God is always free to act according to his will and wisdom. Although God acts in accordance with human needs, we in no way control the acts of God. However, we are relatively involved therein. It is the divine intent that our involvement shall be voluntary as well as deliberate. Joshua indicated that we do have the right of choice. He said as he was preparing the children of Israel to cross the Jordan into Canaan:

And if it seem evil unto you to serve the Lord, choose you this day whom you will serve; whether the gods which your fathers served that were on the other side of the flood, or the gods of the Amorites, in whose land you dwell; but as for me and my house, we will serve the Lord.—Jos. 24:15.

From the creation forward this right of choice is God's gift of agency. God's sovereignty is pervasive. He chooses the appropriate time for his salvation activity, according to his will, on our behalf.

The nature of God's purpose was affirmed by Malachi: "For I am the Lord, I change not; therefore, ye sons of Jacob are not consumed" (Mal. 3:6). This affirmation was a part of Malachi's plea that the people make ready for the Lord's coming. It implies clearly that God's covenants with Abraham and his descendants were not to be thwarted by the sins of the sons of Jacob. The Lord did come to cleanse the temple and to purge the sons of Lehi. This text also may imply a future coming of the Lord to complete that task.

G. A. Buttrick expresses a meaningful principle: "Faith in Christ is the clue of the meaning of history."[3] One may ask, what about the problem of unnecessary disaster and pain? Persons and even civilizations do tend to repeat the sins and the mistakes of their predecessors, but history extends itself far beyond the recurring cycle. History is emergent. In the arena of pain comes the cross, which is the focal point between sin and redemption. The price of sin is always measured in suffering. God's willingness to suffer for our sins becomes his grace in our redemption. In the victory of Calvary, God in Christ's death took upon himself the worst that sin can do to us and conquered. Surely if history has purpose, God must be directing it; and the atonement of Christ is at its center.

God's Plan as Seen in History

Faith is the clue to our perception of God's activity. He is directing history. His purpose is redemption. If the soul is to be redeemed, then history also needs to be redeemed, for our existence is within the framework of history. We cannot get out of this framework, no matter what we do or how hard we try.

"The redemption of history must come from within history. Yes, from beyond it also. . . redemption must come from transfusion of blood."[4] "The Biblical view of history gives life dimension. . . and the persuasion that history shall be fulfilled beyond the gates of time."[5] God is fulfilling history, but human history is recorded in relation to dates and time. God is not controlled by the time limitations of our experience because he is infinite and eternal. Yet it is his design continually to project himself within the structure of history's time limitations.

Since God is directing and fulfilling history purposefully, this should be demonstratable. However, it must be recognized that any such demonstration will need to be based upon faith in God's eternal movement translated within the limits of time. One needs to have faith that the events of history give evidence that the Almighty, as the sovereign Lord, works according to his plan and objectives. As we see "the fullness of the time" within this perspective, life and meaning are given to the chronicles of time in their totality. We must see the movement of God within the full range of history as his eternal purposes become evident to us; this is a revelatory process.

Objective Action Through His People Israel

The Israelites attached great meaning to their deliverance from bondage in Egypt. As they looked backward they saw God's miracle in relation to that which had taken place. Their deliverance from Egypt was a divinely performed act of salvation. The mighty acts of God in their salvation became the focal emphasis of the preaching of Moses, Joshua, and succeeding prophets.

From the records of the Israelites in the Bible, we derive these principles of God's design: (1) God called specific persons for special tasks. (2) He made a covenant with the people through whom he intended to demonstrate his purpose. (3) He chose lands in which his people were to develop their faith and fulfill their covenant with him. (4) God chose the time and the conditions for his specific action. (5) God commanded his people according to his will and purpose. (6) He enticed them to voluntary action. (7) Finally he preserved his people through most hazardous conditions, in spite of their rebellion—and, we may add, he is still doing so.

One of the greatest evidences of an eternal design is in the survival of the Jewish race. Max Dimont wrote: "It happened only once in history."[6] No other people have been able to survive famine, oppression, apostasy, war, captivity, dispersion, and persecution as have the Jews. They have maintained their racial identity and monotheistic beliefs during a period of more than 1,800 years without any central government or a land to call their own—this in spite of such attempts as Hitler made to exterminate them. During World War II up to six million Jews perished in the gas chambers of Germany. Nevertheless, immediately after Hitler's defeat, the autonomous State of Israel was set up in Palestine. We need to give serious thought to the fact that there are now more Jews in Israel than there have been in any previous time in their history. In 1967 2,700,000 Jews defended themselves victoriously against the Arab world of more than 90,000,000. Strenuous efforts are being made to reach a peaceful settlement following the more recent war between Jew and Arab. As we evaluate that which we have been able to observe in our own time, little room is left for doubt that the Almighty has not forgotten, but is fulfilling, the covenant which he made with Abraham, Jacob, Moses, and the prophets.

The architecture of the eternal design was forecast from the beginning of time and it is still visible. The Creator will never forsake his intent or promise.

The Call of Abraham

Abraham was called out of idolatrous Mesopotamia to go into the land of Canaan, some time during the early part of the second millennium B.C.* The Lord covenanted with Abraham to make him a great nation, with the promise that in him all of the families of the earth would be blessed (Gen. 12:1-2). At that time Abraham had no children and Sarah, his wife, was past the age of childbearing. God fulfilled his covenant in giving posterity to Abraham through Sarah, and the exalted concept of monotheism reestablished through Abraham and his posterity has remained to the present day. This latter fact in itself was sufficient and urgent reason for God to issue the call to Abraham. Today Judaism, Christianity, and Moslemism all maintain the Abrahamic and Melchizedekic theology of one supreme God (Gen. 14). Of course, this must be regarded as preservation rather than the first introduction of monotheism into the world. Nevertheless, one can conjecture what the world would be like now if the Lord had not moved as he did at strategic times to call and to enlighten men and women as he maintained his cause in

---

*Due to the recent discovery in Northern Syria of the Ebla texts, this date may need to be adjusted to the Early Bronze Age. This would date it about 500 years earlier, or the middle of the third millennium B.C. (see *The Biblical Archaeologist*, Dec. 1978, pp. 156-8.)

a world which was filled with idolatry. The question may well be raised here, could Christ have performed effectively his redemptive work in the world of Abraham's time? Abraham's call was a divine step forward in laying the foundation for the work which Christ achieved nearly two thousand years later.

No land could have been better suited to the development of the faith of Israel than that of Canaan. Its geography, geology, topography, climate, and location in relation to the ancient world all contributed to the necessity of complete dependence upon the Almighty for protection and subsistence. Military and trade routes between the northern and eastern nations and Egypt passed through Canaan. The land was almost completely dependent upon rainfall for fertility, whereas in Egypt and Mesopotamia irrigation assured seasonal crops. Much of the soil in Canaan was not rich. Some of it was desert. There was not an abundance of mineral resources. God purposefully chose a people and a land suitable to work out the revelation of his will, not only for Abraham's descendants but as a blessing to all people. The focal point of this blessing was in the sending forth of the Son of God, at the chosen time, from the seed of Abraham.

External and Internal Influences on Israelite History and Culture

A. The Patriarchal Period

In order to be able to preserve the superb monotheistic religion and culture, Abraham, an Aramean, was called forth from a pagan world to the designated land of promise (Joshua 24:2-3 and Deuteronomy 26:5 R.S.V.). Nevertheless, Mesopotamia provided a cultural heritage for Abraham and his posterity. In this culture there had been a blending of many ancient peoples, including the Sumerians, the Akkadians, the Amorites, the Arameans, and the Chaldeans. The Arameans, in ancient times, occupied Syria. The Chaldeans were eventually included with Babylonia. From the Aramean culture came the wives of Isaac and Jacob (Gen. 24 and 29). Few civilizations have surpassed that of the Sumerians.[7] However, Sumerian culture declined about the time Abraham left Haran for Canaan. Would it be merely conjecture to assume that God specifically chose the time for Abraham's departure from Haran to the land of promise?

Abraham made an important contact in Canaan which greatly strengthened his faith and helped to develop that of his posterity. There he met Melchizedek who was king of Salem (later Jerusalem, city of peace) and priest of the most high God (Gen. 14). Abraham honored Melchizedek as the priest of God by paying tithes to him. Contemporary scripture represents Melchizedek as a high priest. This is in accordance with Hebrews 5:5-6 where Christ is designated as a high priest after the order of Melchizedek. Here was one exception to polytheistic idol worship in the world of that ancient time. These two great men, Melchizedek and Abraham, left a heritage for Israel which was later evaluated in the Old Testament as well as the New Testament (Ps. 110:4; Heb., chapters 5-7).

B. The Sojourn in Egypt and the Exodus

According to the best calculations based upon biblical texts, the sojourn of the Israelites in Egypt was of sufficient duration to result in considerable Egyptian influence on Israel's religion and culture. Moses was the chief figure of the Exodus. The biblical account gives him an Egyptian background and name. There is no logical reason to dispute this. His Egyptian name, names used for his associates, and some used in the immediate generation of the Levitical genealogy suggest an Egyptian background. Egyptian influence was not limited to the sojourn. This is demonstrated by the biblical accounts of Israel's dealings with Egypt in the succeeding centuries.

Biblical tradition also tells of Moses obtaining refuge in Midian when he fled from Egypt. He met and married a Midianite woman, Zipporah, the daughter of Jethro who was the Midianite priest of Yahweh, Israelite name for God, later changed to Jehovah. This was the second near-eastern exception to ancient pagan pluralistic deism. It was in Midian that Moses had his first confrontation with Yahweh (Exodus 3). How much Yahwehism was derived from the Midianite priest Jethro is still a debatable question among biblical scholars.[8]

The chosen posterity of Abraham through Jacob and his twelve sons had been saved from the ravages of famine by migrating to Egypt. Although it was a brutal act which isolated Joseph from his family, according to his interpretation of that event God prepared the way beforehand for their preservation (Gen. 45:5). Later the Hebrews were forced into slavery by a "new king over

Egypt, which knew not Joseph." This king was most likely Seti the First (sometimes spelled Sethos) or Ramses II of the nineteenth Egyptian dynasty. One may have been the Pharaoh of the oppression, the other the Pharaoh of the exodus.[9] No event in Old Testament history is more important than the exodus of the children of Israel from Egypt to Canaan. From that time forth they acclaimed that their deliverance from Egypt was the mighty act of God in their national salvation. At Sinai the Abrahamic covenant was supplemented by the covenant accompanying the ten commandments (Deut. 5:2-21). Henceforth the total life of Israel was built into the framework of this Sinaitic covenant.

Two things predominated in the time of the Exodus. The first was the urgency for relief from oppression and the lasting effects of slavery. The second was the advantage of the most opportune time for such an undertaking to occur. No doubt both of these were in the forefront of the theophany at Sinai. No time could have been more favorable for the Israelites to take over the land of Canaan. Egyptian power had been weakened in Asia during the heretical reign of Amonhotep IV, 1375-1366 B.C. (also named Akhenaton). He neglected foreign affairs to give attention to a religious revolution at home. He tried to establish a culture based upon belief in a monotheistic sun god. Egyptian power had been further weakened following the overthrow of the Mettani empire in 1370 B.C. by the Hittites. Mettani was an important Northeastern Mesopotamian Empire during this period. The Hittites had achieved great strength in Asia Minor. Subsequently Egypt was involved, and almost overthrown, in war with the Hittites during the reign of Ramses II. Ramses succeeded by a truce in holding the Hittites north of Mount Lebanon. During the period of the conquest of Canaan under Joshua, Egypt was involved in war with the Phoenicians whom they called Sea Peoples. It took all of Egypt's military might to ward off these attacks. Though armed combat was necessary, the Israelites had little difficulty in establishing themselves in Trans-Jordan.

The lands of Edom and Moab had been unsettled nomadic territory between 1900 and 1300 B.C.[10] Therefore, they made little serious difficulty for the children of Israel as they began their march northward. Assyria, Babylon, and Persia had not yet risen to power. Consequently, there was no resistance from these countries which later became great powers. The first two of these later were bitter foes and conquerors of Israel and Judah.

C. Canaanite Influence

After successfully occupying the central portion of the land of Canaan under the leadership of Joshua, successor to Moses, the children of Israel were influenced both for good and evil by the inhabitants of the land. In conquering the land Joshua followed the policy of destroying everything in his sweep, but he was unable to take over all of Canaan. War with the Canaanites continued during the period of the Judges until the time of the victory of Deborah and Barak (Judges 4 and 5). The Israelites learned much from the Canaanites in the arts, in crafts, and in agriculture. Less than half a century earlier the ancestors of the Israelites had been slaves in

Egypt. Therefore, in these skills the Canaanites were much in advance of the children of Israel.

Nevertheless, Canaanite worship of Baal became a lasting problem, affecting Israel's allegiance to Jehovah and to his covenant. Even Elijah's victory at Mount Carmel did not completely obliterate this problem. When David captured the city of Jerusalem from the Jebusites he evidently took the remainder of those people into the Israelite community (see II Samuel 5:5-9). It is interesting to note that David selected as one of his priests Zadok, whom some scholars think may have been a descendant of Melchizedek.[11] If this be true the Jebusites may have made some wholesome contribution to the religion of Israel. We remember that Jerusalem is the same city as Salem over which Melchizedek was high priest and king in the time of Abraham.

The Change to a Monarchy

Some have called the period of the rule of the Judges the dark ages of Hebrew history. There was a decline in all areas of life—economic, political, moral, and religious.[12] Under these conditions the people began to clamor for a king. Though it was with Samuel's fore-warnings of the likely results, which later proved to be justified, God told Samuel to anoint Saul king over Israel. The establishment of the monarchy united the tribes of Israel under one government; such had not been the case during the fragmented rule of the Judges. This enabled David and Solomon, successors to Saul, to extend the territory and influence of Israel into surrounding nations, but unity could not be maintained.

84

After the death of Solomon, Israel was divided into two kingdoms. The ten northern tribes retained the national name of Israel. The two southern tribes of Judah and Benjamin became known as the Kingdom of Judah. According to the best calculations this division occurred in 931 B.C.[13] The northern kingdom finally built a strongly fortified capital at Samaria during the reign of King Omri. Judah retained Jerusalem as its capital city and center of worship. Jeroboam, the first king of the northern tribes, built high places of idol worship at Dan and at Bethel, with a golden calf at each. Division caused rivalry between the two kingdoms which led to almost continuous war.

At times there was some little cohesiveness against foreign foes. However, this lack of unity contributed to the downfall of both kingdoms. During the divided monarchy both nations were generally corrupt. Intermarriages with foreign women led to pagan altars and pagan worship. The prophets vigorously protested and warned against this corruption. At the time of Jeroboam II (782-753 B.C.) Israel had achieved prosperity which led to complacency, pride, immorality, and social injustice of the worst kind. The warnings of the prophets Amos and Hosea went unheeded. As these prophets saw the rising power of Assyria they pled for repentance and trust in God as the only hope of salvation.

Downfall, Captivity, and Exile

The land of Palestine geographically was in a precarious situation. Palestine provided the land route between the ancient empires to the east and north and west and Egypt. This meant that the dominant powers, in order to attack Egypt, had to send their armies through Palestine. Assyria invaded Israel after conquering the northern part of Syria. For a time Israel capitulated as Assyria cleared the route through the Philistine territory, what is now the Gaza strip, then turned back and conquered Damascus. Judah, under the reign of Ahaz, was already paying tribute to Assyria. This left the northern kingdom to fight alone against one of the greatest powers of the ancient world. After a three-year siege, Samaria fell to Sargon II of Assyria in 721 B.C. Great numbers of the rich and nobility were taken into captivity, never to return. The northern kingdom was obliterated. Sennacherib, the son of Sargon II, invaded Judah, destroying forty-six of her walled cities. Only a miracle spared Jerusalem from captivity at that time. On his famous prism Sennacherib wrote that he destroyed forty-six of Judah's walled cities and shut up Hezekiah, king of Judah, "like a bird in a cage."

The ministry of the prophets Isaiah, Micah, and later Jeremiah had little effect on Judah's religious life. These prophets saw a new threat with the impending fall of Assyria and the rise of Babylon. As Amos and Hosea had pled with Israel to repent and place trust in God, so the prophets of Judah, especially Jeremiah, with warnings, called upon all the people to repent and trust God for deliverance. After three sieges, Jerusalem, including the temple, was destroyed by the Babylonians under Nebuchadnezzar in 586 B.C. Rich and noble Jews were taken into Babylonian captivity. Jeremiah remained in Jerusalem and continued his prophetic ministry among the remaining Jews. Ezekiel became the prophet of the exiles in Babylon. Division ended in downfall and captivity.

The Assyrians were ruthless and very cruel in all military campaigns. The Babylonians, too, were cruel and disrespectful of the religion of the exiles. Nevertheless, it is evident that the Jews were allowed to practice their worship to some degree in Babylon. There also appears to have been some communication between the exiles and those who remained in Palestine. The exiles complained that those whom God had used to punish them were more sinful than they. Ezekiel reminded them of their unfaithfulness and that God was just (Ezekiel 18:20 f.). Then came a period of reflection in which a degree of faithfulness to Jehovah was observed by the captives. With the exiles there was always a longing to return to their homeland. However, those who remained in Judah fared little better and sometimes worse than did the captives.

Persian Deliverance

Babylon was overthrown by Persia under Cyrus in 539 B.C. The Babylonians received Cyrus gladly since Nabonidus, their king, had neglected his responsibility in giving leadership in the observance of Babylonian religious worship. Cyrus had great respect for the religions of the nations he conquered. He revived the Babylonian worship. He liberated many who had been held captive in Babylon. Among these were the Jews. His influence, along with that of his once removed successor, Darius the Great, did much for the Jewish economical, political, and religious life. This was very important in the return of the "remnant." The Persian leaders provided funds from their treasury to help rebuild the Jerusalem temple and the walls of Jerusalem. This was done under the leadership of Sheshbazzar, Zerubbabel, and Nehemiah. Isaiah referred to Cyrus as God's anointed (Isaiah 45:1), but this was still a time of considerable distress for the Jews. Those who had not been taken into captivity were unable to offer much help in rebuilding the temple. Also many Jews who were now well settled and had become rich remained in Babylon which minimized the help so much needed at Jerusalem.

Nehemiah, Ezra, and Malachi were deeply distressed to find that during the exile many of the Jews in Judea had married foreign women and were yielding to their idolatrous practices. This was detrimental both to the people and to their religion. The prophets of the post-exilic period spoke out against these conditions (see Malachi, chapters 1, 2, 3). Ezra dealt with the problem much more firmly than Nehemiah had done. His reform was rigid and even dictatorial, but it was effective. Even though the Jews were treated mercifully and were helped by the Persians in their economic and religious reestablishment, they were never again free from foreign domination except for the period of the Hasmonean (also called Maccabees) leadership, 163-63 B.C.

The Hellenistic Period

Persia in turn was overthrown by the Greeks under Alexander the Great of Macedon, one of the Hellenic states. The Greek empire was made up of separately governed city states. These were called the Hellenic states. The eastern world, as far as the Indus River, was brought under Hellenistic control. Alexander's real purpose in his conquest was to spread Greek culture to the whole world. This he did, after his military victories, by the infiltration of Greeks into conquered territory and by building great cities, such as Alexandria in North Africa. He settled soldiers, who were no longer useful in war, in the conquered territories. Many of these married native women which helped to establish Hellenistic culture.

Leading up to and during the period of Alexander's campaigns, great cultural changes had been taking place in Greece. Under the influence of such philosophers as Socrates, Aristotle, and Plato, superstitious mythology and polytheistic deism had been dealt a fatal blow. Following Alexander's conquest the Greek language became the official language throughout the world. Hellenistic influences spread westward to include Rome. The Romans were not equal to the Greeks scholastically, yet they were greatly attracted to Greek learning, so that while Rome finally conquered Greece in the Roman world conquest Greek culture eventually despoiled Roman virtue and vitality.

Alexander gained control of Palestine in 332 B.C. Many Jews were attracted to the ideals of Greek philosophy. Alexander had great respect for the religion of the Jews. There is a story that he worshiped in the Temple at Jerusalem. He extended favors to the Jews who offered him little resistance. As stated, in Egypt he built the city of Alexandria and settled many Jews in that great city of North Africa. There later the Septuagint version of the Jewish Bible was produced in the Greek language.[14]

The Maccabean Period

After the death of Alexander the Great in 323 B.C., his empire was divided under four separate rulers. Here we need to be concerned only with two of these—the Ptolemies, who ruled in North Africa, and the Selucids, who gained control of most of Asia. Each of these lines of rulers contended for control of Palestine. While at first Palestine passed into the hands of Ptolemy I (king in Egypt, 305-283 B.C.), that territory finally came under the rule of the Selucids.[15] Antiochus IV, sometimes called Epiphanes, a later Selucid ruler, was an ardent devotee of the Greek god Zeus. As he tried to force the worship of Zeus on the Jews, he favored those who were known to be Hellenizers—Jews who had succumbed to and favored Greek culture. He accepted bribes from contenders among the Jews for the high priest's office, giving that office to Menelaus who promised him the larger sum of money. The defeated candidate Jason thought that Antiochus had been killed during a campaign in Egypt and sought to take control of Jerusalem. Antiochus, hearing of this, returned and savagely attacked Jerusalem. Then he returned to Egypt but was met by the Romans, who by this time were invading North Africa, and was forced to leave. He decided that Jerusalem, the center of Jewish worship, should be destroyed and colonized with Greeks.

In the meantime Mattathias, a priest, had moved from Jerusalem to Modin, a city northwest of Jerusalem. After refusing to offer sacrifices to Zeus, and seeing a Jew about to obey the orders of Greek officers, sent by Antiochus, to engage in this act of profane worship, he killed both the Jew and a Greek deputy.[16] Mattathias and his sons fled to the desert hills. Many faithful Jews followed them, and they organized guerrilla warfare. Mattathias commanded the Jews to fight on the Sabbath rather than to be cut down, which of course was against Jewish law and practice. He circumcised children and otherwise restored Jewish law (I Maccabees 2 ff.).

This was the beginning of the Maccabean revolt and the commencement of what is usually called the Hasmonean leadership. Never before in the history of the world had so many people come under the influence of a dominant culture as did those of Asia and Africa in relation to Hellenism. The Jews, because of their beliefs and practices, became more involved than any other ethnic, religious, or political group. As a result of this revolt, with its counter-Hellenistic influence, Judaism became the sole survivor of all the cultures with which Hellenism came in contact.

At the head of the revolt to preserve Judaism were the Maccabeans, the sons of Mattathias. Judas followed his aged father as leader. For a time he was highly successful against a much stronger foe. During this time he entered into a pact with Rome. Finally in a losing battle, with 800 men against 20,000 of the enemy, Judas was killed. His brother Jonathan became leader and also high priest. After Jonathan was tricked into capture and killed, his younger brother Simon completely liberated the Jews (144-143 B.C.). In the meantime the temple at Jerusalem had been cleansed and Jewish worship restored. The Jews remained free until 63 B.C. After Simon and two of his sons were slain, his young son John Hyrcanus became governor and high priest. He extended Jewish territory east and north. He compelled the Idumeans to become Jews. This created problems in the time of Herod the Great. The Jews were never happy with the arrangement. John also made a useful treaty with Rome.

It was during this time that the opposing political parties, the Sadducees and the Pharisees, arose. The Sadducees were largely from among the rich and the nobility and were known to be Hellenizers. The Pharisees were of the poorer class but held tenaciously to Jewish law and practice. John Hyrcanus transferred his sympathies from the Pharisees to the aristocratic and politically minded Sadducees. Contrary to the simple ideals of his predecessors, by these acts he paved the way for one of the most disreputable power struggles in Jewish history. This struggle finally emerged into three appeals to Pompey, who by this time was the Roman commander at Damascus. While Pompey was making up his mind, Aristobulus II, one of the contenders for the high priesthood, seized the fortress of Alexandria. Pompey attacked and conquered Alexandria and Jerusalem. This brought the Hasmonean leadership to an end and gave Rome control of Palestine.

The Roman Period

Palestine came under the control of Rome in 63 B.C. After desecrating the holy of holies in the temple, Pompey again allowed Jewish worship. Under Julius Caesar in 47 B.C. Antipater, an Idumean involved in the power struggle, was appointed Roman procurator of Palestine. Herod the Great, Antipater's son, married Mariamne, a Hasmonean princess, and later succeeded his father as king of the Jews. This was very distasteful to the Jews. He ruled until shortly after Jesus' birth in 4 B.C. Herod carried on an extensive building program. He rebuilt the Jerusalem temple, making it one of the most magnificent buildings in the world. It was in this temple that Jesus taught and worshiped. It was from the vicious design of Herod that Mary and Joseph fled into Egypt with their young child, Jesus.

The Development of the Messianic Expectancy

The threads of the hope of the coming of the Messiah as they are found entwined with this background of history need to be evaluated. The Dead Sea Scrolls reveal that the hope of the Messianic kingdom reached a new level of expectancy with the establishment of the Qumran society of the Essenes during the rule of the Maccabeans.[17] From the time of the establishment of the monarchy in Israel there appears to have been a growing anticipation of the time when the ideal king would rule in righteousness in Israel and become the redeemer of the nations. The Essenes were highly eschatological in their belief and outlook. They withdrew into the wilderness to help prepare the way of the Lord. They felt they were fulfilling Isaiah 40:3, "Prepare ye the way of the Lord, make straight in the desert a highway for our God." Scholars have differed in their interpretations of Messianic texts in the writings of Israel's prophets. To the Christian, these Messianic predictions were fulfilled in Jesus Christ. There is no concrete evidence, as was at first thought, with the discovery of the Dead Sea Scrolls, that Christianity was based upon or had its origins in the Essene sect.

The prophets of the exile strengthened Messianic expectations in words of comfort such as are found in Isaiah's writings. The fact that Jesus quoted Isaiah 61:1-2 as being fulfilled in him makes it difficult to give such passages any other than Messianic interpretations. John the Baptist strengthened this point of view when he designated Jesus "the lamb of God" (John 1:29-31, in harmony with Isaiah 53:7). The post-exilic prophets proclaimed the coming of the Messiah. Zechariah 9:9-10 gives the Messiah a future worldwide rule. Such was also characteristic of original Messianic expressions (Isaiah 2:1-4; 9:6-7; Psalm 72:8). Late Judaism saw a continuation of these Messianic ideas, coupled with the hope of the resurrection. The Messiah was to be of the lineage of David. He would arise to rule in righteousness and would free Israel. Jesus had to combat this narrow nationalistic concept. Apocryphal and apocalptic literature contain expressions such as the Son of Man and the Son of David designating the looked-for Messiah. Jesus chose the former in self-designation. An excellent example in non-canonical literature is to be found in the

Psalms of Solomon, chapters 17 and 18. Jews today still look forward to the coming of the Messiah, who will sit on the throne of David. Christians now look forward to his second coming in order to consummate the establishment of the kingdom of God.

The Conditions of the World at the Time of Christ's Birth

George P. Fisher, one-time professor of ecclesiastical history at Yale University, wrote: "The condition of the civilized nations at the birth of Christ was propitious for the introduction and spread of a new religion in its nature adapted to all mankind." After setting forth a brief summary of the influence of Greek culture and Roman law on the ancient world, Fisher stated:

There was a craving, more or less obscurely felt, for a new regenerating force that should enter with life-giving efficacy into the heart of ancient society; the age was ripe and ready for the incoming of such an effort. In the fulness of time God sent forth his Son.[18]

In order to properly understand such an analysis which is representative of conclusions reached by many other biblical scholars, historians, and theologians, it is necessary to appraise three major points of world history, predating and leading up to the time of the birth of Christ. These involve elements and influences of Greek philosophy, Roman law, and the monotheistic concepts of Hebrew religion. At the time of Christ's birth all three were more or less in a state of decadence. They lacked interrelating unity and no one of these influences possessed vitality by itself to undergird a highly moralistic world society.

For centuries the Hebrews had struggled for national freedom while their prophets had combated pagan influences from the outside world. Following the overthrow of Persia by the Greeks, Judaism under Hellenising influences had been greatly weakened; it was saved from complete collapse by the Maccabean revolt. New hopes which had arisen during the period of independence under early Maccabean rule were dashed against a demoralizing power struggle which developed in its later leadership. When the Romans took over, Judaism was divided into conflicting sects and political parties. The Idumean Herod the Great shortly thereafter was made king in Palestine. He played a dual role, courting the favor of both Romans and Jews, but contributed nothing to the revival of Jewish religion. Judaism had not been under any influence of prophetic revivalism from the time of Malachi to the preaching of John the Baptist.

Rome had developed a highly moralistic civilization during the time of the Republic. In 46 B.C. under Julius Caesar, the old Republic was replaced by an emperor state. Two years later Julius Caesar was assassinated. Octavius, who was emperor when Christ was born, succeeded in stabilizing the empire politically, but as Rome came in contact with Eastern culture, moral corruption ensued and continued to increase.

In the Greek world the revolutionary philosophies of Socrates, Plato, and Aristotle, pointing more definitely toward a monotheistic concept, destroyed the old mythical ideas of Greek polytheism. However, in the following centuries preceding the birth of Christ the succeeding philosophies of the Stoics, Neo-Platonism, and Epicurianism had done nothing to establish a vital, challenging faith to replace the existing void caused by the loss of faith in mysticism.

Under these conditions the world situation, which could have looked promising for the greatest advancement up to that time in the history of mankind, had reached a fatal stalemate. W. F. Albright has written:

Meanwhile the civilized world had achieved unity and prosperity under Graeco-Roman culture and Roman domination only to discover that its material and intellectual life was so far ahead of its spiritual development that the lack of integration became too great to permit future progress on the old lines. Jesus Christ appeared on the scene, just when Occidental civilization had reached a fatal impasse.[19]

If ever there was a time when it was needful that God should move in world affairs this was surely the time. The time was right for God to send his Son into the world. Jesus gave reinvigoration to Old Testament Judaistic monotheism at the time that it too had reached a fatal impasse. He gave new and vital interpretations to the teachings of the law and the prophets. No period in world history was more opportune nor presented a greater need for the coming of Jesus Christ.

The Spread of Christianity

Christianity sprang from Judaism by God's redemptive act in Jesus Christ. During the long period of history which we have reviewed, God was preparing everywhere for the reception of the New Testament faith.

Jewish contacts and relationships spread into all parts of the known world. Especially from the time of the exile forward, Jews by captivity and for cultural and economic reasons moved into all major centers of the world. In many Gentile cities, synagogues had been established in which the Christian apostles preached and taught. Persecution had its influence on the spread of Christianity. The first Gentile Christian church at Antioch was established because of migrations of Jewish Christians from Jerusalem during a time of persecution.

Hellenism made its greatest contribution in preparation for the spread of Christianity in the establishment of a universal language in which the gospel could be preached and written. Though the Romans persecuted the Christians, they assisted in the spread of the Christian gospel by establishing peace in a militarily unified world. In this united world the apostles of Christ could pass freely from nation to nation; this would not have been possible in previous centuries. Within three centuries Christianity had been declared a legal religion in the Roman world. Constantine in A.D. 325 called and presided at the first Nicean council to settle theological disputes which had arisen within Christianity. As emporer and at least as a nominal Christian, he saw the need to unify the Christian church for political reasons essential to the unity of the state. God prepared the world beforehand for the great Christian event. The time had fully come for God to send forth his Son.

---

1. George A. Buttrick, *Christ and History* (New York and Nashville: Abingdon Press), pp. 20, 27.

2. Merle D'Aubigne, *History of the Reformation of the Sixteenth Century* (London: Ward, Lock and Company), Preface, p. iv.
3. *Christ and History*, p. 63.
4. *Ibid.*, p. 39.
5. *Ibid.*, p. 13.
6. Max I. Dimont, *Jews, God and History*, a Signet book published by the New American Library, p. 14 ff.
7. See Samuel Noah Kramer, *History Begins at Sumer* (New York: Doubleday Anchor Books).
8. For lineage of priesthood see Doctrine and Covenants 83:2.
9. John Bright, *A History of Israel*, Westminster Press, p. 113.
10. *Ibid.*, p. 37.
11. Walter Harrelson, *Interpreting the Old Testament*, p. 177.
12. H. I. Hester, *The Heart of the Hebrew History* (Liberty, Missouri: Quality Press), p. 155.
13. See *The Mysterious Numbers of the Hebrew Kings*, pp. 39-52.
14. *The Interpreter's Dictionary of the Bible*, Vol. 1, p. 77.
15. See *A History of Israel*, pp. 397-399.
16. See Flavius Josephus, *Antiquities of the Jews*, (Boston: D. Lothrop and Company), p. 323, or Book XII, Ch. VI:2.
17. G. Earnest Wright, *Biblical Archaeology* (Philadelphia and London: Westminster Press), pp. 235-236.
18. George P. Fisher, *History of the Christian Church* (New York: Charles Scribner's Sons), pp. 7-8.
19. William F. Albright, *From the Stone Age to Christianity* (Garden City, New York: Doubleday Anchor Books), p. 403.

THE ATONEMENT AS THE 6 EXPRESSION OF DIVINE LOVE

In this chapter we shall consider the atonement as a Christian doctrine. It is inseparable from the eternal design of God in our behalf. Since God at the appropriately chosen time sent forth his Son into the world, an event divinely planned beforehand and divinely executed according to that plan, it is important that we understand his purpose for doing so and what was achieved by it. Also we must understand something of the process by which this purpose was achieved.

Early Christian Thinking About the Atonement

It seems fairly evident that theologians have found it difficult to establish an explicitly defined dogma of the atonement. Quotations are attributed to Jesus and interpretations expressed on New Testament writings, but these have appeared to many theologians as somewhat fragmented.[1] Early post-apostolic Christian writers were more concerned with establishing a clear Christology and defining the doctrine of the Trinity.[2] From the second century onward efforts were made to establish a dogma of the atonement, especially as relating to the purposes and merits of the death of Jesus. The results are comprised in a number of theories, among which were the classical idea, the Latin theory, the ransom theory, and the satisfaction theory.

The classical theory, Aulen tells us, was never developed concretely, but remained in the state of an idea.[3] The essence of this idea is that God is reconciled with the world only because he himself, through Christ, reconciles the world with himself and himself with the world. Here the emphasis seems to be solely on God's action by his grace, a one-sided proposition in which the demands of justice are not satisfied.[4] The Latin theory is quite different. Satisfaction is offered by Christ as the sinless man on behalf of sinful humanity. God is still the director in that he planned the atonement, but Christ as man voluntarily acts on our behalf.

The ransom theory is based upon Jesus' statement in Mark 10:43-45 and Matthew 20:26-28, "For even the Son of man came, not to be ministered unto, but to minister, and to give his life a ransom for many." The death of Christ was the ransom paid to purchase our freedom from the bondage of sin. But the question has to be dealt with, to whom was the ransom paid? Since sin, by the fall, placed us in bondage to the devil, God must have bargained with Satan to purchase our freedom by the death of Christ. Therefore, according to this theory the ransom was paid to the devil. This ransom theory appears to have been introduced by Irenaeus. Origen went so far as to proclaim that God tricked Satan into believing that by Christ's death, Satan would be conqueror and would hold Christ too in bondage.[5] Strange and even shocking as it may seem, this theory became the prevailing teaching of the Christian church down to the twelfth century.

Anselm, archbishop of Canterbury in the late eleventh century, advanced the theory that the Adamic transgression and human disobedience were an offense to God, for which the demands of justice must be satisfied.[6] God's honor, which had been debased by human sin, found satisfaction in the death of Christ.[7] Anselm's idea at least was a breakthrough on the previously widely accepted hideous ransom theory. Peter Abelard, a contemporary of Anselm (1070-1142), challenged Anselm's satisfaction theory with what seems to be closer to New Testament teaching. The key to Abelard's thinking was that people were moved to repentance as they recognized the suffering and death of the innocent Son of God. Thus the forgiveness of God was invoked and granted.[8]

The preceding is about the briefest possible survey of the history of the doctrine of the atonement from the second to the twelfth century. However, the battle of ideas and theories has continued through the Reformation to our time. Space will not permit further historical consideration here. It is interesting to note, nevertheless, that the ransom theory was advanced in an age when the freedom of slaves could be purchased for a ransom; and that the Anselm satisfaction theory came forth in the age of chivalry, where when people felt their honor was at stake in face of insult, they must demand satisfaction—usually by dueling with offenders. Thus the culture of the time had its influence on the formulation of dogma.

102

The Meaning and Nature of Atonement

The word *atonement* is used only once in the earlier English translations of the New Testament (Romans 5:11) and not at all in the Revised Standard Version which substitutes "reconciliation" for "atonement" in this passage. Nevertheless, the existence of the doctrine of atonement is affirmed in its historical background, as well as in the New Testament teachings of our Lord and the apostles. Atonement (at one ment with God), thus became an adopted Christian theological term. However, the word has wide usage in the Old Testament, where teachings set forth expiation by sacrifice. There is little doubt that the use of the term *atonement* in Christian doctrine obtains its derivation from the Old Testament, but it is used to designate a principle of doctrine clearly involved in the ministry of our Lord. Atonement is more than a teaching; it is an act—an act of divine intervention on our behalf based squarely on the love of God for his created children.

The unassailable character of the love of God involves our reconciliation to God and God with us (II Corinthians 5:19) which we cannot achieve by ourselves, and God cannot achieve without us. Hence in order to understand the atonement we must begin with the doctrine of incarnation. Infinite and finite attributes were joined in the earthly existence of Jesus. The divine nature was revealed through him, who at the same time was both human and divine. In this way God was able to manifest his omnipotent love by a medium comprehensible to us who, though totally finite and by sin estranged from God, were created in his image and likeness, with the potential to become wholly his. Jesus, who was with the Father and shared fully in his glory from before the foundation of the world, became incarnate (John 17:5) that by his own willingness and by the will of the Father reconciliation might be effected.

God loved the world. He did not send Jesus into the world to condemn the world but that the world through him might be saved (John 3:14-17). Jesus came in the flesh, from eternity into time, to do for us that which we could never do for ourselves. Dr. Findley B. Edge has written:

If the nature of man is such that in his "natural" condition he is alienated from God, then the fundamental need of man is to be brought into a saving relationship with God. Since man cannot solve his human predicament within himself, his salvation must come from a source outside himself. God has acted uniquely in Jesus Christ in behalf of sinful man: thus man must come into a saving relationship with God through Christ.[9]

Sin and its concomitant death are our two ultimate enemies. These had to be encountered in totality in order that this relationship might have everlasting value for us. No one who is human has the power to forgive his or her sins, or to bring to pass his or her own resurrection. For this reason the atonement must include the life of Christ, who is the only begotten of the Father in the flesh, his death upon the cross, and his resurrection. Otherwise we would not have the assurance of forgiveness and the hope of immortality and eternal life through the resurrection. The incarnate Son of God had to meet temptation, suffer, and die in order to be resurrected victoriously over sin and death. All three—incarnation, suffering temptation and death, and the resurrection—were essential for our salvation. Thus, the very nature of the atonement is that God, in Christ, took upon himself human nature, suffered as we suffer, and arose victoriously. By this process every obstacle to the possibility of human redemption was removed through divine action. God did for us that which we never could do for ourselves. Sin demands divine action or we perish and God fails.

Atonement as Divine Counteraction

God acts upon foreknowledge in dealing with situations as they have occurred and as they are now. Hence, there is no point in speculating on what might have happened if Adam and Eve hadn't fallen to temptation. We also must realize that the human problem called original sin is a constantly recurring event. The evidences of sin are all about us. No arguments are needed to prove its existence. The history of mankind indicates that human nature remains unchanged in a changing world. This fact in itself provides evidence that the fall is an ever present reality, or in other words the fall has been perpetuated in evil deeds to the present day. The most devastating thing about this fact is that we live far beneath our potentiality. The whole world is an inestimable distance from reaching the full measure of its God-given potentiality. John W. Rushton used to say, "Sin is the measurement of the distance between man and God." Sin alienates us from God. It alienates us from our own better selves, and it often places enmity between us and others.

There are at least three levels of human experience at which sin has taken a devastating toll. The first of these is at the personal level. This is the point at which the fall began, and it has been perpetuated at this level. The fall is not only a historical event; it is an ever present reality and it will be so until the work of redemption has been wholly consummated. The prophet Ezekiel made it clear that people are accountable for their own sins and not those of others (Ezekiel 18:20). Personal sins may be graduated downward, all the way from settling for the second best to total self-destruction.

Second, sin affects the society in which we live. This is experienced in interpersonal, intercommunal, and international relationships. Those who have seen the Berlin wall separating West from East Berlin, even though they may not have been witnesses to any of the atrocities committed there become aware of how human deeds separate people from each other. Such separation is based on hate, and it is most destructive. Race rioting, conditions in the ghettos, sexual perversion and promiscuity, and lust for power have become diseases of our present society. They threaten its security and even now they project the threat of total annihilation.

Third, the whole world of history has been adversely affected by the evil deeds of nations. Never was this truth brought more vividly to my attention than when I looked upon the ruins of ancient Rome, visible at the Roman Forum and at the Colosseum. Here crumbled palaces and walls, broken statues, broken pieces of art, and broken altars are strewed about to remind us of the mighty empire which is no more. The same thing may be said of a series of world empires beginning with ancient Sumer and Egypt. That which caused the downfall of ancient empires and nations both small and great, including Israel and Judah, may be described with one word—sin.

The sins that destroyed Egypt, Israel, Assyria, Babylon, Persia, Greece, and Rome are the same as those which threaten us with destruction at these three levels in our world today. This is a dilemma with which we have never demonstrated the capacity or the will to successfully cope. No human system ever has proved itself adequate to cope with this persistent predicament. Since we cannot extricate ourselves from our plight, it is imperative that we successfully deal with this self-imposed evil and overcome it at all levels of our existence and relationships. Lust and hate produced the dilemma. Only love can conquer it. It is comforting to know that God has prepared the way beforehand for that which he knew would take place.

Thomas Hayward wrote, "The world's a theater, the earth a stage, which God and nature do with actors fill."[10] Because people had neither the ingenuity nor the power to save themselves or the world, God entered earth's stage early in history, warning beforehand of the consequences of yielding to temptation. He gave such warnings to Adam and to Cain (Gen. 2:16-17; 4:6-7). These were warnings before the event. But as Adam and Eve fell and humanity continued to sin, God proceeded to manifest redeeming grace. He called the patriarchs, beginning with Abraham, to a special work involving a covenant and promise to all people (Gen. 12:1-3). He sent prophets among his covenant people to proclaim his word and his will, calling them to penitent living

(Micah 6:6-8). These ministered under the law as given by God, while people encountered him on history's stage. Thus, the acts of God's love and concern are portrayed for us. "But when the fullness of the time was come, God sent forth his Son, made of woman, made under the law, to redeem them that were under the law, that we might receive the adoption of sons" (Gal. 4:4-5). Under this arrangement the Son of God became incarnate in order to play the leading role in our redemption. Since God placed us in the world, where we are subject to the powers of evil, God, in Christ, has taken upon himself the responsibility for our redemption.

Atonement and Human Response

Persons must enter with God into the drama of redemption. Efficacious atonement is not, by any means, a dramatic monologue. Our participation in the act of our redemption is possible by the grace of God through Jesus Christ (Romans 5:8-11). Jesus began his ministry by preaching the kingdom of God and calling for repentance (Mark 1:12-13). Our response must be one of trust and obedience. We must be willing to risk our lives in the hands of God. In so doing, our wills must become reconciled to the will of God, for *our* willfulness is at the very heart of our sinning. Thus, sin is basically rebellion against our loving Creator. Whether the sin is committed knowledgeably or ignorantly, the act is done by the human will and not by the will of God. James wrote:

Let no man say when he is tempted, I am tempted of God; for God cannot be tempted with evil, neither tempteth he any

108

man; but every man is tempted when he is drawn away of his own lust, and enticed. Then when lust hath conceived it bringeth forth sin; and sin, when it is finished, bringeth forth death.—James 1:13-15.

This is more than a physical death. It is spiritual death in that sin separates us from God.

Jesus does not require us to fulfill any role in which he himself is unwilling to participate. He gave unreserved allegiance to the will of God. Who is to say that it was any less difficult for him to do so as the Son of God in the flesh than it is for us? Matthew informs us that three times in his agony at Gethsemane Jesus prayed, "Oh, my Father, if it be possible, let this cup pass from me." Each time he concluded his prayer with the victorious expression of obedience, "Nevertheless not as I will, but as thou wilt" (Matt. 26:36-41). The cross is the symbol of Christ's victory over the flesh. The resurrection is the guarantee of Jesus' triumph over death.

These victories over the flesh and death, and the meaning of human obedience to God, are symbolized in the ordinance of baptism.

Know ye not that so many of us as were baptized into Jesus Christ were baptized into his death? Therefore we are buried with him by baptism into death; that like as Christ was raised up from the dead by the glory of the Father, even so we also should walk in the newness of life. For if we have been planted together in the likeness of his death, we shall be also in the likeness of his resurrection; knowing this, that our old man is crucified with him, that the body of sin might be destroyed, that henceforth we should not sin. For he that is dead to sin is freed from sin.—Romans 6:3-7.

Salvation for us is the work of God. I have already affirmed that God in Christ has done for us that which we never could have done for ourselves. But in order to remain under God's grace, wholly united with him in Jesus Christ, we must faithfully continue to manifest works of righteousness in our daily living. Jesus said to his disciples:

I am the vine, ye are the branches. He that abideth in me, and I in him, the same bringeth forth much fruit; for without me ye can do nothing. If a man abide not in me, he is cast forth as a branch, and is withered; and men gather them, and they are cast into the fire, and they are burned.... If ye keep my commandments, ye shall abide in my love; even as I have kept my Father's commandments, and abide in his love.—John 15:5-6, 10.

Our role is to yield faithful obedience always to that which Jesus has commanded. This principle is expressed in the following words: "And because iniquity shall abound, the love of many shall wax cold. But he that remaineth steadfast, and is not overcome, the same shall be saved" (Matt. 24:10-11).

Atonement as Sacrifice in Our Redemption

Paul wrote, "You are bought with a price" (I Cor. 6:20). Paul was saying Christ has purchased our freedom from the enslavement of sin in a manner similar to that which, under certain circumstances and for a price, a slave's freedom could be purchased. But this price frees us only from the bondage of sin; now we are obligated, as belonging to Christ, to continue in his service. In Acts 20:28 Paul admonished the elders at Miletus to "feed the church of God which he hath purchased with his own blood." If we regard the church as

110

those redeemed by Christ, the price was paid in his own blood. Paul elsewhere indicates the efficacy of the blood of Christ on our behalf. John wrote: "The blood of Jesus Christ his Son, cleanses us from all sin" (I John 1:7).

The idea of expiation and redemption by the offering of sacrifice persists throughout both the Old and New Testaments. Whatever variations of meaning there may be between sacrifice and redemption in the Old Testament, in the New Testament it is clear that the eternal and supreme sacrifice was made once for all in the death of Jesus Christ upon the cross. In the light of this fact one can neither ignore nor evade the validity of sacrifice in the plan of redemption.

No aspect of atonement is more difficult to understand and explain than that which deals with this element. Since the idea of sacrifice is prevalent in both testaments of the Bible, theological controversy has persisted as to the nature and meaning of sacrifice in relation to the atonement. The following is very helpful at this point:

Wherefore, redemption, cometh in and through the holy Messiah; for he is full of grace and truth. Behold, he offereth himself a sacrifice for sin, to answer the ends of the law, unto all those who have a broken heart and a contrite spirit; and unto none else can the ends of the law be answered. Wherefore, how great the importance to make these things known unto the inhabitants of the earth, that they may know that there is no flesh that can dwell in the presence of God, save it be through the merits, and mercy, and grace of the holy Messiah, who layeth down his life according to the flesh, and taketh it again by the power of the Spirit, that he may bring to pass the resurrection of the dead, being the first that should rise. Wherefore, he is the first fruits unto God, inasmuch as he shall make intercession for all the children of men; and they

111

that believe in him, shall be saved.[11]

A number of questions may arise which seem to have no answer. Is sin so terrible as to demand so much to make forgiveness and salvation possible? Is God so demanding that he required so much in order that he might be appeased or reconciled? Is justice so exacting that God had to pay a ransom to the devil, who by the fall of man held him as hostage? If these questions are valid, why such a cruel, horrible ordeal as the crucifixion of the Son of God? By reading and meditating upon the preceding quotation, including its entire context, one may see that all such questions are really unrelated to the main issue. The issue is centered in what sin has done to our relationship with God and what God has done to reestablish that broken relationship. It was not God or anything he had done or demanded that nailed Jesus to the cross. It was a sinful world full of hate and violence which did this. Here God himself suffered for our sins. This was no ransom paid to the devil. As Gustaf Aulen states, "God's sacrifice of himself was offered to himself in Jesus Christ."[12] This was done for our sake that we might be reconciled to God, and not that God should be appeased or reconciled to us (II Cor. 5:17-19). God, in Christ, gave himself to us for our sakes because we need his redeeming love and grace in order to bring about our reconciliation to him.

This is an entirely different approach to atonement than those which are made by attempts at finite rationalization. Basically, the atonement is infinite and eternal action. It does not subscribe ultimately to finite measurements or limitations. Even though the Word became flesh in Jesus Christ, he still retained his divine nature. Therefore, we understand the atonement only by an encounter with God through the Holy Spirit. In this kind of experience we know it is real and that forgiveness and redemption are real. The eternal qualities essential to complete atonement were retained and demonstrated in the resurrection of Christ. Paul stated to the Corinthians, some of whom were arguing that there is no resurrection: "If Christ be not raised, your faith is vain; ye are yet in your sins" (I Cor. 15:17). In Romans 5:10 Paul makes it clear that we are reconciled to God by the death of Jesus Christ, and we shall be saved by his life.

Atonement is the divine process of reconciliation. Love is the foundation of redemption. Jesus taught us even to love our enemies. Will God do less than this? Sin placed us at enmity with God, but this did not stop him from loving us. Furthermore God did not force the crucifixion upon Jesus. He laid down his life voluntarily. The pre-crucifixion events demonstrate this truth. Jesus "steadfastly set his face to go to Jerusalem," even though he knew that it meant death to do so. Only Christ, who had the power over life and death, could manifest the love of God adequately to redeem sinners.

Therefore doth my Father love me, because I lay down my life that I might take it again. No man taketh it from me but I lay it down of myself. I have power to lay it down, and I have power to take it again. This commandment have I received of my Father.—John 10:17-18.

God and Christ equally love mankind so much that the plan of redemption was fully agreed upon by them mutually. J. G. Whittier wrote:

The Eternal Goodness

I know not what the future hath
Of marvel or surprise,
Assured alone that life and death
His mercy underlies. . . .

I know not where his islands left
Their fronded palms in air
I only know I cannot drift
Beyond his love and care.[13]

Atonement is God's action to redeem us from our self-indulgence to become that which God purposes by his eternal will and love.

---

1. See the following citations: Gustaf Aulen, *Christus Victor* (New York: Macmillan Company), chapter 1; Vincent Taylor, *The Atonement in New Testament Teaching* (London: Epworth Press), pp. 11-13; Hastings Rashdall, *The Idea of Atonement in Christian Theology* (New York: Macmillan), pp. 3-5; Paul Tillich, *Systematic Theology* (Chicago: Harper and Row), Vol. 2, p. 170; *The Interpreter's Dictionary of the Bible*, Vol. 1, p. 312 par. 6 f; E.Y. Mullins, *The Christian Religion in Its Doctrinal Expression* (Nashville: Broadman Press), p. 304.
2. *Christus Victor*, p. 1.
3. *Ibid.*, p. 157.
4. *Ibid.*, pp. 145-146.
5. *The Interpreter's Dictionary of the Bible*, Vol. 1, p. 312.
6. *The Idea of Atonement in Christian Theology*, p. 323.
7. *Ibid.*, p. 350 f.
8. *Ibid.*, pp. 358-359.
9. Findley B. Edge, *A Quest for Vitality in Religion* (Nashville: Broadman Press), p. 156.
10. John Bartlett, *Familiar Quotations* (New York: Blue Ribbon Books), p. 69.
11. Book of Mormon, II Nephi 1:71-77.
12. *Christus Victor*, p. 77.
13. James Dalton Morrison, Ed., *Masterpieces of Religious Verse* (New York: Harper Brothers). From the poem "The Eternal Goodness" by J. G. Whittier, p. 69.

SECTION 11

**EXPECTATIONS
AND HOPES OF
THE KINGDOM
OF GOD**

THE KINGDOM OF GOD: IDEALISM OR REALISM?

Idealism Versus Realism

E. Stanley Jones tells of a conversation which he had with a highly intelligent actress in Russia in which she said: "I suppose you are a religious man?" Jones replied in the affirmative. "You want God to hold your hand," said the actress as she took his hand in an endeavor to demonstrate that religion made him weak, dependent, and created a lack of self-reliance. Jones described religion as adequacy, not weakness. The actress then commented, "I suppose you are an idealist?" Again, though Jones hesitated, he replied, "I suppose I am." The actress abruptly ended the conversation with the word "Au revoir. I am a realist."[1] With a great deal of consternation, this renowned missionary began to search for answers as to whether Jesus was actually a realist. The results of his work in this regard are contained in his book, *Is the Kingdom of God Realism.*

In each of the words idealism and realism, "ism" is a suffix. This means that we are dealing with the marginal difference between the significance of the words *ideal* and *real* as they relate to the kingdom of God.

Truth and Reality

Since truth and reality are in many ways synonymous, one may well pose Pilate's question to Jesus: "What is truth?" (John 18:38). The following is a good summarization of the nature of truth: "Truth is knowledge of things as they are, and as they were, and as they are to come."[2] We may build our meritorious ideals on the reality of such knowledge. However, if our ideals are not undergirded by the truth, they may be meaningless or even destructive. For instance, Nietzsche's philosophy of the ruthless use of power to produce his superman and his ideals concerning the emergence of the super race destroy all that is ennobling in both divine and human natures. He regarded Christianity as being the very opposite of his ideals. To him Christianity arose and grew among the poor, whom Nietzsche regarded as being weak and therefore unworthy to survive.[3] The philosophy of Jesus expressed in John 12:8, "For the poor ye have always with you," is factual and morally realistic in the sense that they ought not be permitted to perish as having no value because they are poor.

Again, adverting to the intelligent Russian actress, what did she mean by saying, "I am a realist"? Burnett Hillman Streeter states that Marxist Communism has officially adopted a dialectical materialism as contrasted to mechanical materialism. The dialectical materialism implies a logical or theoretical premise, whereas mechanical materialism implies no planned process.

Materialism asserts that nothing but matter is ultimately real . . . dialectical materialism asserts that the character of the

117

universe is such that all things, whether in inanimate nature or in the evolution of human history, move in accordance with a certain rhythm or law to which the name of dialectic is given. This dialectic rhythm is of such nature that it necessarily results in progress—the conflict of opposites leading to a new and higher synthesis.[4]

This adopted definition of Marxist Communism makes of it a sort of religion without God. The whole matter here boils down to the question as to whether realism is confined exclusively to that which is material or whether it also has justifiable spiritual aspects.

Truth and Spirit

A number of important questions arise out of this query: (1) Is there a spiritual realm or are all things solely material in nature? (2) Are the spiritual and material realms independent of each other or are they interrelated? (3) Are there spiritual formulae or laws? (4) If so, what is the nature and function of spiritual law?

These and many other questions are so interrelated that I shall not attempt to deal with each one separately here. We know that law pervades and controls the material universe. Many of these laws have been discovered and their uses learned by humans. We are still in the process of daily discovering new laws in the material realm. Available illustrations at this point are almost innumerable.

Let's take water as a simple example of law. Pure water consists of two parts hydrogen and one part oxygen. No other formula known can produce pure water except H_2O. The same principle pervades all chemical substances. The prevalence of law is confirmed in contemporary scripture:

All kingdoms have a law given: and there are many kingdoms; for there is no space in the which there is no kingdom; and there is no kingdom in which there is no space, either a greater or lesser kingdom. And unto every kingdom is given a law; and unto every law there are certain bounds also, and conditions.[5]

If there is law it is justifiable to concede that there also must be a Maker or Giver of the law. This requires intelligence and a question must be dealt with: Is intelligence merely mechanical and material or is it spiritual? It can hardly be conceded that human intelligence is completely mechanical or material.

Spirit Is Real

I may hold a stone in my hand, in which case I know two things. First, I know the stone is there. Second, I know that it is materialistic in substance and nature. But how do I know this? There is a consciousness within me, which I did not place there, by which I am able to recognize the truth in regard to material things insofar as I am trained to do so. This case, however, assumes that I have the use of sight and feeling. That inner consciousness, which is not materialistic although it operates totally within a material body, gives me perception. The stone, which has no cognitive ability, does not know it is in my hand. My hand communicates the sensation of the presence of the stone to my brain; my eyes communicate its image to my brain; but neither

119

hand nor eyes know the stone is there, although they do communicate its presence through a nervous system. It is my inner consciousness which makes me aware that the stone is in my hand. Then what is that inner consciousness and from whence is it derived?

Job exclaimed: "There is a spirit in man and the inspiration of the Almighty giveth him understanding" (Job 32:8).

The Genesis account of creation informs us that after God had formed man from the dust of the ground, He "breathed into his nostrils the breath of life; and man became a living soul" (Gen. 2:7).

It is important to remember that this was the breath of God which gave life to man (God breathed). This was much more than an act of artificial animation. Breath is used in this passage in its broadest sense. The same root word has many times been translated "spirit" in the Bible. Job, then, was saying that body and spirit make a complete being, and that the Almighty communicates with him through his inner consciousness which is spirit.

I may die holding that stone in my hand, but the body which is made from the ground now is dead and does not know it is there. What has made the difference? The spirit which gives and maintains life within the body has departed. I take the liberty to suggest that this does not mean I cease to exist. It simply means that my body and spirit are no longer combined and that body without the spirit cannot continue to exist in its present form. Is then the spirit, which the corporal man neither originally possesses nor finally controls, any less real than the material body?

Rene Descartes, the well-known French mathematician and philosopher, for years struggled with the problems of relating to reality. Early in life he believed largely what he had been taught, including honor for and belief in God. Then he began to question the foundations of his belief. He meditated upon the proposition as to how one could sort truth from error and know for a certainty what is absolutely true. At this point, Descartes resolved to believe everything false except that which could be proved beyond any question of doubt. By this method he arrived at what he considered to be the foundation of truth. "Cogito ergo sum"—I think therefore I am. Descartes concluded that he could not doubt without thinking and because he could think there must be reality to his being. Further, he concluded that this conscious part of his being must have a Cause beyond himself and more perfect than he. Descartes concluded that he had a soul which could be independent of his body and that its Cause is God.[6] Prudence requires us to recognize that Descartes' method of arriving at truth, while admitting that he manifested deep contrition and honesty, was completely philosophical. While recognizing the soul as coming from God, he later used an existential proposition to make the distinction between the soul (spirit) and body, as he concluded:

. . .My essence consists solely in the fact that I am a thinking thing or a substance whose whole essence or nature is to think. And although I possess a body with which I am very intimately conjoined, yet because, on the one side, I have a clear and distinct idea of myself inasmuch as I am only a thinking and unextended thing, and as, on the other, I possess a distinct idea of body, inasmuch as it is only an extended and unthinking thing, it is certain that this (that is to say, my soul by which I am what I am), is entirely and absolutely distinct from my body, and can exist without it.[7]

Such a conclusion evokes some very vital questions as to the character and structure of that which is material, the human body, and that which is spiritual. First we need to be aware that human reasoning is a finite process and has its limitations. Second, that which is distinctly spiritual is infinite and eternal. Third, He who is and ever shall be eternal, the "I Am" to all generations (Exod. 3:14-15), wills "to bring to pass the immortality and eternal life of man."

Jesus Taught Spiritual Reality

In essence it was a spiritual truth which Jesus shared with Nicodemus when He said, "Except a man be born again he cannot see the kingdom of God" (John 3:3). Nicodemus was baffled because he thought only in material terms. "Can a man enter the second time into his mother's womb and be born?" (John 3:4). At this point, Jesus began to introduce to Nicodemus the relationship of that which is spiritual to the material person.

Except a man be born of water and the Spirit, he cannot enter into the kingdom of God. That which is born of the flesh is flesh, and that which is born of the Spirit is Spirit.... The wind bloweth where it listeth [wills, R.S.V.], and thou hearest the sound thereof, but canst not tell whence it cometh and whither it goeth; so is everyone who is born of the Spirit.— John 3:5-8.

One must be born of the Spirit in order to comprehend that which is spiritual.

122

This is usually an unostentatious force from God working quietly within the soul. But Nicodemus was still puzzled as he inquired, "How can these things be?" Jesus clearly intimated that as a master in Israel Nicodemus should know these things. Then he spoke affirmatively of spiritual realities; he continued the conversation by informing Nicodemus of the nature of Jesus' own mission and of the love and justice of God exhibited in our behalf, assuring him that condemnation rested only upon those who believe not on him. Refusing to love truth he said: "They come not to the light" but "he who obeyeth the truth, the works that he doeth they are of God" (John 3:10-22).

One may derive further understanding in regard to spiritual truth from Jesus' visit with the Samaritan woman at Jacob's well. Jesus was tired and no doubt thirsty as he rested, sitting on the well. It was natural that he should ask the woman who came to the well to draw water to give him a drink. Quite another question perplexed her than that which had troubled Nicodemus. Why should a Jew ask a favor of her, a Samaritan, since Jews in general despised the Samaritans? In answer to her question of concern over this, Jesus used water, a material substance, analogically in regard to eternally spiritual truth. The water which he would give to those who desired and merited it would become a well within them, springing up into everlasting life. When the woman asked Jesus to give her this water, he proceeded to tell her how she had lived with five husbands, and as she had said she had no husband, he told her the man with whom she was then living was not really her husband. Perceiving him to be a prophet, she asked him concerning a question of great controversy between Jews and Samaritans: Should they worship God "in this mountain," Mount Gerizim, or at Jerusalem as the Jews maintained? The summary of Jesus' answer was that the true worshiper must worship the Father in spirit and in truth. Here he synonymously related Spirit and truth. This relationship was affirmed wherein he said: "The Spirit of truth is of God. I am the Spirit of truth."[8]

Truth Is Power

Spirit and truth as reality, quite appropriately, may be used interchangeably. Truth and power may also be used in opposition theologically. Jesus prayed for his disciples, saying, "Sanctify them through thy truth; thy word is truth" (John 17:17). And to Moses, God said concerning creation, "For mine own purpose have I made these things. Here is wisdom, and it remaineth in me. And by the word of my power have I created them, which is mine Only Begotten Son, who is full of grace and truth."[9] These quotations are in full agreement with Hebrews 11:3 which states: "Through faith we understand that the worlds were framed by the word of God, so that things which are seen were not made of things which do appear." Spirit, truth, Word which is Christ, and power may all be equated and are instruments at the use and command of God in the accomplishment of his purpose which is "to bring to pass the immortality and eternal life of man." And eternal life will be fully realized in and through the kingdom of God.

Quoting Zorobabel or Zerubbabel, who returned

from Babylon to Jerusalem under Darius I of Persia to become governor and to give leadership in rebuilding the temple at Jerusalem, Josephus wrote:

I have already demonstrated how powerful women are; but both these women themselves, and the king himself, are weaker than truth: for although the earth be large, and the heaven high, and the course of the sun swift, yet are all these moved according to the will of God, who is true and righteous, for which cause we also ought to esteem truth to be the strongest of all things, and that which is unrighteous is of no force against it. Moreover, all things else that have any strength are mortal, and short-lived, but truth is a thing that is immortal and eternal. It affords us not indeed such a beauty as will wither away by time, nor such riches as may be taken away by fortune, but righteous rules and laws. It distinguishes them from injustice, and puts what is unrighteous to rebuke.[10]

We need to understand the circumstances in which Zerubbabel's comments were made in order to fully appreciate what he said and why he said it. Josephus tells us that after a great feast Darius asked questions of his three guards as to which was the most powerful—wine, kings, women—or whether truth was not the strongest of them all. To the one who made the wisest speech he promised great gifts and honors. The king was so pleased with Zerubbabel's speech that he granted him an additional request. It was thus upon his request that Zerubbabel was permitted to go to Jerusalem to rebuild the temple. Zerubbabel was fully aware that lives must be built upon the spiritual foundation of truth in order that the rebuilding of the Jerusalem temple might have true significance.

Reality in the Scriptures

A basic knowledge of the sacred literature is vital to our true comprehension of God's eternal design for his people. I had an uncle who for years was captain of a Canadian Pacific Railroad ship which ferried trains across the Detroit River. From earlier associations I had judged him to be an atheist. However, during the last visit I had with him, which lasted most of a day, he talked freely about his beliefs. I learned from him that day that he was not skeptical about the existence of God. His quarrel was with the Bible as containing revelation or the word of God. He was skeptical because of what appeared to him to be mythological concepts, human errors, and inconsistencies. One cannot begin to enumerate all of the instances in which such have appeared to occur, let alone deal with each in seeking conciliatory explanations.

However, honest and unbiased scholarship and especially archaeological findings have done much to erase inconsistencies and supposed elements of myth. Through archaeological research and findings, major empires, nations and their cities, and even places of secondary importance mentioned in the Bible are now identifiable. The Rosetta Stone found in Egypt and the engravings on the Behistun rock made by Darius the Great of Persia have given us the keys for translating the ancient languages of Egypt and Mesopotamia. Records have been found which have made available much of the history from New Testament times as far back as 4,000 B.C. In consequence of these findings, we have definite information of peoples and places such as

Sumer, Akkad, the Hittites, Assyria, Babylon, Egypt, Elam or Persia, Canaan, and Phoenecia, etc. Much of the nature of Baal worship, so vigorously opposed by Elijah (I Kings 18:18), has come to light with the discovery in 1929 of the Ras Shamra tablets on the northeastern Mediterranean coast. (Ras Shamra was also called Ugarit.) Thus archaeology has done much to make the scriptures become alive and real. This includes the Book of Mormon in America as well as the Bible in the ancient Near East. I wish to make it clear, however, that archaeological findings illuminate the text rather than offer absolute proof of the veracity of these scriptures. Full acceptance must be by faith. But, then, faith is an essential law of living. "Faith is the assurance of things hoped for, the evidence of things not seen" (Heb. 11:10).

The kingdom of God can be built only by faith in the reality of the principles I have set forth. This requires combined human and divine action. As Paul wrote, "We are laborers together with God" (I Cor. 3:9). The kingdom for which Jesus said we should pray (Matthew 6:11) is a fellowship of saints, here upon the earth, in which the will of God predominates by being fully observed. What can be more realistic than that the will of God shall be done upon earth as it is now being done in heaven? This will be the human situation when his kingdom has fully come. Then it will be more than an ideal toward which to look and hope. It truly will be practical and real when God's people are fully in accord with his will.

1. E. Stanley Jones, *Is the Kingdom of God Realism* (New York and Nashville: Abingdon-Cokesbury Press), p. 13.
2. Doctrine and Covenants 90:4b.
3. See William Durant, *The Story of Philosophy* (New York: Simon and Schuster, 1952), pp. 318-335.
4. Burnett Hillman Streeter, *The God Who Speaks* (New York: The Macmillan Company, 1937), pp. 7-8.
5. Doctrine and Covenants 85:9.
6. Ralph M. Eaton, Ed., *Descartes Selections* (New York: Charles Scribner's Sons), pp. 28-31.
7. *Ibid.*, p. 152.
8. Doctrine and Covenants 90:4c.
9. *Ibid.*, 22:21 a,b.
10. *Antiquities of the Jews*, pp. 230-231 (Book XI, Ch. III, par. 6).

KINGDOM 8 RESOURCES

God and Creation

In the Inspired Version of the Holy Scriptures the earliest stages of creation are related with some additional unique perceptions, yet these do no violence to other translations.[1] God is represented in the first person. He speaks and reveals himself to Moses "concerning this heaven and this earth" (Gen. 1:1 I.V.). Then God introduces himself to Moses by name and tells how he proceeded with the creation (Gen. 1:2 I.V.).

I am the Beginning and the End; the Almighty God. By mine Only Begotten I created these things. Yea, in the beginning I created the heaven, and the earth upon which thou standest. And the earth was without form, and void; and I caused darkness to come up upon the face of the deep. And my Spirit moved upon the face of the waters, for I am God. And I, God, said, Let there be light, and there was light. And I, God, saw the light, and that light was good. And I, God, divided the light from the darkness. And I, God, called the light day, and the darkness I called night. And this I did by the word of my power; and it was done as I spake. And the evening and the morning were the first day.—Genesis 1:2-8 I.V.

Our concern here is not with the effort to define the word *beginning* except as it relates to God's eternal action. The key point is that beginning represents God's initial movement toward the definite yet mysterious achievement of creation. In all versions of the Bible, the absence of a definite date or a definable chronology for creation points to the fact that when creation took place is by no means of primary importance to our understanding. Nor is it essential that exactly how it happened should be spelled out for us. God is announced as having eternal Being. He ordered that which took place and still is engaged in the purposeful, ongoing process of creation. Some call this evolution but it is not without purpose. An evolutionary process of creation without an intelligent Director would be meaningless and devoid of design.

God is the primary source and cause of creation. By his own existence and power he created all things necessary to the fulfillment of his purpose in our existence upon the earth. This creation is God's earthly kingdom. He gave men and women dominion over it. Both external matter and internal endowments are the Creator's gifts with which to fulfill his divine purpose in humanity. He is moving, in history and in the lives of those who receive and obey his gospel, to translate this earthly kingdom into a celestial dominion.

However, we need to perceive that God is not confined to that which now is humanity's domain. He is working his plan and design in other areas than those which are known to us. But a great question will persist: How much of that which in God's wisdom and good judgment is unknown to us still relates to his eternal design for us now, and hereafter? Perhaps the best answer to this question was expressed by Paul in his interpretation of Isaiah 64:4: "Eye hath not seen, nor ear heard, neither have entered into the heart of man, the things which God hath prepared for them that love him" (I Cor. 2:9). Nevertheless, all that God has prepared is not left entirely to the imagination of those who love and serve him. Under the influence of the Holy Spirit, the human mind and heart at times may be liberated sufficiently from their finite limitations to discern and understand truth which pertains to the Infinite, but which otherwise is hidden in the mysteries of the Almighty. Significantly the same apostle states in that which immediately follows: "But God hath revealed them unto us by his Spirit; for the Spirit searcheth all things, yea, the deep things of God. For what man knoweth the things of man, save the spirit of man which is in him? even so the things of God knoweth no man, except he has the Spirit of God" (I Cor. 2:10-11). The gift of a spiritually liberated consciousness in this kind of divine self-disclosure is truly a kingdom resource.

It is quite evident from the Genesis account, no matter what translation one may wish to use, that God was not acting alone in creation. This is borne out wherein he said: "Let *us* make man in our image, after our likeness." The Inspired Version does not represent *us* and *our* as a council of heavenly beings to whom God was speaking. Rather God was speaking to his Only Begotten, and it is in God and Christ's image and likeness that we are made (Gen. 1:27, 29 I.V.). Furthermore, when darkness reigned in a chaotic void, "The Spirit of God moved upon the face of the waters" (Gen. 1:2 K.J.V.; Gen. 1:5 I.V. . . . . "The Spirit of God was moving over the face of the waters" [Gen. 1:2 R.S.V.]). All three versions are in full agreement in regard to the movement of the Spirit of God. The Inspired Version represents a holy union of the Father, Son, and Holy Spirit working harmoniously in eternity, under the direction of the Father. "Father, Son, and Holy Ghost are one God, infinite and eternal, without end."[2] Such boundless unity of action should be an absolute as well as a symbolic resource for building the kingdom of God.

All three comprising the one God participated significantly in the order of creation. His presence and action are most important to our faith in and knowledge of God and of things as they are or are yet to be. It is comforting and should be strengthening to our faith to have the testimony that all three persons, comprising one God, acted unitedly to initiate the kingdom of God from the earliest beginnings.

Science has demonstrated repeatedly that light is vital to all life. Now it is believed that light is also the source of all energy. By his unfathomable intelligence, power, and will the Creator spoke to say: "Let there be light," and light prevailed where darkness was reigning. It should be obvious to all believers that light and truth are indispensably annexed. The following analysis of light and truth is both spiritual and scientific.

This Comforter is the promise which I give unto you of eternal life, even the glory of the celestial kingdom; which glory is that of the church of the Firstborn, even of God, the holiest of all, through Jesus Christ, his Son; he that ascended up on high, as also he descended below all things, in that he comprehended all things, that he might be in all and through all things, the light of truth, which truth shineth. This is the light of Christ. As also he is in the sun, and the light of the sun, and the power thereof by which it was made. As also he is in the moon, and is the light of the moon, and the power thereof by which it was made. As also the light of the stars, and the power thereof by which they were made. And the earth also, and the power thereof, even the earth upon which you stand. And the light which now shineth, which giveth you light, is through him who enlighteneth your eyes, which is the same light that quickeneth your understandings; which light proceedeth forth from the presence of God, to fill the immensity of space. The light which is in all things; which giveth life to all things; which is the law by which all things are governed; even the power of God who sitteth upon his throne, who is in the bosom of eternity, who is in the midst of all things.[3]

Light and truth will stand on their own merits regardless of what our conceptions may be. In no way will my thinking or that of anyone else alter the facts of truth. But what a blessing it is to be able to clearly comprehend, and to interpret beneficially, the principles of truth when we are exposed to them. The preceding quotation beautifully associates the light by which we see with our eyes and by which our understandings are quickened with the Comforter (Holy Spirit), with God and Jesus Christ his Son, as the power of God by which all things were made and are governed. This interpretation of light makes of it a major resource of his kingdom. And think, "light proceedeth forth from the presence of God to fill the immensity of space." Who can define the dimensions of space or proclaim where it does not exist? Truly we may declare with the psalmist: "I will praise thee; for I am fearfully and wonderfully made; marvellous are thy works; and that my soul knoweth right well" (Psalm 139:14 K.J.V., I.V.).

God's Will and Action on Our Behalf

God has acted on man's behalf in creation and from creation forward. There is no doubt that his action was divinely ordained beforehand. The whole of creation portrays both the resourcefulness and the purposefulness of God; it also manifests his matchless intelligence, power, and glory. The axiom, "This is my work and my glory, to bring to pass the immortality and eternal life of man," had its origin long before it found expression in the recorded word of God.[4] The principle expressed arises out of the nature of God and is no less eternal than is he. The Genesis account affirms clearly that each phase of creation was pronounced good by the Creator. God makes no mistakes. He does all things well and according to his predetermined purpose and everlasting will. The ultimate and greatest attribute of God is his goodness. Without his goodness there could be no hope for our future. The kingdom of God is to be composed of persons who have become good in the likeness of God's goodness.

The kingdom of God is our God-given environment in which to achieve, according to his purpose and by his grace, immortality and eternal life. God has provided for us and within us the resources essential to the achievement of his will. It must not be assumed, however, that because God has an everlasting will, and plans beforehand the means to accomplish his will, that all things which happen do so because God has willed it. It has been argued that God predestines or wills all that happens on the premise of his unassailable foreknowledge. Therefore, since God has a perfect foreknowledge, that which happens must be in consequence of the immutability of his foreknowledge. This idea has been extended by some to mean that God predestines some souls to be saved and others to be damned without regard to merit. This idea is inconsistent and immoral even though it was advanced and upheld by such great Christian theologians as St. Augustine and John Calvin.[5]

Martin Luther implied that we are unable to act by our own free will but are in bondage to the will of God. He attempted to rationalize this idea as bondage rather than freedom of the human will by distinguishing between the revealed or preached word of God as found in the scriptures and the inscrutable or unrevealed and unfathomable will of God into which it is not our right to inquire.[6]

God's Investments in Us

God not only created the universe adequate to human physical needs but he invested himself in us so as to have made us in his image and after his likeness. In Genesis 1:26 K.J. it is stated, "And God said, Let us make man in our image, after our likeness." The Inspired Version of the Holy Scriptures attributes the pluralism of "us" and "our" to "mine Only Begotten, which was with me from the beginning" (Genesis 1:27 I.V.). This interpretation is most enlightening, not only in that it designates the eternal unity between God and Christ prior to and in the creative endeavors but also implies clearly the divine intent that we also should be joined with them in like unity. The potential of our unity with God and

Christ in the kingdom of God relationship existed in the processes of creation and with the Creator.

These attributes of the divine nature invested in us are the resources with which we have been endowed, and they are to be employed in making the kingdom a reality here upon the earth. In the sermon on the mount Jesus challenged his disciples in these words: "Seek ye first to build up the kingdom of God, and to establish his righteousness." This commandment was prefaced by the statement, "Seek not the things of this world," and was followed with the promise that all other needful things "shall be added unto you" (Matthew 6:38 I.V.). Above all else, the kingdom of God enterprises have prior claim upon us. His kingdom shall become a reality only when we fully cooperate with our Maker in the use of the giftedness which he has bequeathed us. The establishment of the kingdom of God is not a separate sort of divine miracle in which he does it all and we do nothing. It is an act in which God, by his own image and likeness in us, shares with us the challenges, the work, and the glory of our achievement. Neither is the building up of the kingdom of God an objective to be sought solely by human activism. The human race has demonstrated constantly its inadequacy for the task of shaping its utopian existence.

Human Progress Is Inadequate

Emil Brunner has aptly pointed out that Western humanity is today experiencing an acute sense of hopelessness. He further declares that this hopelessness began as the Western European man, from the time of the Renaissance forward, developed confidence in his own powers to control and to construct his future. And he further states, "That man is very far from being the unqualified arbiter of his future."[7] Brunner discusses at length the futility of belief and trust in human progress. He states:

Modern man, who, for the sake of his freedom emancipated himself from God and became godless, thus became inevitably the destroyer of the divine order of creation, the destroyer of life and finally the destroyer of himself. The greater the resources which progress places in his hands, the more dreadful must be his work of destruction. This is the lesson which humanity has had to learn in recent decades, and in awful contemplation of the nothingness of its optimistic hopes of progress. The monstrous increases in the scientific means of conquering nature have been exposed as dangerous possibilities of universal suicide. Science and technics in the atom bomb, social political organization in the totalitarian state, and state education in totalitarian uniformity have seen the dreadful unfolding of their truly daemonic potentialities. And at the same time the charm of the idea of progress has vanished and humanity, in the full flower of its development, has fallen a prey to the panic of nihilism.[8]

Doctor Brunner has given us a brilliant analysis of the situation, which, while he applies it chiefly to Western man, is prevalent throughout the whole world.

All Are Uniquely Gifted

Nevertheless, even though we have continuously prostituted the resources with which God has endowed us these are not to be ignored or pushed to one side with the hope of substituting a better way. God placed them within us with no other intent than that of accomplishing his purposes through us as his sons and daughters whom he loves passionately and without reservation. God's way is not only "the best way"; it is the only way. Therefore, each must learn what his or her God-given gifts are and then use these gifts in accordance with his will. Contemporary revelation enlightens us and helps at this point:

All are called according to the gifts of God unto them; and to the intent that all may labor together, let him that laboreth in the ministry and him that toileth in the affairs of men of business and of work labor together with God for the accomplishment of the work entrusted to all.[9]

There is certainly no hint here that God by election, according to his will, chooses some for the blessedness of eternal life while others, by that same will, he chooses to leave under eternal damnation. "God so loved the world that he gave his only begotten Son that whosoever believeth in him should not perish but have everlasting life" (John 3:16). Even though no two may be exactly alike, all are impartially gifted by God. As our unique gifts are combined voluntarily and used under the direction of God, there is provided, from our side of the issue, all that is required to build his kingdom.

The Gifts of Companionship and Procreation

As we again pick up the biblical account of creation, we discover that God created, in the image of his Only Begotten, male and female. What an endowment he gave when he blessed them and instructed them to be fruitful, to multiply, and to replenish the earth and subdue it! Furthermore, this blessing was extended in giving to the man and the woman dominion over the remainder of that which God had created (Gen. 1:29-30 I.V.). God's first gift to man, beyond that of life in the image and likeness of God, was in providing for him a helpmate. This second gift not only involved another beautiful person for companionship but with this companionship they together were endowed with the power to reproduce their own kind. The monogamous relationship for procreation and the maintenance of a saintly home atmosphere are imperative in the kingdom of God society. God said that for this cause "shall a man leave his father and his mother, and shall cleave unto his wife; and they shall be one flesh" (Gen. 2:30 I.V.).

This monogamous relationship was upheld by our Lord when he was questioned by the Pharisees on the matter of divorce (see Matthew 19:4, 5). The term one flesh may well relate to offspring as well as to the marriage relationship itself. Our flesh together is transmitted to and becomes one in our offspring. This could not hold true in the same sense in a polygamous relationship. Without reproduction there could not be a continuity of any kind of society, but in the society of the kingdom of God the sacredness of monogamous marriage must be upheld.

Dominion, Intelligence, and Obedience

Dominion over the earth and every living thing our

heavenly Father has created is a priceless gift. This is a resource essential to human subsistence and to the existence and the growth of society. The type of society which thus evolves will depend upon how that dominion is exercised. We must learn how properly to control and utilize the dominion awarded to us. The power which can be used to bring about heavenly conditions on the earth can, if misused, destroy us. God's power is as the two-edged sword. It cuts both ways. If proper control is to be exercised in the utilization of the gift of dominion the intelligence which coexisted with humankind and God in creation is required. But obedience to the commandments of God is also required. In spite of Martin Luther's arguments that our will is in bondage to the will of God rather than being totally free, which freedom Luther says belongs only to God, we were created free to act by choice. Otherwise we would be under the necessity of struggling with the proposition that God commanded our first parents not to do something which he willed that they should do and therefore had to do. Our freedom of choice, even when we choose evil rather than good, is maintained throughout the scriptures. Joshua said: "And if it seem evil unto you to serve the Lord, choose you this day whom ye will serve; whether the gods which your fathers served that were on the other side of the flood, or the gods of the Amorites, in whose land you dwell; but as for me and my house, we will serve the Lord" (Joshua 24:15).

The scriptures give us the following statement which should be proportionately enlightening and spiritually rewarding in our understanding of available resources for righteous living:

And now, verily I say unto you, I was in the beginning with the Father, and am the Firstborn; and all those who are begotten through me, are partakers of the glory of the same, and are the church of the Firstborn. Ye were also in the beginning with the Father; that which is Spirit, even the Spirit of truth; and truth is knowledge of things as they are, and as they were, and as they are to come; and whatsoever is more or less than this, is the spirit of that wicked one, who was a liar from the beginning. The Spirit of truth is of God. I am the Spirit of truth. And John bore record of me, saying, He received a fullness of truth; yea, even of all truth, and no man receiveth a fullness unless he keepeth his commandments. He that keepth his commandments, receiveth truth and light, until he is glorified in truth, and knoweth all things.[10]

This proclamation depicts clearly the relationship of Jesus Christ with the Father in the beginning, and our relationship to our Creator through Jesus Christ and the Holy Spirit. The fruit of the garden of Eden which was forbidden to man was the fruit of the tree of knowledge of good and of evil. If Adam and Eve had chosen to obey God they would have been glorified in his truth, eventually coming to know all things. What a marvelous insight and promise! This elucidates the question as to what might have happened had our first parents been obedient to God from the beginning. Nevertheless, we are held accountable, not for their disobedience but for our own. As men and women have chosen to be disobedient throughout the ages, they have spurned and forsaken the resources by which the kingdom of God could have been their everlasting inheritance.

Following the preceding quotation there is another striking principle:

Man was also in the beginning with God. Intelligence, or the

light of truth, was not created or made, neither indeed can be. All truth is independent in that sphere in which God has placed it, to act for itself, as all intelligence also, otherwise there is no existence. Behold, here is the agency of man, and here is the condemnation of man, because that which was from the beginning is plainly manifest unto them, and they receive not the light. . . . The glory of God is intelligence, or, in other words, light and truth; and light and truth forsaketh that evil one.[11]

There is a Latin expression frequently used in defining creation, *creatio ex nihilo*. The implication of this phrase is that God created all things out of nothing. But alongside this may be placed the principle of co-existence—that is, that some attributes as well as things always coexisted with God. Certainly the theological hypothesis of *creatio ex nihilo* could not rule out those things which pertain to the very nature of God himself such as intelligence, or the light of truth. The scripture I quoted declares that intelligence or the light of truth was not created or made, neither indeed can be. It was through this intelligence, which is declared to be the glory of God, that men and women had their beginning. In order that they may be in the image and the likeness of their Maker, they too were gifted with intelligence, otherwise there could be no existence. Intelligence carries with it the need of opposites between which choices may be made. Therefore intelligence and agency are inseparably entwined in the eternal design.

We have the freedom under our right of choice to become what God has designed that we should be; otherwise we remain separated from God and under the condemnation of being less than that which God intended us to be. Truth makes us accountable for the choices which we make. We must accept the consequences of those choices unless ultimately we heed the counsel of God to repent; in which case joy is shared both with humanity and with God and the angels, through the forgiveness of sins, which God freely bestows by his grace. Thus "truth is independent in that sphere in which God has placed it, to act for itself," either to our condemnation or to the achievement of the divine purpose in us.

Resource and Stewardship

Responsibility runs parallel with resources which we have portrayed. Stewardship involves all of the elements previously discussed in this chapter, but it is especially related to accountability. There are three areas in which accountability applies: (1) Time is our method of measuring that part of eternity which is allotted to us here in this life. And yet we cannot help commenting on the magnificence of God's creation in that he has placed in the firmament heavenly bodies moving freely within their orbits by which time can be computed with minute accuracy. Since we pass through this life only once, it is vital that we shall make the best possible use of this part of our stewardship. (2) Each of us possesses unique gifts, to be discovered, developed, and used constructively, not only for our benefit and to God's glory but for the benefit of all humanity. (3) Basically all things belong to God. Since we are stewards under him, we are accountable to him for the use we make of the temporal possessions which he has granted to us. Our involvement in stewardship is encompassed within the divine plan and has been revealed by God who made us.

---

1. Joseph Smith, Jr., Inspired Version, The Holy Scriptures (Independence, Missouri: Herald Publishing House).
2. Doctrine and Covenants 17:5h.
3. *Ibid.*, 85:2-3.
4. *Ibid.*, 22:23b.
5. See Van A. Harvey, *A Handbook of Theological Terms* (New York: Macmillan Company), pp. 187-188.
6. Martin Luther, *The Bondage of the Will*, Fleming H. Revell Company, pp. 169-171.
7. Emil Brunner, *Eternal Hope* (Philadelphia: Westminster Press), pp. 7-8.
8. *Ibid.*, p. 23.
9. Doctrine and Covenants 119:8.
10. *Ibid.*, 90:4.
11. *Ibid.*, 90:5a-c, 6a.

9

AGENCY AND FREEDOM OF THE WILL

Components Are Elusive and Debatable

Agency and freedom of the will are among God's own most precious endowments. These have been transmitted to us and will be eternally safeguarded by him. Each contains elements which need to be considered in relationship to the other. Theologically, agency is the active power of the God-given right of choice—the right to free exercise of the human will in response to God's will in achieving his eternal design. Thus, stewardship and agency are joined in fulfillment of the awaited promise of the kingdom of God. These aim at the solution of world problems through the salvation of souls, both for time and eternity.

Yet freedom of the will is one of the most elusive tenets within the framework of Christian theology. It has been given a great deal of attention by Christian scholars, both in the present and in the past. Great debates occurred among those viewing the question from opposite sides. Briefly some highlights of these debates are as follows:

Sharp differences developed between Peter and Paul at Antioch, arising out of Peter's actions to bind the wills of certain Gentile Christians to Old Testament

Jewish practices (Gal. 2:11-21). Peter took the side of Jews who attempted to deny the Gentiles "our liberty which we have in Christ Jesus, that they might bring us into bondage" (Gal. 2:4).

The effect of Peter's action at Antioch to withdraw himself from these Gentile Christians and consort with dissident Jews was to deny the Gentile Christians the freedom of justification by faith in Christ and at the same time bind them to the Old Testament law of circumcision. Paul felt this would take the very heart out of the message and ministry of Jesus; he protested vigorously and stated that he "withstood Peter to the face because he was to be blamed" (Gal. 2:11). He contended that all believers must have free access to justification by the grace of Christ through their faith in him, and they were not subject to the law of circumcision as practiced under the Old Testament regime. The saintly will must be free from the bondage of a spiritually impotent and time limited ceremonial law.

St. Augustine and St. Jerome took a firm stand against the Pelagians who attributed all redemptive power to the will of man, or to the freedom of the human will. This appears to have been an extreme interpretation pointing in the wrong direction. The Pelagians denied the efficacy of the grace and atonement of Jesus Christ in the process of salvation.[1]

Luther opposed Erasmus on the subject of free will and published a reply to *The Diatribe*, a work written by Erasmus upon the nature of freedom of the will. Luther entitled his reply, *The Bondage of the Will*. Other theologians such as John Calvin and John Knox, with Luther, portrayed beliefs relating to this subject in their position of total predestinarianism.[2]

It is interesting and important to note that those participating in the struggle to set forth the truth pertaining to freedom of the will, no matter on which side of the issue they stood, were and are men of renown. Perhaps no two apostles had more influence than Peter and Paul in the promulgation of the Christian Church and the spread of primitive Christianity. Both Augustine and Jerome were highly recognized by the church in their time. Erasmus has been classified as a great scholar and, in many respects, a forerunner of the Reformation. Pelagius, though excommunicated for his views, received considerable recognition.

Presupposition and perhaps, prejudicial concepts are held by some scholars who have written upon this doctrine. In spite of the fervent expression of their ideas, serious doubt remains as to whether their conclusions are correct. The viewpoints of other extremists are out of harmony with rational truth and the scriptures.

One may ask, "Where does this topic fit into the Christian faith? Does it have a legitimate place in Christian theology? Is it of sufficient importance to warrant the time to study it?"

These questions persist in spite of the tremendous backlog of thought, discussion, debate, and literature which is available on the subject. If answers to these questions are affirmative, as I believe them to be, then we must endeavor to determine the topic's value and place in Christian doctrine. I am convinced that agency and freedom of the will, correctly understood, interpreted, and applied, are inseparably related to the principles of eternal salvation.

What Is Involved

First, we need to have clearly in mind definitions of two main words in the topic, *freedom* and *will*, both of which are shared in the meaning of agency. Since words have different variations of meaning, we need to understand the sense in which these words are used in the topic and adhere to their meaning throughout this study.

The topic involves the nature of God and also the nature of persons as God created them. God's purposes and the way and means by which those purposes are to be achieved are at the very heart of each element of the theme. Keeping these simple factors in mind may not resolve every problem but it will enhance our studies.

Will can be both a verb and noun. As a verb it is an auxiliary usually used to express futurity with determination. It can imply power, as well as determination, to act when it is used in this manner. However, in our subject *will* is used in the nominative sense rather than as a verb.

Webster's New Twentieth Century Dictionary includes in its definition of will: "The power of self-direction or self-control. The power of conscious and deliberate action or choice."[3] From the theological standpoint there are two levels of the will—infinite and finite. Infinite will is exclusively characteristic of Deity. Finite alludes to the human will. It is important that these two levels of the will not be confused. The issue here is concerning questions of the limitations and extent of powers of the human will. This should be contrasted with the purpose and power of the will of God in relation to achievement of his purposes in us. We are confronted with determining the manner and extent in which God moves and acts in the process of salvation and the part the human will plays in the process of our salvation.

Some maintain that the will of persons has no function whatsoever in the process of salvation; that persons' freedom to act has no bearing thereupon and that their status in life now and hereafter is predetermined by divine will. Election is often used to designate this purported principle.

We now seek a similar appropriation of the word *freedom*. Like *will*, it is a word which has numerous applications. Included in *Webster's New Twentieth Century Dictionary*, the definitions of freedom are (1) "A being able to act, move, use etc., without hindrance or restraint." (2) "A being able of itself to choose or determine action freely."[4]

Since these issues are theological, the ultimate proposition before us is determining how persons may become spiritually free. Do they have any freedom of the will in selecting their course? Do they do this on the basis of their right of self-determination or are they subject at every point to the divine will, without freedom of choice? Do persons do what they do in every instance because God wills it or because they choose to do so whether or not their choices harmonize with the will of God? On what basis is true and ultimate freedom realized and where does it begin in the experience of humankind?

Freedom Is Based on Truth

The Lord's teachings emphasize the direct relationship existing between freedom and truth. Christ bases ultimate freedom, the freedom of the soul, upon our acceptance of truth revealed in his word. Jesus said: "If ye continue in my word, then are ye my disciples indeed; and ye shall know the truth, and the truth shall make you free" (John 8:31, 32). The introductory statement, "If ye continue in my word," clearly suggests that they were free to choose either course—to continue or not to continue in his word. The promise of freedom was attached conditionally to the choice they were yet to make.

Ultimate and eternal freedom is more than the right of choice or the right of self-determination. I may exercise my freedom of will in choosing to place my soul in bondage to sin, such as stealing, murdering, or even sinning against the Holy Ghost. My choice does not make me free beyond the point of the original freedom I had to make such a choice. However, if I do not have this original freedom, I have no agency. Original freedom, therefore, is very important because it assures us the right of choice, without which there is no purpose to intelligence.

In modern scripture we find the following statement:

All truth is independent in that sphere in which God has placed it, to act for itself, as all intelligence also, otherwise there is no existence. Behold, here is the agency of man, and here is the condemnation of man, because that which was from the beginning is plainly manifest unto them, and they receive not the light.[5]

The beginning of our freedom is in our divinely endowed gift of intelligence.

The preceding statement sets forth the nature of the movement of God in the performance of his will. Truth and intelligence must be free and independent to act as such. Otherwise, things could not be as they are. All existence is based upon this principle. We are granted not only freedom of choice but guaranteed the perpetuation of agency in the total experience of living. God wants us to be good not alone because he wills it so but because he wants us to choose to be good.

The principle which guarantees our agency carries with it tremendous responsibility. This fact was elucidated by the Master:

For God sent not his Son into the world to condemn the world; but that the world through him might be saved. . . . And this is the condemnation, that light is come into the world, and men love darkness rather than light, because their deeds are evil.— John 3:17, 19.

This implies that it is in the nature of things that we possess agency. Also, that both truth and intelligence have freedom of expression. This freedom provides God with the opportunity of entrance and movement in the lives of people as they choose the light which comes from him. Thus from the beginning, God placed upon us the responsibility for our own actions. Intelligence makes us free, but we must learn the proper exercise of that freedom.

Freedom of Choice Versus the Use of Power

Freedom of the will pertains to our freedom of choice

but is exercised within the limits of our humanity. Only God is omnipotent. It was he who gave us the right of choice. Therefore, we must recognize the supremacy of God. Surely no one among us is foolish enough to say that he or she is free by any choice or act of the human will to achieve the forgiveness of sins. Neither would we dare to say that we can, by our own wills, bring to pass our resurrection from the dead. These acts are limited to the Deity and are extended from the Father through his Only Begotten Son.

Jesus said, "I have the power to lay my life down, and I have the power to take it again." He also successfully defended, before his enemies, the power which he possessed to forgive sins. It is apparent that we do not possess this power by right of agency. Therefore, we must differentiate between the powers of the will of God and those of our own will. We do not have freedom of will relating to the exercising of redemptive powers. Our own strength cannot bring about our redemption. This is accomplished only by means of divine grace through the atonement of the Lord Jesus Christ. Lehi states:

Wherefore, redemption cometh in and through the holy Messiah: for he is full of grace and truth. Behold, he offereth himself a sacrifice for sin, to answer the ends of the law, unto all those who have a broken heart and a contrite spirit; and unto none else can the ends of the law be answered. Wherefore, how great the importance to make these things known unto the inhabitants of the earth, that they may know that there is no flesh that can dwell in the presence of God, save it be through the merits, and mercy, and grace of the holy Messiah, who layeth down his life according to the flesh, and taketh it again by the power of the Spirit, that he may bring to pass the resurrection of the dead, being the first that should

rise. Wherefore, he is the first fruits unto God, inasmuch as he shall make intercession for all the children of men; and they that believe in him, shall be saved.[6]

There is a fine line between the terms "redemption" and "salvation." The preceding quotation, along with many other passages of scripture, indicates clearly that the power of redemption belongs to God. The redemption of our souls from the curse of sin and the penalty of death is solely by the grace of God. Nothing that the human soul can perform or do contributes to that grace. We are utterly dependent upon it.

However, while the application of the principles and power of the redemptive grace of God comes first by divine will, it also comes second by human choice. The person must subscribe to the will of God and abide the conditions upon which salvation is contingent. Belief, repentance, and obedience are all acts of human will. The presence of these principles in the gospel of Jesus Christ and the ordinances which accompany them make it possible for our human wills to be united with the divine will in the acceptance of redemptive grace. From this point on, the person is in partnership with God—a steward—in working out his salvation.

If we have no freedom to choose God, it follows that we do not have partnership with God. Thus, God has denied himself the channel of free admittance into the lives of those whom he is attempting to redeem. He must enter by force. The scriptures teach that God offered us salvation when he gave his Only Begotten Son to the world. Salvation becomes effective when we choose to believe on and obey him.

God Has Agency

God of all beings must be free. In the beginning he chose to make humankind in his image and likeness. The only qualifying principle of freedom which God possesses in the exercising of his will is that of his own nature, the essence of which is truth, intelligence, goodness, and love. Since we are made in the image and likeness of God, the divine nature must be potentially within us. This principle of the nature of God pertaining to freedom provides the right of choice. If we have no such right of choice then this fact attributes clearly and definitely the plight of the damned to the divine will. This is no less than preposterous.

Luther answered this conclusion, as he wrote against freedom of the will. Erasmus in *The Diatribe* is deceived in that he makes no distinction between God preached and God written—that is, between the word of God and God himself. God does many things not shown in his word, and he wills many things which his word does not show he wills. Thus, he does not will the death of a sinner—that is, in his word; but he wills it by his inscrutable will. At present, however, we must keep in view his word and leave alone his inscrutable will; for it is by his word and not his inscrutable will that we are guided. Who can direct himself according to a will that is inscrutable and incomprehensible? It is enough simply to know that there is in God an inscrutable will; what, why, and within what limits it is wholly unlawful to inquire or wish to know or be concerned about or touch upon; we may only fear and adore!

So it is right to say that if God does not desire our

death, it must be laid to the charge of our own will if we perish. He desires that all men should be saved in that he comes to all by the word of salvation, and the fault is in the will which does not receive him. He says in Matthew 23: "How often would I have gathered thy children together and thou wouldst not." But why the Majesty does not remove or change this fault of will in every man (for it is not in the power of man to do it) or why he lays this fault to the charge of the will when man cannot avoid it, it is not lawful to ask and though we do, the answer will never be found, for Paul says in Romans 9:20, "Who are thou that repliest against God?"[7]

The Will of God Versus the Will of Man

The powers of the will of God and those of people must be clearly differentiated. Luther declared that the freedom of the will is a nonentity, existing in name only. He also upheld the position that the human will has power to go only in one direction—toward evil.[8] This point of view nullifies, if not totally denies, the power of the will of God, for he offers redemptive grace to all. The first requirement in our salvation is to recognize the extent of the efficacy of the will, the power, and the grace of God made manifest in the atonement. The atonement is not contributed to nor brought about by the human will. It is solely by the will of God that salvation is offered to us through the redemptive processes of atonement. The second requirement for us to recognize is equally valid which is that belief, repentance, and obedience are all acts of the human will, albeit they are stimulated by the Holy Spirit.

The truth is that people may and even must be influenced to make their choices. Nevertheless, they are free to exercise their own wills in these choices. Election to salvation is dependent therefore upon both the will of God (for he wills that all should be saved) and the will of the person who has the right to accept or to reject the redemptive grace of God.

Book of Mormon writers emphasize the agency of man, its efficacy and place in the life of man and in the purposes of God. A summary only is given here:

> It must needs be that there is an opposition in all things. If not.... righteousness could not be brought to pass; neither wickedness; neither holiness nor misery; neither good nor bad..... Wherefore there would have been no purpose in the end of creation.... If... there is no law... there is no sin. If... there is no sin... there is no righteousness. If there be no righteousness, there be no happiness.... If these things are not, there is no God. And if there is no God, we are not.... For there is a God, and he hath created all things,... both things to act and things to be acted upon....
>
> The Lord gave unto man that he should act for himself.... Man could not act for himself, save it should be that he was enticed by one or the other.... All things have been done in the wisdom of him who knoweth all things.
>
> Adam fell, that men might be; and men are, that they might have joy. And the Messiah cometh in the fullness of time, that he may redeem the children of men from the fall. And because that they are redeemed from the fall, they have become free forever knowing good from evil; to act for themselves, and not to be acted upon, save it be by the punishment of the Law, at the great and last day, according to the commandments which God hath given. Wherefore, men are free according to the flesh; and all things are given them which are expedient unto man. And they are free to choose liberty and eternal life,

**through the great mediation of all men, or to choose captivity
and death, according to the captivity and power of the devil.**[9]

Restrictions placed upon human will mean that we
are not free to accomplish the divine purpose in our own
way. We are free to choose our own way, but we must
accept the consequence which is to place ourselves in
bondage by our own actions. We are also free to accept
the will of God and anticipate the joys and blessings of
this choice.

God Is Supreme

This fundamental reasoning impresses the fact that
God eternally seeks to influence us by his will with confidence in its ultimate triumph. The choice that many
make against God or against doing his will does not
prevent ultimately the accomplishment of his design.
This assertion does not uphold or deny universal
salvation. It is simply stating the divine principle that
the will of God is supreme. Therefore, his designs will
not be circumvented. We are reminded that

**The works, and the designs, and the purposes of God, can not
be frustrated, neither can they come to naught, for God doth
not walk in crooked paths; neither doth he turn to the right
hand nor to the left; neither doth he vary from that which he
hath said; therefore his paths are straight and his course is one
eternal round.**[10]

The following also indicates how God eternally works
his will: "Surely the wrath of man shall praise thee; the
remainder of wrath shalt thou restrain" (Psalm 76:10).

157

When we willfully rebel against God, we not only sin against him as the Supreme and Perfect Being; we reject light and truth and every other counterpart of the divine nature. Such rejection cannot be charged to the will of God as it must be if we have no freedom of the will. It is rather the result of a will which, by its own free choice, places itself in the bondage of being either deliberately or ignorantly at cross-purposes with God.

1. F. L. Cross, Ed., *The Oxford Dictionary of the Christian Church* (London, New York, Toronto: Oxford University Press), p. 1040.
2. Marvin Halverson and Arthur Cohen, *A Handbook of Christian Theology* (Cleveland and New York: World Publishing Company), pp. 271-272.
3. Noah Webster, *Webster's New Twentieth Century Dictionary*, Wm. Collins and World Publishing Company, p. 2092.
4. *Ibid.*, p. 710.
5. Doctrine and Covenants 90:5b, c.
6. Book of Mormon, II Nephi 1:71-77.
7. *The Bondage of the Will*, pp. 170-171.
8. *Ibid.*, pp. 142-143 and 271.
9. Book of Mormon, 1970, pp. 83-86.
10. Doctrine and Covenants 2:1.

Predestination and Necessity

Freedom of the will and some assumed ideas of predestination as relating to salvation by divine election are in absolute opposition. These ideas exclude both the purpose and the efficacy of human choice based upon our right of agency. This becomes quite unreasonable when it commits to the will of God the fate of the damned. Such fallacy was taught by a number of the Reformers, among whom was Martin Luther. These Reformers used the synonyms "predestination" and "foreordination" in a distinctly inadequate sense. This is not to question their integrity nor to impugn their motives.

There is a genuine principle of predestination. Three questions come into focus therewith: (1) Upon what is predestination based? (2) To what extent does it apply in the work of God? (3) What relationship does predestination have to our eternal salvation?

Paul Tillich seems to have developed a logical premise about this. After reasoning against double predestination in mankind's eternal destiny, he states: "...God's act always precedes and, further,...in order to be certain of one's fulfillment, one can and must look at God's activity alone. Taken in this way, predestination is the highest affirmation of Divine love, not its negation."[1] God's love is not inadequate to his purpose; neither can it be debased in any respect in relation to creation, purpose, or redemption, all three of which correlate with the eternal design of God.

Some may deny any legitimacy to predestination due to incorrect interpretations and lack of understanding. Therefore, we are obligated to discuss objectively both the use and the efficacy of predestination in the workings of God.

Predestination is scriptural. Even though Peter and Paul differed on the question of the enforcement of certain aspects of the Jewish law, they were in agreement that some things are predestined of God. Predestination is based upon necessity and the foreknowledge of God. God has the ability to foresee and to understand the future in the same degree that he understands the past and present. Therefore, he acts upon that which his foreknowledge necessitates.

Peter's concept of predestination is expressed in these words:

But with the precious blood of Christ, as of a lamb without blemish and without spot; who verily was foreordained [*destined*, R.S.V.] before the foundation of the world, but was manifest in these last times for you, who by him do believe in God, that raised him up from the dead, and gave him glory; that your faith and hope might be in God.—I Peter 1:19-21.

Paul took the principle which was expressed by Peter pertaining to Jesus Christ and pursued the predestined will of God by making this will apply also to those who are justified and glorified in Jesus Christ. He said:

160

And we know that all things work together for good to them that love God, to them who are called according to his purpose. For him whom he did foreknow, he also did predestinate to be conformed to his own image, that he might be the firstborn among many brethren. Moreover, him whom he did predestinate, him he also called; and him whom he called, him he also sanctified; and him whom he sanctified, him he also glorified.—Romans 8:28-30.

This, of course, applies to Christ. It is well to consider a second significant statement made by Paul.

According as he hath chosen us in him before the foundation of the world, that we should be holy and without blame before him in love; having predestinated us into the adoption of children by Jesus Christ to himself, according to the good pleasure of his will, to the praise of the glory of his grace, wherein he hath made us accepted in the beloved.... That in the dispensation of the fullness of times he might gather together in one all things in Christ, both which are in heaven, and which are on the earth; even in him; in whom also we have obtained an inheritance, being predestinated according to the purpose of him who worketh all things after the counsel of his own will; that we should be to the praise of his glory, who first trusted in Christ. In whom ye also trusted, after that ye heard the word of truth, the gospel of your salvation; in whom also, after that ye believed, ye were sealed with that Holy Spirit of promise, which is the earnest of our inheritance until the redemption of the purchased possession, unto the praise of his glory.—Ephesians 1:4-6, 10-14.

The writers were saying in essence that the spiritual blessings which we enjoy in Christ are not an afterthought of the Creator or an accident of some evolutionary process. They make clear that God planned (predestined) "before the foundation of the world" the fulfillment of his eternal purpose; that is, "that in the dispensation of the fullness of time he might gather together in one all things in Christ, both which are in heaven, and which are on the earth." There is no hint here that those who may not attain "the good pleasure of his will" were discriminated against by divine choice, or that it was the intent that they should be predestined by the will of God to condemnation.

Some things are firmly fixed by the will of God on the basis of their necessity. The passages quoted indicate the necessity of the atonement which was made voluntarily through Jesus Christ. They point out, too, the divine calling of those who are accepted of God by virtue of their obedience and faith in him. In both instances the law of necessity prevails. No one can come to Christ except he is drawn to him by the Father (John 6:44). This is not to say that all whom God seeks come, nor that any who seek to come to God will be turned away because he has chosen not to elect them to salvation. These quotations are dealing only with one phase of the issue. They should not be projected to indicate more than intended. Paul did not say that those who are not called to eternal salvation are elected to eternal damnation by action of the divine will, without equal opportunity to accept salvation through the grace of God as revealed in the gospel of Jesus Christ.[2]

Nephi stated that "there must be an opposition in all things."[3] This, too, points out the law of necessity. The principle is inescapable. One cannot have a wall which does not have opposite sides. Heat and cold are opposite extremes of temperatures. One cannot have electrical illumination without an element which resists the passing of the electric current so vigorously that the friction caused produces heat sufficient to make light.

That which is predestined is established thus on the basis of its unavoidability. The Book of Mormon makes clear that you cannot have sin without having righteousness. You cannot have either of these without law, for without law there is no transgression; hence, there would be no sin if there were no law.[4] Since law is necessary, the possibility of violation must exist. But law was not predestined to make men sinners. It was provided to offer righteousness which cannot exist outside of that law and its observance.

The Psalmist wrote: "The law of the Lord is perfect" (19:7). James informs us, "Whoso looketh into the perfect law of liberty, and continueth therein, he being not a forgetful hearer, but a doer of the work, this man shall be blessed in his deed" (1:25). Law alone, though necessary to establish righteousness, is not sufficient. The life and ministry of Jesus, through whom both grace and law are offered, are imperatives to salvation equal with our obedience to his commandments. (See Romans chapters 5-8.)

Predestination and Foreknowledge

Predestination accompanies intelligence and reality. Every doctrine or precept must be based upon a principle of truth. There is no freedom of either divine or human will outside the bounds of truth. Upon what truth does the doctrine of predestination depend? Predestination is based upon the foreknowledge of God. Paul indicated this in the eighth chapter of Romans. The simple fact is clearly stated that God acted according to his foreknowledge of that which is necessary to "make our calling and election sure." He predestined Christ to be our Redeemer in order to provide all things needful for our redemption. He foreknew both Christ and our needs. He knew beforehand that man would fall; hence, he knew also that redemption must be provided and that this could be done only by divine atonement. The will of man does not and cannot possess nor exercise the means or power of his own redemption. We have already emphasized that free will applies only to the right of choice and not to freedom of the use of omnipotent power. God chose Christ to be our Redeemer because he knew he was totally worthy of the trust and adequate to our needs. By Jesus' own proposition God possessed the foreknowledge that Christ would not fail (Gen. 3:13 I.V., Matt. 26:39, 42, 44).

This raises the question as to how inclusive the foreknowledge of God actually is. Certainly he knows all things needful to be the Creator and to perpetuate his creation. He also knows everything necessary in order to redeem and to save his creation. Truth is a knowledge of things as they are, as they were, and as they are to come. Jesus stated that the word of God is truth (John 17:17). By the word of God's power he brought about the creation (Hebrews 11:3). The word of God is creative, revelatory, and redemptive. How then can there be any restrictions or limitations on that which God knows and on that which he designs by necessity of his foreknowledge? Knowledge, purpose, and destiny must come within the bounds of will and law. I refer to the previous quotation: "All things have been done in the wisdom of him who knoweth all things."[5] Moreover, "He that keepeth his commandments, receiveth truth and light, until he is glorified in truth, and knoweth all things."[6]

Doctrine and Covenants provides some good examples of the infinite foreknowledge of God. The Lord revealed to Moses the principles by which he created the earth. He also stated that he had created many worlds, even worlds which are not numbered to man. They are known to God, for he created them by the word of his power. But he revealed to Moses only that which pertained to this world.[7] Also, there is the account of a revelation given to Enoch in which God portrayed to Enoch his eternal design reaching beyond the end of time far into eternity.[8] These are further indications that there are no restrictions on either the knowledge or foreknowledge of God.

The question is often asked, "What would have happened if—Adam had not sinned? Christ had not come into the world? he had not been crucified or, being crucified, had not been resurrected?" Such questions are actually irrelevant. The facts are Adam did fall; Christ did come into the world; he did rise from the dead. God deals with reality, both as he knows it and foresees it, and not with supposition or with what might have been. Our security, our redemption, is assured and conveyed in the fact that God foreknew what would happen, planned accordingly, and has revealed that plan in Jesus Christ and in his word. We have the assurance that his will shall prevail. The foreknowledge of God is adequate to the development and the perpetuation of his predestined will.

The Reformers who recognized the principle of predestination did not adquately interpret it. This is not difficult to understand when we take into account their motivations. Their chief objective was to refute the inordinate emphasis placed upon works in contrast to divine grace by the Roman Church. Luther with utmost integrity endeavored to combat this perversion. In doing so he extended the principle which had set his soul aflame—"The just shall live by faith"—into realms of inconsistency which made him a pronounced predestinarian. He claims to base his conclusions chiefly on the writings of Paul and St. Augustine in his attempt at refutation of the freedom of the will as represented in Erasmus' *Diatribe*. It appears he approached his treatise with some bias which, in spite of his greatness, led him into a dangerous fallacy. He excluded the human will, in its final analysis, at every point. This he did in an attempt to declare that works of any sort have no merit whatsoever, either in man's justification, or in his salvation. According to Luther man is saved by election only because God wills it so. He is damned by the same means and can do nothing about it.[9] Luther maintained that Erasmus straddled the fence, endeavoring to uphold the medieval Roman theology while at the same time sharing in many ideas of the Reformers.

It was natural for Luther to adopt such an extreme position when taking into account the fact that the emphasis of Roman theology was upon external acts rather than upon the internal working of divine grace in the process of salvation. Roman theology attributed to the power of free will the performance of acts necessary to attain salvation. Luther's contention was against this whole system because of the disproportionate emphasis upon works as contrasted with the doctrine of salvation by grace. In the Roman system saints were substituted for Christ and his atonement. The Romans prayed and gave homage to these saints as intermediaries. This was a clear perversion of the truth.

Since Luther claimed to base his conclusions chiefly upon the writings and teachings of the apostle Paul and those of St. Augustine, here again we need to recognize the motivations behind the statements of these men. For instance, when Paul emphasized justification by faith as against the works of the law, what was his chief purpose or design? Was his debate more against a group of discordant Christian Jews who would bind all to the observance of the Old Testament law of circumcision, or was his primary purpose that of a clearer enunciation of the Christian doctrine of salvation by grace? If the latter is the case, he still was evidently using the term "law" in a restricted sense as applying to the Old Testament practice of circumcision. Luther does not clearly enunciate between the law of circumcision and the irrevocable law of God based upon his righteous design expressed in creation and in redemption.

This, for instance, would not be in accord with the use of the term "law" in the writing of the prophet Joseph Smith:

And again, verily I say unto you, that which is governed by law, is also preserved by law, and perfected and sanctified by the same.

That which breaketh a law, and abideth not by law, but seeketh to become a law unto itself, and willeth to abide in sin, and altogether abideth in sin, can not be sanctified by law, neither by mercy, justice, or judgment; therefore, they must remain filthy still.

All kingdoms have a law given: and there are many kingdoms; for there is no space in the which there is no kingdom; and there is no kingdom in which there is no space, either a greater or lesser kingdom.

And unto every kingdom is given a law; and unto every law there are certain bounds also, and conditions.

All beings who abide not in those conditions, are not justified; for intelligence cleaveth unto intelligence; wisdom receiveth wisdom; truth embraceth truth; virtue loveth virtue; light cleaveth unto light; mercy hath compassion on mercy, and claimeth her own; justice continueth its course, and claimeth its own; judgment goeth before the face of him who sitteth upon the throne, and governeth and executeth all things: he comprehendeth all things, and all things are before him, and all things are round about him; and he is above all things, and in all things, and is through all things, and is round about all things: and all things are by him, and of him; even God, for ever and ever.

And again, verily I say unto you, He hath given a law unto all things by which they move in their times, and their seasons; and their courses are fixed; even the courses of the heavens, and the earth; which comprehend the earth and all the planets; and they give light to each other in their times, and in their seasons, in their minutes, in their hours, in their days, in their weeks, in their months, in their years: all these are one year with God, but not with man.

The earth rolls upon her wings; and the sun giveth his light by day, and the moon giveth her light by night; and the stars also giveth their light, as they roll upon their wings, in their glory, in the midst of the power of God.

Unto what shall I liken these kingdoms, that ye may understand?

Behold, all these are kingdoms, and any man who hath seen any or the least of these, hath seen God moving in his majesty and power.[10]

The preceding recognizes an extensive range as well as application of law. This point of view Luther missed entirely in his predestinarian approach to the gospel, which he in fact recognized not as law but solely as divine grace in which only the will of God functions. Salvation, therefore, according to Luther is a matter of divine election in which human will or agency has no part.

I have found little in the writings of St. Augustine to indicate that Luther fully agreed with his beliefs and teachings. St. Augustine wrote in favor of freedom of choice. "Now wherever it is said, 'Do not do this,' and 'Do not do that,' and wherever there is any requirement in the divine admonitions for the work of the will to do anything or to refrain from doing anything there is sufficent proof of free will."[11] This plainly attests to freedom of the will. Augustine does not place the fact nor the blame for our evil choices on any other. St. Augustine's views were written against the Pelagians who denied the necessity of divine grace, emphasizing absolute freedom of the will in salvation.

As much as we respect the sincerity and good intentions of those who held or hold to the theory of total predestination, we are left to conclude that in this they erred. The scriptures proclaim, "In vain do they worship me teaching for doctrine the commandments of men" (Matt. 15:9).

Clear Concepts Are Necessary

Christian theology exists for the purpose of keeping our concepts of the deity and salvation clear. Worship is the keynote of redemption and salvation. We worship truly only as our concepts of the total personality of God and the processes of salvation are clarified and kept clear. "The true worshipers shall worship the Father in spirit and in truth" (John 4:25, I.V.). Perversions distort our concepts; hence, they make vain our efforts of worship.

After a careful examination of Restoration theology over a long period, we are led to the conclusion that the right of choice or of free agency is a divine gift to mankind. In this the Almighty is endeavoring to carry out his initial purpose in our creation wherein he said: "Let us make man in our image and after our likeness." If we do not possess freedom of the will, we are not in the image of him whose will is free, nor can we grow into any substantial likeness of our Creator. From the start we would be denied the attributes essential to such development. These attributes are essential to the working out of the divine purpose within us, on a voluntary basis, both as to the will of God and the operation of the human will as a response.

The history of the human race indicates that people, though generally religious by nature, are inclined to be in rebellion against God and are very much sinners. This again affirms that they have not the power to save themselves. Redemption comes by the grace of God. But to say that God grants this grace to some and denies it to others solely on the basis of his choice or the expression of his will, without regard to justice or purpose, is clearly a perversion of truth.

The only feasible answer as to why some are denied salvation by the grace of God is that they do not make themselves available for salvation. Either they are ignorantly unaware of their need of God's grace to save them or else they willfully choose not to accept it. This does not say that God has failed to place in us the potentialities which when touched by his grace are free to respond to that divine touch. Otherwise redemption would be ineffective and salvation nonexistent.

1. Paul Tillich, *Systematic Theology* (New York and Evanston: Harper and Row), Vol. 1, pp. 285-286.
2. See George A. Buttrick, Commentary Editor, *The Interpreter's Bible* (New York and Nashville: Abingdon Press), Vol. 10, pp. 614-623.
3. Book of Mormon, II Nephi 1:81.
4. *Ibid.*, II Nephi 1:88-92.
5. *Ibid.*, II Nephi 1:114.
6. Doctrine and Covenants 90:4e.
7. *Ibid.*, 22:20-21.
8. *Ibid.*, 36.
9. *The Bondage of the Will*, pp. 169-171.
10. Doctrine and Covenants 85:8-12c.
11. J. G. Pilington, Ed., *Basic Writings of St. Augustine* (New York and Toronto: Random House), Vol. 1, p. 736. In order to get a clear conception of St. Augustine's views of will and predestination, read "On Grace and Free Will" and "The Predestination of the Saints," *ibid.*, pp. 733-817.

COVENANT **11** WITH PROMISE

Righteousness Versus Will

F. Henry Edwards has written, "The work of God would have been aimless unless it had been made fruitful by his continuing care."[1] The reason is that God is holy. He is a righteous God. All of his "mighty acts" are based upon his righteousness. God pronounced every act of creation good. Consequently, the righteousness of God should be considered in relation to his nature and his will. E. Y. Mullins states, "...righteousness is grounded in the nature rather than in the will of God."[2] God is free to choose to function as he wills but his will is subject to his nature. What God wills, he wills because he is who he is and, by nature, what he is.

We are created in his "image and after his likeness" (Gen. 1:26). Therefore, this principle is also true of us. We will to do what we do because we are free to do so by the gift of agency. Agency is a counterpart of intelligence (Doctrine and Covenants 90:4b, c) which means that both responsibility and accountability are involved in this freedom. Otherwise, agency and intelligence would be pointless.

Since God is spiritually and infinitely righteous, what he wills is right. What we do is not always right because, though spiritual by creation, we are also finite and fleshly. Incarnation means that Jesus became fleshly in the same degree that we are. In the atonement he demonstrated that, if one so wills, the Spirit can triumph over the flesh (Luke 22:42). Jesus also commanded that we should become perfect even as our Father in heaven is perfect (Matt. 5:48). God never has forgotten and never will forsake his purpose in creation. In his righteousness he wills that all mankind shall seek him and do his will. He has done everything in his power, and by his will, to secure our salvation. (See Isaiah 55:6-11.) His covenants are made with promise for our welfare and when observed by us our salvation is made secure by his immutable will.

Creation and Spread of Wickedness

The Old Testament account of creation by no means tells everything in detail. Many questions are left unanswered. However, a number of basic truths are currently in evidence. For instance, God said he saw that light was good and he divided light from darkness, making day and night. Another axiom resides in the following quotation:

And I, God, said, Let the earth bring forth grass; the herb yielding seed; the fruit tree yielding fruit after his kind; and the tree yielding fruit, whose seed should be in itself, upon the earth; and it was so, even as I spake.—Gen. 1:15, I.V.

In the Inspired Version of the Bible, some questions are answered not only in regard to creation but also pertaining to that which followed. There was a spiritual

173

creation in heaven before inanimate and animate life appeared upon the earth. The natural creation followed this spiritual creation (Gen. 2:5, I.V.). All versions of the Bible agree that Eve and Adam yielded to temptation, disobeyed the commandment of God, resulting in a loss of status. This loss of status was chiefly in changes from Edenic paradise to earthly existence. They were driven from Eden to a world of struggle, pain, and sorrow. They were no longer in the direct presence of God. The woman would bear children in sorrow and pain. Weeds, thistles, and thorns grew up, and man was destined to earn bread by the sweat of his brow. From the time Cain murdered his brother, Abel, wickedness spread throughout Adam and Eve's posterity. The world of sin could not maintain the celestial law of Enoch's city of righteousness so the city was taken from the earth (Gen. 7:27, I.V.). In spite of Noah's preaching, wickedness was accelerated into deplorable corruption and violence until God determined to destroy this world of corruption by a flood (Gen. 8:17-18, I.V.; Gen. 11-12, R.S.V.).

God Projects Himself into Human Affairs by Covenant

God also determined to make a new start with Noah, his sons, and their families. After the flood the command given to Adam to multiply and replenish the earth and subdue it was repeated to Noah. This was not the only fresh start God has made, yet he never has broken the covenant made with Enoch, which he repeated to Noah, symbolized by the rainbow.

And the bow shall be in the cloud; and I will look upon it,

that I may remember the everlasting covenant, which I made unto thy father Enoch; that, when men should keep all my commandments, Zion should again come on the earth, the city of Enoch which I have caught up unto myself.

And this is mine everlasting covenant, that when thy posterity shall embrace the truth, and look upward, then shall Zion look downward, and all the heavens shall shake with gladness, and the earth shall tremble with joy; and the general assembly of the church of the firstborn shall come down out of heaven, and possess the earth, and shall have place until the end come. And this is mine everlasting covenant, which I made with thy father Enoch.—Gen. 9:21-23, I.V.

As we study the Old Testament some imperative doctrinal truths are made to stand out clearly. Knowledge of these is essential to understanding God's covenant with his people in any age, for they are entwined into his marvelous works. Chief among these are monotheism and monogamy. The first relates to the nature of God. The second affects and is the basis of a righteous society.

Monotheism

Monos is the Greek word for one; *theism* is derived from the Greek word *theos* meaning God. Monotheism, therefore, means belief in one God. In the broadest sense, monotheism is not entirely unique with the Bible. For instance, the major emphasis of the reign of Amenhotep IV (also called Ikhnaton, 1370-1358 B.C.) in Egypt was devoted to the worship of one god, but this god was Aton, the Sun God.[3] Paul, as he came to Athens, found an altar with the inscription written upon it, "To the Unknown God." The apostle declared, "Whom ye ignorantly worship, him declare I unto you." He told of the true nature of God and preached Christ to an audience on Mars Hill (Acts 17:22-31).

Moslemism or Islam is monotheistic in belief and worship. The god of Islam is Allah. Though in some respects Moslemism relates itself to the Judaic and Christian concepts, it contains theology as well as historical practices which are not fully in accord with either. Christianity on the other hand had its origin in Judaism and is the fulfillment of Judaism. This was attested to by Jesus when he said, "Think not that I am come to destroy the law, or the prophets [upon which Judaism is founded]. I am not come to destroy but to fulfill" (Matt. 5:17). No such claim was made by Mohammed or his successors. Early in life Mohammed began to believe that there is only one true God. In spite of persecution from his native Meccans, he tenaciously held to this theology. After purported revelations in visits from the angel Gabriel, he proclaimed himself to be a prophet. He declared that he was the greatest of all major prophets, among whom were Adam, Noah, Abraham, Moses, and Jesus. He also declared himself to be the last of the prophets, "Sent with the Sword." He said, "The sword is the key to heaven and hell; all who draw it in the cause of the Faith will be rewarded."[4] Even Jesus was a lesser prophet than he, according to his teaching. Mohammed and his followers uprooted idolatry first at Mecca and later wherever it was found as the Islamic religion spread. His original loftier ideals of reformation deteriorated into corruption, plundering, conquest, and violence. He spread the Islamic religion by means of armies and the sword.

The Bible portrays monotheism as the earliest form of religious belief. God called the earth into being. He created, and communicated with, the first man and first woman, Adam and Eve. Although wickedness spread, resulting in unbelief, violence, and idolatry, there were always those who responded to the call of God and, acting as his prophets and preachers, called upon the people to repent by reminding them of God's laws and his covenant with them.

God has projected himself into human affairs at the most appropriate times. Coursing through all divine action was a "called out" people with whom God made covenants having both promise and warning. Hence, we have the covenant made with Abraham concerning him and his seed. This covenant was symbolized by circumcision (Genesis 18:7-14). The Sinaitic Covenant was based upon the Ten Commandments. Then there was the promise of the new covenant (Jeremiah 31:31). In regard to the Abrahamic Covenant, we must not overlook the promise made to Hagar concerning Ishmael and his descendants (Gen. 21:9-18).

Perhaps the strongest and most explicit example in regard to one Supreme Being is to be found in Moses' experience at Mount Horeb, where he saw a bush on fire which was not being consumed. As he approached it to see why the bush was not consumed, a voice spoke to him saying:

> . . . Moses, Moses. . . . Draw not nigh hither; put off thy shoes from off thy feet; for the place whereon thou standest is holy ground. Moreover he said, I am the God of thy father, the God of Abraham, the God of Isaac, and the God of Jacob. And

Moses hid his face; for he was afraid to look upon God.—Exodus 3:4-6.

Then God called upon Moses to return to Egypt to deliver his people from bondage and lead them to Canaan, the land promised by covenant to Abraham and his seed after him. After a short debate in which he expressed reluctance to undertake such a gigantic mission:

. . . Moses said unto God, Behold, when I come unto the children of Israel, and shall say unto them, The God of your fathers hath sent me unto you; and they shall say to me, What is his name? what shall I say unto them?

And God said unto Moses, I AM THAT I AM; and he said, Thus shalt thou say unto the children of Israel, I AM hath sent me unto you.

And God said moreover unto Moses, Thus shalt thou say unto the children of Israel, The Lord God of your fathers, the God of Abraham, the God of Isaac, and the God of Jacob, hath sent me unto you; this is my name forever, and this is my memorial unto all generations.—Exodus 3:13-15.

There could be no hint of polytheism here. God named himself, "I am." "I" is the *singular pronoun* of the first person, that is, the person speaking. "Am" is that part of the verb "to be" expressing existence, or being, in the present tense. "This is my name forever and this is my memorial to all generations" may very well apply to the past, present, and future.[5]

The sign promised to Moses was that when he had brought forth the people out of Egypt, "you shall serve God upon this mountain" (Exodus 3:14). In the fulfillment of that promise, the ten commandments were given. The very first commandment is, "Thou shalt have no other gods before me." The second commandment established an irrevocable rule against idolatry. Later as he sought to prepare them to enter the Promised Land, Moses repeated these commandments to the children of Israel and added:

. . . Hear, O Israel, the statutes and judgments which I speak in your ears this day, that ye may learn them, and keep and do them.

The Lord our God made a covenant with us in Horeb.

The Lord made not this covenant with our fathers, but with us, even us, who are all of us here alive this day.—Deut. 5:1-3.

The covenant was between the one holy God and the people on terms that they would keep his laws. Both God and Moses knew the polytheistic idolatry practiced by the inhabitants of the land into which they were going and by those of surrounding nations with whom they would have dealings.

Not until 1929, with the discovery of the Ras Shamra Texts, was the real nature of Canaanite Baal worship understood. While plowing near the Mediterranean coast in 1928 a Syrian peasant struck a stone on which were Mycenaen (a form of Greek) markings. This led to the later discovery nearby of a mound, called by the Syrians "Ras Shamra" because of the flowers which grew on it. Excavations proved this to be the ancient Syrian city of Ugarit. Here a library and several temples were found. One temple was dedicated to the god Baal who has been mentioned so many times in the Old Testament. The texts when translated disclosed the licentious and mythological nature of Baal worship.

We cannot cover all the details here, but this much is known and will serve our purpose. Baalism was a cultic fertility worship. There are two seasons during the year in the larger part of the eastern Mediterranean coast and in Palestine: the rainy season, spoken of in the Old Testament as the former and latter rains, and the dry season. Baal was worshiped as the rain god. According to legend, he is confronted with a bitter enemy, the god Mott, whom some sources say kills Baal at the beginning of the dry season. His mate is the fertility goddess named Anat in the Ras Shamra texts, who is probably Ashtarath, mentioned a number of times in the Old Testament. Anat subdues Mott and Baal is resurrected. He begins sexual activity with his female goddess and the rains return, making the land fertile so as to maintain all forms of life. It was believed that human sexual activity assisted Baal and his consort in blessing the earth with fertility. Temple festivals were held, which ended in debauchery and all kinds of sexual orgies.[6] Unfortunately, at times this invaded the Israelite society in Canaan. It was often introduced through intermarriage with foreigners as was the case with Ahab, King of Israel, and Jezebel, a Sidonian princess who induced Ahab to establish and maintain Baal worship in Israel throughout his reign (I Kings 16:30; 19:18).

With this background information, one can well understand Elijah's reason for standing up to Ahab and the prophets of Baal at Mount Carmel (I kings, chapter 18). These prophets had to be slain in order to cleanse Israel from such a destructive religious practice.

Canaanites maintained sacred prostitutes in their temples. God forbade the Israelites to indulge in such practice before they entered Canaan (Deut. 23:17-18). Allegiance to and the worship of the one true and holy God is imperative to a happy, moral society in any age.

We need to be aware that humanity needs to be fore-warned, taught, and always conscious of this everlasting truth. In face of the growing widespread perversion of sex today, surely the voice of God is speaking to the whole world now "out of the ground" (Isa. 29:4, I.V.) by knowledge such as has been brought to light through the Ras Shamra texts. Another source from the ground gives us this happy result of a morally clean society:

Behold, the Lamanites, your brethren, whom ye hate, because of their filthiness and the cursings which hath come upon their skins, are more righteous than you; for they have not forgotten the commandments of the Lord, which were given unto our fathers, that they should have, save it were one wife: and concubines they should have none; and there should not be whoredoms committed among them.

And now this commandment they observe to keep; wherefore because of this observance in keeping this commandment, the Lord God will not destroy them, but will be merciful unto them; and one day they shall become a blessed people.

Behold, their husbands love their wives, and their wives love their husbands, and their husbands and their wives love their children.[7]

Monogamy

"Monogamy is the basic principle on which Christian married life is built."[8] This principle was laid down by the Almighty to be observed from the beginning: "Therefore shall a man leave his father and his mother, and shall cleave unto his wife; they shall be one flesh" (Gen. 2:30, I.V.).

Lamech, a descendant of Cain four times removed, was the first to violate this law (Gen. 4:19). He had two wives at the same time. When questioned by the Pharisees about divorce, Jesus quoted Genesis 2:24 K.J.V. and 2:30 I.V., using words to the effect that monogamy was the divine intention from the beginning. Thus Jesus strongly upheld monogamy (Matt. 19:5-6). In contemporary revelation the principle of monogamy is also strongly upheld:

Thou shalt love thy wife with all thy heart, and shall cleave unto her and none else; and he that looketh upon a woman to lust after her, shall deny the faith, and shall not have the Spirit; and if he repents not, he shall be cast out.[9]

The following is the joint vow taken by those who are married by a Reorganized Latter Day Saint minister:

You both mutually agree to be each other's companion, husband and wife, observing the legal rights belonging to this condition; that is, keeping yourselves wholly for each other, and from all others, during your lives?[10]

Perhaps the most explicit of all scripture on this subject is found in the Book of Mormon:

For behold, thus saith the Lord, This people begin to wax in iniquity; they understand not the scriptures: for they seek to excuse themselves in committing whoredoms, because of the things which were written concerning David, and Solomon his son.

Behold, David and Solomon truly had many wives, and concubines, which thing was abominable before me, saith the Lord, wherefore, thus saith the Lord, I have led this people forth out of the land of Jerusalem, by the power of mine arm, that I might raise up unto me a righteous branch from the fruit of the loins of Joseph.

Wherefore, I, the Lord God, will not suffer that this people shall do like unto them of old.

Wherefore, my brethren, hear me, and hearken to the word of the Lord: For there shall not any man among you have save

it be one wife; and concubines he shall have none: For I, the Lord God, delighteth in the chastity of women.

And whoredoms are an abomination before me: thus saith the Lord of hosts.[11]

The Old Testament indicates that men highly honored of God entered into polygamy and concubinage. How is this to be explained against the clarity with which the divine law is expressed? Some were caught up in the culture of their land, the practices and even the civil law of their day. Others, in addition to the prestige of foreign cultures, were influenced by ignorance and weaknesses of the flesh. David and Solomon are examples of the latter. The fact that God used such men does not say that he condoned all their actions.

The discovery of the Nuzi tablets throws light on polygamy and concubinage in the age of the patriarchs. Nuzi was an ancient city southeast of Ninevah whose inhabitants were Horites mentioned in Genesis 14:6; 14:5, I.V., as the Hivites.[12] Haran, where Abraham dwelt after leaving Ur of the Caldees, was also in this land of the Horites.[13] According to Nuzi custom and law, if a couple had no son they could adopt someone as their son, who was to take care of them as long as they lived and see that they had a proper burial. In return for this service he became heir to their property. (This very likely accounts for the presence of Eliezer in Abraham's home. See Genesis 15:1-4.) Or if the wife so desired she could give her handmaiden to her husband to raise up children for her, which very well may account for Sarah's act of giving Hagar to Abraham, from which relationship Ishmael was born to Abraham and Hagar (Gen.

16). In the event that later a son should be born to the legal wife, the bondwoman was not to be cast out. Little wonder Abraham was reluctant to follow Sarah's demands that Hagar be cast out after Isaac was born to her.

The Nuzi law code also accounts for Jacob's agreement with Laban to work for him seven years to obtain Laban's daughter, Rachel, whom Jacob loved at first sight. But at the end of seven years, Laban gave him his elder daughter, Leah. When Jacob complained, Laban retorted that, "It must not be done in our country, to give the younger before the firstborn" (Gen. 29:26, I.V.). Then Laban agreed to give Rachel to Jacob in one week, for which Jacob was to serve Laban another seven years, so Jacob now had two wives. In bearing children, rivalry arose between Rachel and Leah because Rachel was barren, while Leah, for a time, was bearing children regularly. Their rivalry led to each of them giving Jacob her handmaiden, as Sarah had done with Abraham.

It is most likely that when Jacob arrived at Laban's home, Laban had no son of his own. When Jacob was leaving, Laban claimed Jacob's wives and children as belonging to him, which indicates that he had adopted Jacob as his heir (Gen. 31:43). Laban had sons of his own born later. For them he must provide an additional inheritance or else disinherit Jacob and his own daughters. These sons complained that Jacob was, by yet another bargain with Laban, "stealing him blind." Whereupon the Lord told Jacob to return to his father's land. As Jacob prepared to leave, Rachel stole the household gods. Then they all left while Laban was away shearing sheep. When he learned of their departure, Laban pursued them. It is interesting to note that he was more concerned about retrieving the stolen images than arguing over the flocks which Jacob, according to his agreement with his Uncle Laban, had taken. The reason for Laban's concern was that whoever possessed the household gods had legal claim as heir. This story is found in detail in Genesis, chapter 29-31. As one reads the Old Testament narratives, he is led to see that there is no cover-up. It tells it as it is.

All of this seems to say quite clearly that God deals with and uses people—in spite of their ignorance, their peculiar culture, and their sins—at the point where he may reach them and obtain response. His purpose is to lead them, while bearing with their ignorance and sins, to a higher code of ethics and morality, ever striving toward the perfection of society which is experienced in the kingdom of God.

Thus God moves to achieve his purposes, and it is vital that we understand the manner in which he moves among us. It should be our joy to be motivated thereby in our cardinal responsibility of taking the gospel, in its purity, to all peoples, ministering to them in the spirit and love of the Lord Jesus, to lift them into realms of joy they have not known before. Then they, too, will be inspired by the hopes and expectations of the kingdom of God.

Covenants and Commandments

A covenant is an agreement between two or more

parties which all involved pledge to keep. Since God is infinite and we humans are finite, it is necessary that there shall be a self-disclosure of the divine nature and will. We need to know what the Lord wills for us; hence we must be instructed in regard to what we should do. God performs his part in giving us directions by way of counsel and commandments.

Authority to command belongs to the Commander. Many of us would like to have this authority so that we might use it in our own way. This is in nature rebellion, which leads to sin and self-destruction. It may lead to the misuse of the best gifts that God has placed within us. One of our greatest sins is to settle, by choice, for the second best while God is seeking perfection in our lives. The Psalmist wrote:

The law of the Lord is perfect, converting the soul; the testimony of the Lord is sure, making wise the simple. The statutes of the Lord are right, rejoicing the heart; the commandment of the Lord is pure, enlightening the eyes. —Psalm 19:7-8.

The covenant made with Israel through Moses at Mount Sinai was based upon the Ten Commandments. The first four of these commandments deal with our concept and honor of our heavenly Father. Briefly they are no other gods; no handmade images of anything which would ascribe worship to other than God who led Israel out of Egypt; no taking of his name in vain; and keeping the Sabbath day holy, a day set apart for rest and worship. The last six commandments deal with our social relationships. They are honor thy father and thy mother; do not kill (commit murder); do not commit adultery; do not steal; do not bear false witness; and do not covet. These ten commandments are the framework of a law code based upon love for God and for our brothers and sisters. The scriptures commanded: "Hear, O Israel; The Lord our God is one Lord; and thou shalt love the Lord thy God with all thine heart, and with all thy soul, and with all thy might" (Deut. 6:4-5). Jesus said: "This is the first and great commandment. And the second is like unto it; Thou shalt love thy neighbor as thyself. On these two commandments hang all the law and the prophets" (Matt. 22:37-39).

Jesus knew the scriptures. In this instance, he combined two commandments, one from Deuteronomy 6:4-5 and the other from Leviticus 19:18, declaring that these are central to all the law and the prophets. In the Jewish canon the law and the prophets are two categories of Old Testament scripture.

Commandments have come from God, to man, through his revelatory processes. While the Ten Commandments form the core of the Israelite law to be lived by, many explanatory additions and interpretative appendages have been included in other places of the entire Old Testament. These will be dealt with in part as we proceed. There are also other commandments which are circumstantial, dealing with specific situations. These are too numerous to epitomize. Nevertheless, a good example is afforded when God told Noah a flood was impending and that he should build an ark. He gave Noah all necessary instructions in regard to the entire situation.

The giving of commandments was characteristic of God from creation forward. Adam was commanded that he should not eat of the fruit of the tree of the knowledge of good and evil, which God had planted in the Garden of Eden, with the warning that if he disobeyed he would surely die. Forewarning of the consequences of disobedience often accompanied the giving of a commandment. After Eve and Adam partook of the forbidden fruit, and were driven out of the garden, Adam offered sacrifices to the Lord. Upon one of these occasions he was met by an angel who asked him why he did so. Adam replied: "I know not save the Lord commanded me." The angel explained, "This thing is a similitude of the sacrifice of the only Begotten of the Father" (Gen. 4:6-7 I.V.). In this there is a clear semblance of the greatest of all divine covenants.

The prophets often upbraided the people for not keeping the commandments of the Lord and reminded them of the consequences of not doing so. Isaiah, chapter 1, is an example of this type of prophetic ministry.

Hear, O heavens, and give ear, O earth; for the Lord hath spoken; I have nourished and brought up children, and they have rebelled against me.

The ox knoweth his owner, and the ass his master's crib; but Israel doth not know, my people doth not consider.

Ah sinful nation, a people laden with iniquity, a seed of evildoers, children that are corrupters; they have forsaken the Lord, they have provoked the Holy One of Israel unto anger, they are gone away backward.

Why should ye be stricken any more? ye will revolt more and more; the whole head is sick, and the whole heart faint.—Isaiah 1:2-5.

Wash ye, make you clean; put away the evil of your doing from before mine eyes; cease to do evil; learn to do well; seek judgment, relieve the oppressed, judge the fatherless, plead for the widow.

Come now, and let us reason together, saith the Lord; though your sins be as scarlet, they shall be as white as snow; though they be red like crimson, they shall be as wool.

If ye be willing and obedient, ye shall eat the good of the land; but if ye refuse and rebel, ye shall be devoured with the sword; for the mouth of the Lord hath spoken it.—Isaiah 1:16-20.

Prophetic ministry not only gave warnings of the consequences of evildoing and called for obedience but it also contained promises of blessings which would follow obedience.

The psalmist, in poetic style, reminds us of the mercy of the Lord and the joy which attends keeping his covenant and commandments.

But the mercy of the Lord is from everlasting to everlasting upon them that fear him, and his righteousness unto children's children; to such as keep his covenant, and to those that remember his commandments to do them.—Psalm 103:17-18.

Covenants and commandments are associated in all three categories of the Old Testament literature. Covenants and commandments were carried over into the ministry of Jesus and the apostles. The New Testament literature is basic to all scripture. It is the first of all accounts of God's revelations.

Covenant and Priesthood

The relationship of priesthood to covenant and to worship is an extensive study. Here we will consider briefly a few pertinent items relating to this topic. Much material is found in the Old Testament in regard to the ministry of priesthood. However, to get the broader perspective we will not be confined to Old Testament scripture. All people called of God in every age, have a covenant obligation to witness for God.

The key to this part of our discussion is couched in the following statement: "The government of the church is by divine authority through priesthood."[14] In *Cruden's Complete Concordance* is the statement: "There were priests in every nation since the term is used of all who have charge of the religious life of the people."[15] While priesthood was established and functioning from the time of Adam forward, the Jewish priesthood began in the time of Moses. Jehovah gave him instructions in regard to the call and ordination of Aaron and his sons (Exodus 28). It is to be remembered that Moses already had contact with Jethro, the priest of Midian, through whom he received the priesthood. In the epistle to the Hebrews it is written concerning the high priest, which principle presumably, in the total context, applies to all priesthood: "And no man taketh this honor unto himself, but he that is called of God, as was Aaron" (Hebrews 5:4). A holy priesthood was in existence prior to the time of Aaron's ordination. Abraham was blessed by Melchizedek, "king of Salem" and "priest of the most high God" (Gen. 14:18-20). Abraham paid tithes to Melchizedek.

The epistle to the Hebrews makes clear that there are two orders of the priesthood, the Melchizedek and the Aaronic (Hebrews 7:11). Melchizedek was of the Order of the High Priesthood, since Christ is designated as belonging to this same order (Hebrews 5:5-6). This assumption is further confirmed in these words:

190

For it is evident that our Lord sprang out of Juda; of which tribe Moses spake nothing concerning priesthood. And it is yet far more evident; for that after the similitude of Melchizedek, there ariseth another priest, who is made, not after the law of a carnal commandment, but after the power of an endless life. For he testifieth, Thou art a priest forever after the order of Melchizedek.—Hebrews 7:14-17.

The above leads to three indisputable conclusions. First, priesthood is very sacred and is conferred only by divine authority or by a call from God. Second, the same priesthood to which Christ belonged was conferred upon Melchizedek and upon others. Third, in Old Testament times the priesthood became lineal through the descendants of Aaron, but this was no longer thus considered after the time of Christ (see Hebrews 7:14).

Priesthood was not intended to be temporary or by interim arrangement. It is everlasting in duration and nature even though there may have been times when, because of sin, God did not call men to function therein. "Thou art a priest forever after the order of Melchizedek" (Psalm 110:4). As further confirmation of the eternal nature of priesthood, consider the following: "And thou shalt anoint them, as thou didst anoint their father, that they may minister unto me in the priest's office: for their anointing shall surely be an everlasting priesthood throughout their generations" (Exodus 40:15). "Behold, I give unto him my covenant of peace: and he shall have it, and his seed after him, even the covenant of an everlasting priesthood; because he was zealous for his God, and made an atonement for the children of Israel" (Numbers 25:12-13).

The last quotation involves the covenant of an everlasting priesthood. Nehemiah also makes reference to the covenant of the priesthood. He said: "Remember them, O my God, because they have defiled the priesthood, and the covenant of the priesthood, and of the Levites" (Neh. 13:29). Here Nehemiah is pleading with God to remember those who had defiled the covenant of their priesthood. The Inspired Version of the scriptures states that the gospel began to be preached from the beginning by holy angels, and that the "same priesthood which was in the beginning, shall be in the end of the world also" (Genesis 5:44; 6:7 I.V.). Contemporary revelation affirms the bestowal of both priesthoods with an oath and covenant "of [the] Father which he can not break, neither can it be moved; but whoso breaketh this covenant, after he hath received it, and altogether turneth therefrom, shall not have forgiveness of sins in this world nor in the world to come."[16]

The succeeding imposing statement by Joseph Smith, the martyr, on priesthood emphasizes most vividly its sacred usages:

. . . The rights of the priesthood are inseparably connected with the powers of heaven, and the powers of heaven cannot be controlled nor handled only upon the principles of righteousness. That they may be conferred upon us, is true; but when we undertake to cover our sins, or to gratify our pride, or vain ambition, or to exercise control, or dominion, or compulsion upon the souls of the children of men, in any degree of unrighteousness, behold, the heavens withdraw themselves; the Spirit of the Lord is grieved; and when it is withdrawn, Amen to the priesthood, or to the authority of that man . . . no power or influence can or ought to be maintained by virtue of the priesthood only by persuasion, by longsuffering, by gentleness and meekness, and by love unfeigned.[17]

The prophet here not only sets forth how sacred the covenant of the priesthood must be esteemed but he also portrays how deep his own insight and how great his personal stature in relation to his exercise of priesthood ministries.

Covenant and Promise

Redemption is predicated first on the fact that Jesus is the anointed one, foretold in Old Testament predictions; and, second, on our unreserved acceptance of him as Lord and Savior. Thereby we, being born again, are able to see his kingdom and become subjects thereof. This new birth is the entrance to the road leading to our final destiny in the kingdom of God (see John 3:3-8).

God acts by covenant with his people. (See Genesis 9:22, 23 I.V., Deuteronomy 5:2-21; Jeremiah 31:31; Hebrews 8:6-13.) In covenant relationship we pledge to serve Jesus Christ with all that we are and possess, in time, in talents, and in temporalities. We take up our cross to follow him and pledge to keep his commandments as we become people of the covenant. Otherwise God's covenants become one-sided and are ineffective.

The efficacy of water baptism is in its symbolism of the cleansing power of the Holy Spirit in the remission of our sins. By this covenant we symbolically express before him, before the world, and before those of the faith our desire to follow him and to be obedient to his commandments. Its importance, therefore, cannot be overemphasized. By the gift of the Holy Spirit working in our lives, he achieves in us what we never could do for ourselves. Hence, the Holy Spirit comes with power and assurance as the gospel of the kingdom of God, fulfilled in Jesus Christ, is preached (see I Thess. 1:5).

No one truly comes to Jesus Christ except he is drawn by the influence of the Holy Spirit. Nevertheless, all are invited to come to Jesus and no one who seeks to come is denied (see Revelation 22:17). No one can experience the joys of eternal life unless he is baptized by the Holy Spirit. Repentance and faith must accompany one's acceptance of Jesus Christ. Our covenant to accept and serve him must be expressed in deep contrition and humility.

All those who humble themselves before God and desire to be baptized, and come forth with broken hearts and contrite spirits, and witness before the church that they have truly repented of all their sins, and are willing to take upon them the name of Jesus Christ, having a determination to serve Him to the end, and truly manifest by their works that they have received of the spirit of Christ unto the remission of their sins, shall be received by baptism into the church.[18]

In making this covenant with God through Jesus we have the joyous anticipation of going on to perfection (Hebrews 6:1-2). The Revised Standard Version uses the word maturity in place of perfection. The process leading to perfection is one of maturation.

Covenant and Remembrance

In the process of maturation we must have assistance. Jesus was well aware of this need as he led the disciples to the upper room and said to them:

With desire I have desired to eat this passover with you before

I suffer; for I say unto you, I will not anymore eat thereof, until it be fulfilled which is written in the prophets concerning me. Then I will partake with you, in the kingdom of God. —Luke 22:15-16, I.V.

The first three of the synoptic writers indicate that as Jesus gave the bread and the wine to the apostles his central emphasis was that they were to partake of each in remembrance of him. The Lord's Supper is to keep us in remembrance of him and to remind us of the promise that we have made in our covenant to serve him. Our remembrance of him is to be verified in keeping his commandments, in loving him, and in loving all mankind, even our enemies. We are not to overlook the fact that Jesus made an eschatological promise in Luke's account of this event: "For I say unto you that I will not drink of the fruit of the vine until the kingdom of God shall come" (Luke 22:18). Matthew and Mark are in agreement with Luke. As a matter of fact Matthew is even more specific than the other two: "I say unto you, I will not drink henceforth of this fruit of the vine, until that day when I drink it new with you in my Father's kingdom" (Matt. 26:29).

Our communion prayers contain these emphases: (1) They are willing to take upon them the name of God's Son. (2) Always remember him. (3) Keep his commandments, (4) "that they may always have his Spirit to be with them."[19]

The Book of Mormon records the observance of the communion as Jesus appeared to his people in ancient America. It is to be remembered that this was after his resurrection. Here, then, they saw what Jesus prayed for at Gethsemane: "Father, I desire that they also, whom thou hast given me, may be with me where I am, to behold my glory which thou hast given me in thy love for me before the foundation of the world" (John 17:24, R.S.V.).

Several things were emphasized by Jesus at that time: (1) The importance of baptism in water; (2) the provision for authoritative serving of the bread and wine by one ordained to do so; (3) the bread and wine to be served in remembrance of him; (4) the Holy Spirit promised on the same conditions that he had made the promise to his disciples in Palestine.[20]

The evidence is clear that remembrance and promise predominate the ordinance of the Lord's Supper. Partaking thereof worthily must always enhance our testimony of Jesus. Therefore, in summary, conversion, covenant, remembrance, and promise are central to the qualities required for the more abundant life—the eternal life. God's actions made to the whole world in giving his only begotten Son are the greatest of all his covenants.

1. F. Henry Edwards, *The Joy in Creation and Judgment*, Herald Publishing House, Independence, Missouri, p. 36.
2. *The Christian Religion in Its Doctrinal Expression*, p. 234.
3. Jack Finegan, *Light From the Ancient Past*, Princeton University Press, New Jersey, pp. 104-112.
4. *Cyclopedia of Religious Knowledge*, pp. 623-628. See also Joseph Gaer, *How the Great Religions Began*, a Key Signet book published by the New American Library, pp. 194-214.
5. See "Forever" *Webster's Dictionary of Synonyms* (Springfield, Mass.: G&C Merriam Company).
6. *Biblical Archaeology*, pp. 112-113.

7. Book of Mormon, Jacob 2:54-57.
8. Doctrine and Covenants 150:10a.
9. *Ibid.*, 42:7d.
10. *Ibid.*, 111:2b.
11. Book of Mormon, Jacob 2:32-37.
12. *Interpreter's Dictionary of the Bible*, Vol. 2, p. 645.
13. George Earnest Wright and Floyd Vivian Filson, *The Westminster Historical Atlas of the Bible* (Philadelphia: The Westminster Press), p. 31, map 111 D2.
14. *Rules and Resolutions*, The Reorganized Church of Jesus Christ of Latter Day Saints (Independence, Missouri: Herald Publishing House), Res. 849, p. 77.
15. Alexander Cruden, *Cruden's Complete Concordance* (Philadelphia, Toronto: John C. Winston Company, 1930), p. 512.
16. Doctrine and Covenants 83:6g, h.
17. Edward W. Tullidge, *The Life of Joseph the Prophet*, Board of Publication, Reorganized Church of Jesus Christ of Latter Day Saints, Plano, Illinois, 1880, pp. 272-273.
18. Doctrine and Covenants 17:7.
19. *Ibid.*, 17:22-23.
20. Book of Mormon, III Nephi 8:28-43.

THE NATION ISRAEL 12 AND THE KINGDOM OF GOD

All Are God's People

All people are one under God. Nevertheless, we are indebted to the Hebrews for our Bible. It was written and preserved by them. While narratives such as the serpent and the fall, the flood, the tower of Babel, etc., comparable in some respects to those found in the early chapters of Genesis, are known to have existed in Mesopotamian and Babylonian myths, there is no definite similarity that could possibly justify the conclusion that biblical primeval history was derived from such sources. As already pointed out, the biblical message is monotheistic throughout. Early Mesopotamian and Babylonian legends are based solely on polytheistic myths.

The origin of the Hebrews, commonly called Israelites, reaches far into the past beyond the time of Abraham. The biblical account begins with God. All peoples are descendants from Adam and Eve, the first man and the first woman whom God created. As Peter exclaimed in the household of Cornelius, "God is no respecter of persons; but in every nation he that feareth him, and worketh righteousness, is accepted with him"

(Acts 10:34-35). We are all God's people, whatever our race, color, or national allegiances. In his sermon to the Athenians on Mars Hill, Paul corroborates this truth. "God that made the world and all things therein, seeing that he is Lord of heaven and earth . . . hath made of one blood all nations of men for to dwell upon all the face of the earth, and hath determined the times before appointed, and the bounds of their habitation; that they should seek the Lord, if they are willing to find him, for he is not far from every one of us" (Acts 17:24-27 I.V.). All are under his care and each soul is equally precious with every other soul to him. Among the occasions when Jesus upheld this universal principle against Pharisaical narrowness were the parables of the lost sheep, the woman who had lost a piece of silver, and the prodigal son (Luke 15).

I once heard a seminary professor give a great deal of emphasis to two verses of scripture. The first one is Deuteronomy 32:9: "For the Lord's portion is his people; Jacob is the lot of his inheritance." The second is to be found in Malachi 1:2-3: " . . . Was not Esau Jacob's brother? saith the Lord, yet I loved Jacob, and I hated Esau. . . . " The Old Testament makes it clear that the purpose of the Abrahamic covenant was to be achieved through Isaac's descendants, not Ishmael's, and Jacob's, not Esau's, posterity. But this is not to imply that our heavenly Father was not concerned about any other people. God is the universal God of the cosmos and its inhabitants. He seeks the salvation of all people.

How then are we to explain God's hate for Esau? In this second passage Jacob is used as a symbol of Israel's remnant just returned from Babylonian captivity. Esau likewise is used as a symbol of the Edomites, Esau's descendants. Israel needed assurance of God's love for her. In the time of distress during the Babylonian siege of Jerusalem 586 B.C., Edom had failed to come to the assistance of Israel and may have assisted the enemy. It was actions of the Edomites in the rejection of God and of Israel their brethren that God hated and not the person Esau.

Jesus said, "God so loved the world that he gave his only begotten Son that whosoever believeth in him should not perish, but have everlasting life. For God sent not his Son into the world to condemn the world; but that the world through him might be saved" (John 3:16-17). God does not condemn men because of who they are but for the reason that they "love darkness rather than light, because their deeds are evil" (John 3:19).

The ensuing comment seems like an adequate summarization as well as support of the principle that we are all one people and equal under God.

Their preservation* is the result of the historicizing tendency observable throughout the whole Old Testament. Of great theological significance is the fact that Israel understood the whole human community to derive from Adam and Eve. There are not, in the last analysis, any alien peoples on the earth. Mankind is one.[1]

It is the divine purpose that all races, colors, and nations shall become fully aware of this and shall learn to live as one family in holiness and peace under him. This is a basic kingdom enterprise.

---

*An antediluvian genealogical listing is found in Genesis 4:17-26.

The Nation Israel

Heretofore in Israel's ancestry we have been considering the origin of all humanity, including the Israelites. Now we shall give brief attention to the beginning and development of Israel as a nation and her religious ideals, especially in the light of the scripturally supported theory that they are a people chosen of God.

Israel's ancestry as a nation may be traced to Abraham. Here we need to remember God's covenant with Abram, as he was named at the time the covenant was made:

Now, the Lord had said unto Abram, Get thee out of thy country, and from thy kindred, and from thy father's house, unto a land that I will show thee; and I will make of thee a great nation, and I will bless thee, and make thy name great; and thou shalt be a blessing; and I will bless them that bless thee, and curse them that curse thee; and in thee shall the families of the earth be blessed.—Genesis 12:1-2 I.V.

This covenant which was repeated to Abraham several times in various forms was for a special purpose. He and his posterity were to become a "blessing to all the families of the earth." Abraham through his posterity, Isaac and Jacob and his twelve sons, were to grow into a nation, called to a special mission involving all humanity for which they must be irrevocably responsible.

While the beginning of the Israelites is traceable through Jacob and Isaac to Abraham, they did not reach the full status of nationhood until after the sojourn in Egypt, the exodus, the conquest of Transjordan by Moses, and Joshua's conquest of a large part of Canaan west of the Jordan River. Still, following

Joshua's death during the time of the Judges, the twelve tribes of Israel were not closely united in a common statehood or cause. The Judges were largely charismatic military leaders chosen to assemble and lead the tribes against their troublesome foes. Deborah and Barak soundly defeated the Canaanite General Sisera and overcame the attacks of the Canaanites who remained in the land (Judges 4 and 5). Gideon overcame the Midianite marauders (chapters 6-8). Jephthah drove off the Ammonites who invaded Israel from east of the Jordan River (chapter 11). Samson was a pathetic failure against the Philistines (chapters 14-18). It was not until the time of King David that the twelve tribes of Israel were welded into a union and matured into a strong nation. By political and military leadership, David subdued all internal and external enemies and extended Israel's territory into an empire, reaching from the Gulf of Aqabah in the south close to Hamath in the north. This empire included Edom, Moab, Ammon, and Syria, in addition to the territory already possessed by the Israelites. In spite of his human weaknesses and sins, David held true to the worship of Jehovah and gave spiritual and prophetic leadership in song and poetry. Solomon's achievements were mostly related to building the temple and in the development of industry and foreign trade.

One of the greatest tragedies in Israel's history followed Solomon's reign, and arose largely out of his burdensome taxation which was increased greatly by Rehoboam, his son. The nation divided into two rival kingdoms, Judah and North Israel. This greatly reduced Israel's military strength in a time when it was to be needed most against Syria, Assyria, and Babylon, ending in final captivity and exile for both kingdoms. The Northern Kingdom was never reestablished. By the return of "the remnant," Judah regained nationhood after Babylon was overthrown by Persia in 539 B.C. Prophetic ministry continued to uphold the high ideals which God had called the Israelite community to exhibit. There is no question that the Kingdom of God emphasis found in the New Testament is drawn from the Old Testament in which, from the time of Moses forward, Israel predominated in Old Testament history and religion.

THE RELIGION OF ISRAEL

In order to appreciate the significance of Israel's religion we must understand the nature of the environment and background in which Israel rose to full national status. Paganism prevailed everywhere in the ancient Near East. This paganism partook of the deification of natural phenomena. Pagans saw the powers of nature as divine powers. The universe to them was one of nature gods and goddesses who, though exercising certain magical powers, did not possess sovereign control. They were subject to rather than in control of nature. They ate, warred, cohabited, and reproduced other gods. Their gods gave no moral inspiration or moral laws. The gods themselves were immoral. The Near Easterner's sense of morality and of social justice often superseded his ideas of how the gods conducted themselves.

From the beginning Israel's religion was monotheistic. It arose out of God's revelation in historic situations. God's will was transcendant and he was sovereign over all. Miracles were not attributed to magical powers or credited to the magic working of the prophet. They were performed by the grace and power of God and affected Israel's faith, belief, and worship. Israel's religion postulated the universal rule of purposeful intelligence.

In the religion of Israel, sin is not perpetrated by Deity. Mankind is the source of evil. He is portrayed as a fallen creature who often offers stubborn resistance to the righteous will of God. God is always represented as holy and sinless. Israel's monotheism did not grow out of controversy about idolatry or mythology; rather it waged a constant battle against these concepts and their attendant practices.

Monotheistic concepts which preceded God's call to Abraham and his call to Moses from the burning bush, while scripturally clear, are from outside sources such as archaeology historically vague. Genesis 14 gives a brief account of Abraham's meeting with Melchizedek, priest of the most high God, El Eloyn. Jethro, Moses' father-in-law, was the Midianite priest of Yahweh.[2] A new Israelitish conception of religion began with Moses' experience at the burning bush. God called Moses to deliver Israel from Egyptian oppression. Yahweh expressed his will and revealed his name to Moses at the burning bush. Yahweh thereafter became the Israelite name of God, equivalent of the later name Jehovah. Signs and wonders were manifested at Sinai and continued to attend Moses as he led the Israelites out of their bondage in Egypt. The revelations of Yahweh to

Moses were expounded by him at Sinai, and during the Israelites' desert wanderings they learned of Yahweh's sovereignty over man and nature: ". . . there is none like the Lord our God" (Exodus 8:10).

Israel's relationship to Yahweh was a covenant relationship sealed with the Ten Commandment law. Israel's allegiance to and worship of Yahweh continually gravitated to this Sinai experience and covenant. Through the Sinai covenant the people were to know Yahweh by his everlasting name and by his continuous presence. Their remembrance of deliverance motivated their sacrificial worship. Israel's national and cultural life was the product of the pervasiveness of God's revelation in her history. "I am who I am. . . . This is my name for ever, and thus I am to be remembered throughout all generations" (Exodus 3:14-15 R.S.V.).[3]

Messianic Expectations in the Old Testament

Messianic prophecy is central to Old Testament Scripture. Throughout the Old Testament there is repeatedly expressed a hopeful expectation of the coming Messianic kingdom when the ideal king of the lineage of David will rule in peace. In the patriarchal blessing which father Jacob gave to Judah, he made this pronouncement: "The sceptre shall not depart from Judah, nor a lawgiver from between his feet, until Shiloh come; and unto him shall the gathering of the people be" (Genesis 49:10 K.J.V. and I.V.).

There is some question as to the significance of the word *Shiloh*. In the exegesis of this verse, the

Interpreter's Bible gives two alternatives but states that in either case "the verse has a Messianic significance."[4] The Revised Standard Version translates the verse thus: "The scepter shall not depart from Judah, nor the ruler's staff from between his feet, until he comes to whom it belongs; and to him shall be the obedience of the peoples." The inference is that the sceptre belongs to another than Judah, who is yet to come and rule. This seems to imply that Shiloh, to whom the sceptre really belongs, is the Messiah.

A much disputed text is found in Isaiah 7:13-14:

...Hear ye now, O house of David; Is it a small thing for you to weary men, but will ye weary my God also? Therefore the Lord himself shall give you a sign. Behold a virgin shall conceive, and shall bear a son, and shall call his name Immanuel.

Isaiah had sought out Ahaz, king of Judah and of the Davidic line, to warn him not to fear Rezin of Syria or Pekah of Israel, who had entered into an alliance to invade Judah. It was Assyria that Ahaz needed to fear. The prophet proposes to Ahaz that if he doesn't believe him, he should ask the Lord for a sign. Ahaz makes a flimsy excuse and Isaiah tells him the sign will be given in any event by the birth of a child whose name shall be Immanuel, which means "God with us." Matthew employs this passage in relating to Jesus in an almost indisputable manner as he interprets the events in regard to Jesus' birth (Matthew 1:20-24; 2:3-6 I.V.). The critical problem arises out of the fact that in the original Hebrew of this Isaianic text the word *Almah* is used, which means a young woman of marriageable age.[5] The word for virgin is *Bethulah*. Matthew evidently has used the Septuagint which translates Almah *parthenos*. In the Greek *parthenos* does mean virgin. The fact that Almah in the Hebrew means a young woman does not rule out the possibility that she may have been a virgin. Other than a Messianic interpretation of this passage fails in the proper usage of his name Immanuel. "God with us" conforms ideally with the Christian doctrine of the divine incarnation. It is of interest that while Isaiah 7:14 bolstered the faith of Judah in the time of impending grave danger, Isaiah proclaimed:

The people that walked in darkness have seen a great light; they that dwell in the land of the shadow of death, upon them hath the light shined.... For unto us a child is born, unto us a son is given; and the government shall be upon his shoulder; and his name shall be called Wonderful, Counselor, The mighty God, The everlasting Father, The Prince of Peace. Of the increase of his government and peace there shall be no end, upon the throne of David, and upon his kingdom, to order it, and to establish it with judgment and with justice from henceforth even for ever. The zeal of the Lord of hosts will perform this.—Isaiah 9:2, 6-7.

The prophet is expressing eventual hope, through the Messiah, to a people doomed if they do not repent. If anything, this passage is more explicit than its forerunner. There are four appellations here which give assurance that the Son or child is divine: (1) Wonderful Counselor. (2) The mighty God. (3) The everlasting Father. (4) The Prince of Peace. His government is eternal and it will increase forever.

Isaiah, chapter 11, speaks of a rod to come forth out of Jesse, King David's father, who was of the lineage of Judah. The Spirit of the Lord is to be upon him and righteousness and peace will attend him. An ensign will be set up for the nations and He will assemble the outcasts of Israel. Ephraim (North Israel) and Judah will be rejoined and will dwell without envy in peace. The angel quoted this whole chapter,[6] with other Messianic passages, to Joseph Smith on the night of September 21, 1823, stating that this was soon to be fulfilled.

Micah foretells the place of the Messiah's birth:

But thou, Bethlehem Ephratah, though thou be little among the thousands of Judah, yet out of thee shall he come forth unto me that is to be ruler in Israel; whose goings forth have been from of old, from everlasting.—Micah 5:2.

When the ruthlessly jealous King Herod heard of the birth of Jesus he called the chief priests and scribes of Jerusalem together to inquire of them where the child was to be born. They told him in Bethlehem and quoted this passage from Micah in support of their answer.

Jeremiah foretold the Messianic event as a righteous Branch of David who was to be called "The Lord our Righteousness."

And I will gather the remnant of my flock out of all countries whither I have driven them, and will bring them again to their folds; and they shall be fruitful and increase. And I will set up shepherds over them which shall feed them; and they shall fear no more, nor be dismayed, neither shall they be lacking, saith the Lord. Behold, the days come, saith the Lord, that I will raise unto David a righteous Branch, and a King shall reign and prosper, and shall execute judgment and justice in the earth. In his days Judah shall be saved, and Israel shall dwell safely; and this is his name whereby he shall be called, THE LORD OUR RIGHTEOUSNESS.—Jeremiah 23:3-6.

Then there is the new covenant the Lord promised to make with the house of Israel:

Behold, the days come, saith the Lord, that I will make a new covenant with the house of Israel, and with the house of Judah; not according to the covenant that I made with their fathers, in the day that I took them by the hand to bring them out of the land of Egypt; which my covenant they brake, although I was a husband unto them, saith the Lord; but this shall be the covenant that I will make with the house of Israel; After those days, saith the Lord, I will put my law in their inward parts, and write it in their hearts; and will be their God, and they shall be my people. And they shall teach no more every man his neighbor, and every man his brother, saying, Know the Lord; for they shall all know me, from the least of them unto the greatest of them, saith the Lord; for I will forgive their iniquity, and I will remember their sin no more.—Jeremiah 31:31-34.

The writer of the epistle to the Hebrews comments on this covenant in support of Jesus and the restoration of the Melchizedek priesthood in him (see Hebrews, chapters 7 and 8).

One of the Messianic messages in the Old Testament most frequently used by Christians is the song of the suffering servant. This is found in Isaiah 52:13 - 53:12. The Ethiopian was reading this passage when he was joined by Philip, the Christian disciple. He asked, ". . . of whom speakest the prophet this? of himself, or of some other man?" (Acts 8:34). Philip began at this scripture and "preached unto him Jesus." When the Ethiopian confessed that he believed in Jesus and requested baptism, Philip baptized him.

There is a great deal of controversy today among both Jewish and Christian scholars concerning the interpretation of this and other Isaianic servant passages. One point of view, largely Jewish, is that the servant referred to in Isaiah 52:13 is the nation Israel. In all fairness we

are obligated to evaluate another statement in Isaiah
49:3: "Thou art my servant, O Israel, in whom I will be
glorified." However, we need to take a look at some
other passages in which the term *servant* or its
equivalent is used. Isaiah wrote of Cyrus, king of Persia,
who liberated the Jewish captives in Babylon, "He is
my shepherd, and he shall fulfill all my purpose"
(Isaiah 44:28 R.S.V.). In Isaiah 45:1 Cyrus is called the
Lord's anointed. In Jeremiah 27:6 Nebuchadnezzar,
king of Babylon, is designated as the Lord's servant.
These passages indicate that servant, shepherd, the
Lord's anointed, etc., had a variety of usages. The
question is, can the anonymous servant of Isaiah 52 and
53 be identified with Israel as a nation? It is quite clear
that this servant is a person, not a community or nation.

Bernard Anderson has made a striking chart of the
differences between the claims that this suffering
servant is the nation Israel and that the servant is a
person.[7] Two major points are made by Anderson:
(1) The servant of Isaiah 53 suffers for the sins of others;
Israel suffered for its own sins. (2) This servant is to redeem Israel. Israel did not demonstrate ability without
help to save itself from its enemies, much less to redeem
itself from its sins. As with all humanity Israel's
salvation must come from a higher source than itself,
from outside itself. Christians need to be cognizant of
orthodox Jewish interpretations which are anti-Chris-
tian and anti-Messianic. Christopher R. North has
stated, "With the introduction, a couple of centuries
ago, of the second Isaiah theory Christian scholars
began to adopt Jewish interpretations of the servant
Psalms."[8] North also states, "It is agreed on all hands

210

that the portrait of the servant did ultimately find its actualization in Christ."[9]

Undeniably, Israel had a servant mission to perform (see Isaiah, chapter 49). This mission was written into the covenant God made with Abraham. Three things should be clear to our perception: (1) Israel as a nation, especially in ancient times, was never missionary minded. (2) Israel, the same as all nations, must be redeemed by the ministry of the lowly suffering servant, who is King of Kings and Lord of Lords. (3) The burden is upon us today to take his gospel as a witness to every nation and to all peoples.[10] The burden of that mission was laid upon Christ's church when he said to his apostles,

Go ye, therefore, and teach all nations, baptizing them in the name of the Father, and of the Son, and of the Holy Ghost; teaching them to observe all things whatsoever I have commanded you; and, lo, I am with you alway, even unto the end of the world.—Matthew 28:19-20.

In the eternal design the nation Israel was loved and chosen by God to fulfill the Abrahamic covenant, that of becoming a blessing unto all the families of the earth. Israel was chosen to bring forth the Messianic kingdom of God but rejected and crucified the lowly suffering servant. The Israelites did not discern the mightiest of all the acts of God, when he sent his Son to gather the lost sheep of the house of Israel (Matthew 15:24). This was mightier than their deliverance from Egyptian slavery in the time of Moses. Yet God has not forgotten his covenant nor cast off his chosen people. What could be more demonstrative of this fact than that, after eighteen hundred years of dispersion, the Jews should survive persecution and the threat of extinction, to be again established in their homeland as modern Israel? Prophecy indicates this was to take place. The prophets have also indicated Israel's part in the final dominion of God's kingdom upon the earth.[11]

Ancient Israel, though often unfaithful, at its best under the ministry of the prophets looked forward with hope and expectation to the day of the Lord. Like Israel we are now experiencing the manifestation of divine goodness in the midst of adversity, confusion, crime, and turmoil. We, too, are encouraged by faith to realize that God's design is eternal. He will never forsake his promise. He is preparing his people to seek first to build his kingdom and to establish his righteousness in our time. The witness of Christ, by those who truly have entered his service, must go forth to "all the families of the earth," that the day of the world's redemption may be hastened. There shall be a new Israel composed of Jews, and Gentiles who are adopted into the kingdom of God and who thereby become his chosen people and, by that adoption, the seed of Abraham.

1. *Interpreting the Old Testament*, p. 53.
2. See *Interpreter's Dictionary of the Bible*, Vol. 2, p. 896.
3. See Leo W. Schwartz, Ed., *Great Ages and Ideas of the Jewish People*, (New York: Random House), pp. 3-29.
4. *Interpreter's Bible*, Vol. 1, p. 821.
5. *Ibid.*, Vol. 5, p. 128.
6. Church History, Vol. 1, p. 13.
7. Bernard W. Anderson, *Understanding the Old Testament* (Englewood Cliffs, New Jersey: Prentice Hall, Inc.), pp. 414-429.
8. C. R. North, *The Suffering Servant of Deutero Isaiah* (London, New York, Toronto: Oxford University Press), p. 28.
9. *Ibid.*, p. 216.
10. John Bright *The Kingdom of God* (New York and Nashville: Abingdon Press), pp. 147-155.
11. See Isaiah 11 and Daniel 2:44; 7:26-27.

THE KINGDOM OF GOD 13 AND NEW TESTAMENT TEACHING

THE KINGDOM CONCEPT IS THE UNIFYING LINK BETWEEN THE OLD AND NEW TESTAMENTS

If a true perspective of the kingdom of God is to be obtained, no successful attempt can be sustained to make any segment of Holy Writ stand by itself. As we move more specifically into the New Testament teachings, we are not attempting to sectionalize the word of God in our efforts to substantiate genuine hopes for the triumph of his kingdom. The search of each area of revealed truth is important, but each must be consistent and considered in relation to the whole. Paul wrote: "All scripture given by inspiration of God is profitable. . .for instruction in righteousness" (II Tim. 3:16 I.V.).

The Jews regarded the nation Israel as God's kingdom. Nevertheless, a universal application is implied by the Psalmist and many of the prophets.

All thy works shall praise thee, O Lord; and thy saints shall bless thee. They shall speak of the glory of thy kingdom, and talk of thy power; to make known to the sons of men his mighty acts and the glorious majesty of his kingdom. Thy king-

213

dom is an everlasting kingdom, and thy dominion endureth throughout all generations.—Psalm 145:10-13.

And in the days of these kings shall the God of heaven set up a kingdom, which shall never be destroyed; and the kingdom shall not be left to other people, but it shall break in pieces and consume all these kingdoms, and it shall stand forever.... And the kingdom and dominion, and the greatness of the kingdom under the whole heaven, shall be given to the people of the saints of the Most High, whose kingdom is an everlasting kingdom, and all dominions shall serve and obey him.—Daniel 2:44; 7:27.

And the Lord shall be King over all the earth; in that day shall there be one Lord, and his name one.—Zechariah 14:9.

God's kingdom, eventually, is to envelop the whole world and to be everlasting. John Bright states, "Old Testament prophecy like Old Testament faith itself, had always an eschatological orientation.... The triumph of the divine design... it looked for 'last things.' The effective terminus towards which history moves."[1] This very well may be another way of saying the Old Testament throughout is kingdom of God orientated. Its total outlook portrays a "Messianic kingdom" theology of hope. There was always the hope of the coming of the Messianic kingdom, when the ideal king would rule.

The Old Testament prophets often associated this kingdom with the throne of David which may be symbolic of Jesus' human lineal background. Isaiah declared,

Of the increase of his government and peace there is no end, upon the throne of David, and upon his kingdom, to order it, and to establish it with judgment and with justice from

214

henceforth even forever. The zeal of the Lord of hosts will perform this.—Isaiah 9:7.

Isaiah 11 begins with a rod coming forth "out of the stem of Jesse" and a branch growing out of his roots. Jesse was David's father. The whole chapter deals with the prospective achievements of this Messianic rod and branch upon whom "the Spirit of the Lord shall rest." These achievements are worldwide involving all Israel and the gentile nations as a whole. They are even now in the process of fulfillment.

Jeremiah offers a similar hope:

Behold, the days come, saith the Lord, that I will raise unto David a righteous Branch, and a King shall reign and prosper, and shall execute judgment and justice in the earth. In his days Judah shall be saved, and Israel shall dwell safely: and this is the name whereby he shall be called, THE LORD OUR RIGHTEOUSNESS.—Jer. 23:5-6.

Here again a kingly righteous branch is to be raised up unto David. Ezekiel offers hope to the captive Jews in Babylon, referring to them as cattle to be fed by David, their shepherd, who is to become a prince among them (see Ezekiel 34:22-24).

This language portrays a Messianic apocalyptic symbolism, since David, the second king of Israel, had been dead for approximately four centuries.

The New Testament preaching of the kingdom of God clearly binds it with the Old Testament. The New Testament does not replace the Old Testament. Rather, as Jesus said, it fulfills the law and the prophets. Marcion (a second century A.D. heretic), in a form of Gnosticism, rejected all of the Old Testament. To him the gospel of Jesus was one of love to the absolute exclusion of the law. Marcion may have considered this to his advantage since he is reported to have been the son of a bishop, who excommunicated him for immorality.[2] At any rate his position is a direct contradiction of the words of Jesus wherein he affirmed that he had not come to destroy but to fulfill the "law and the prophets.... Till heaven and earth pass, one jot or one tittle shall in no wise pass from the law, till all be fulfilled" (Matt. 5:17-18).

The Presence of Jesus

We cannot complete the kingdom of God by ourselves. This task requires the authority and presence of Jesus. Jesus may be present in person or by the power of the Holy Spirit. When he said, "I will build my church," he actually meant he would give power to and direct the work of establishing his kingdom. Little else can be implied in light of his total teaching and ministry.

Jesus began his Galilean ministry proclaiming, "The time is fulfilled, and the kingdom of God is at hand: repent ye, and believe the gospel" (Mark 1:15). Mark affirms that Jesus then set about calling disciples (Mark 1:16-20) to whom he later said, "I will build my church" (Matt. 16:18). Authority is expressed in Matthew 16:19: "And I will give unto thee the keys of the kingdom of heaven: and whatsoever thou shalt bind on earth shall be bound in heaven: and whatsoever thou shalt loose on earth shall be loosed in heaven." Evidently this authority was not confined to Peter, to whom Jesus spoke at the time, because Jesus conferred similar authority on all the disciples (Matt. 18:18 and John 20:23).

Mark is considered by some New Testament scholars as the earliest of the gospel writers.[3] His announcement of the preaching of Jesus in Galilee was preceded by references to the ministry of John the Baptist. John the Baptist, in harmony with Isaiah 40:3, declared his message as, "The voice of one crying in the wilderness, Prepare ye the way of the Lord, make his paths straight." And, "There cometh one mightier than I after me. . . . I indeed have baptized you with water: but he shall baptize you with the Holy Ghost" (Mark 1:3, 7, 8).

Jesus was conversant with Old Testament predictions. It may be implied from Mark 1:12-13 that John's imprisonment was the signal that the time had come for Jesus to commence his public ministry. His first announcement was "the time is fulfilled" which indicates that he knew "the fullness of the time" had been reached. He must not delay. Jesus was precise in all his decisions and actions.

When Jesus said, "The kingdom of God is at hand," this was tantamount to saying it is a present fact. Over the centuries among the Jews there had arisen a great anticipation for the time when this would take place. But at least two problems present themselves at this point. One has to do with misconceptions concerning the nature of the kingdom. The other relates to what Jesus himself meant by his assertion, "The kingdom of God is at hand."

The Jews hoped for and expected the restoration of the throne of David when the Messiah came. The apostles had been stimulated by the miracles of Jesus to expect this to happen. Even after Jesus' resurrection, they asked him, "Wilt thou at this time restore again the kingdom to Israel?" (Acts 1:6). Jesus answered that it was not for them "to know the times or seasons which the Father hath kept in his own power." Their job was to be witnesses to him in all the world (Acts 1:7-8). Among some groups of the Jews (especially those known as Zealots) this misconception created a grave danger. Jesus was fully aware that if he submitted to kingship this would be an act of treason against Rome. The result would be that which happened in A.D. 70 when the armies of Rome, under Titus, in order to suppress a Jewish revolt, entirely destroyed Jerusalem and the temple.

Jesus' mission was not to restore the throne of David. This may appear to have been the most likely way he could have proved to the Jews that he is the Messiah; however, in order to do this he would have had to over-throw Roman rule. At his trial, he said to Pilate, "My kingdom is not of this world; if my kingdom were of this world, then would my servants fight. . . . To this end was I born, and for this cause came I into the world, that I should bear witness unto the truth" (John 18:36-37). In order to preserve his higher spiritual aims Jesus carefully avoided any conflict with Rome which would have jeopardized Jewish welfare and made him unfaith-ful to his own mission. The kingdom which Jesus pro-claimed had a much wider and more profound meaning than to restore the Davidic throne to Israel.

The time which he said was fulfilled had no reference to the establishment of a political or nationalistic rule. The mission he assigned to his apostles was

Go therefore and make disciples of all nations, baptizing them in the name of the Father and of the Son and of the Holy

218

Spirit, teaching them to observe all that I have commanded you; and lo, I am with you always, to the close of the age.—Matthew 28:19-20, R.S.V.

No other kingdom commission could be adequate. The church either sustains spiritual life or perishes according to its response to this sound evangelistic foundation and outreach. The apostle Paul wrote concerning this foundation:

You are built upon the foundation by the apostles and prophets, and Christ Jesus himself is the foundation-stone. In him the whole building is bonded together and grows into a holy temple in the Lord. In him you too are being built with all the rest into a spiritual dwelling for God.—Eph. 2:20-22 N.E.B.[4]

The church is built upon Jesus as the foundation stone and maintained by the evangelistic, apostolic, and prophetic ministries.

The Kingdom of God Is at Hand

What did Jesus mean when he proclaimed in Galilee, "The kingdom of God is at hand"? Does this mean that Jesus expected the immediate triumph of his kingdom in all its power and glory? The New English Bible translates this text, "The kingdom of God is upon you," which could be interpreted meaningfully that Jesus was telling them that "the burden of the kingdom of God is on you." Jesus' proclamation that the kingdom is at hand must be related to its antecedent, "the time is fulfilled," which means without doubt, the time has come for that which is happening to happen. And we may add the clear implication, "If you want to be a part

219

of it, repent and believe the good news."

Other sayings of Jesus demonstrate that the kingdom of God is a progressive process in which all of humanity must be involved. It is not an instantaneous miracle brought about by Deity acting alone. One needs only refer to that which is commonly called the Lord's Prayer to substantiate such a position: "Thy kingdom come. Thy will be done on earth, as it is done in heaven" (Matt. 6:10). This is perhaps the clearest definition Jesus is recorded as giving of the kingdom of God, which in no way robs God of his power and glory. "Thine is the kingdom, and the power, and the glory" (Matt. 6:13). The kingdom is God's will being done on earth as it is now being done in heaven.

The kingdom of God, ideally, has always been a truism. It is the ultimate of the eternal design, but Jesus, by his life and ministry, was bringing it into practical reality. It had yet to find acceptance and fulfillment in human lives. The two statements of our Lord, "The kingdom of God is at hand" and "Thy kingdom come, thy will be done on earth, as it is done in heaven," derive correlation and consistency from this view. The idea which developed that Jesus meant and even expected the imminence of the kingdom of God is clearly a misconception arising out of early and successive misinterpretations. Many other texts would bear clarification on this point but those already alluded to will serve our purpose here. The ensuing statement provides a good summary: "The kingdom is the reign of God, his sovereignty over mind and heart and will, and in the world. It is the sonship to God and brotherly relation with men. It is in the future, but whenever human life is brought into harmony with the Father's purpose, it is present."[5] The kingdom then has a conditional fulfillment, based upon repentance, belief, and obedience to the gospel of Christ.

The Teachings of Jesus

Jesus' ministry was kingdom centered in all that he said and did. Yet at no time did he transmit a clearcut definition of the kingdom of God to his disciples, nor do we find his disciples asking him to do so. In both instances, there is a plausible reason. First, such a definition cannot be encapsulated in a few simple words or principles for the guidance of a few people. The kingdom way of life is both complex and eternal in nature and is designed for all mankind everywhere. Second, the disciples, though with the narrow Jewish concept of the time, thought they already understood the full meaning of the kingdom of God (see Acts 1:8). Nevertheless, Jesus accentuated many aspects of God's kingdom and also instructed his disciples, with clarity, regarding their responsibilities to it.

The Sermon on the Mount (Matt. 5-7) embodies many kingdom of God overtures. The beatitudes depict Jesus' challenge to acquire the qualities of the kingdom way of personal living and the blessings accompanying observance of these qualities. We are reminded here of the rich young man who came to Jesus asking, "Good Master, what good thing shall I do, that I may have eternal life?" Jesus answered, "If thou wilt *enter into life*, keep the commandments," to which the young man replied that he had, from his youth up, kept those

221

commandments which Jesus enumerated. What did he lack still? Jesus said to him, "If thou wilt be perfect, go and sell that thou hast, and give to the poor, and thou shalt have treasure in heaven: and come and follow me" (Matt. 19:21). This young man denied himself entrance into the "kingdom of heaven" by failing to follow Jesus' instruction. He also denied himself the riches of that life which leads to perfection. Eternal life is a quality of living, both for here and hereafter.

Immediately following the beatitudes, Jesus graphically described the influence radiating from those who live in compliance with the kingdom's life-style. They shall become "the salt of the earth" and the "light of the world." "Therefore, let your light so shine before this world, that they may see your good works, and glorify your Father who is in heaven" (Matt. 5:18 I.V.).

Next Jesus links himself, his ministry, and our accountability for its laws and teachings to the Old Testament:

Think not that I am come to destroy the law, or the prophets; I am not come to destroy, but to fulfill. For verily I say unto you, Heaven and earth must pass away, but one jot or one tittle shall in no wise pass from the law, until all be fulfilled. Whosoever, therefore, shall break one of these least commandments, and shall teach men so to do, he shall in no wise be saved in the kingdom of heaven; but whosoever shall do and teach these commandments of the law until it be fulfilled, the same shall be called great, and shall be saved in the kingdom of heaven.—Matt. 5:19-21 I.V.

Our righteousness must excel if we are to have part in God's kingdom.

Jesus expanded and gave new, influential meaning to the Old Testament commandments. This was promised in the new covenant of Jeremiah 31:31-34: "I will put my law in their inward parts and write it in their hearts; and will be their God, and they shall be my people." Dr. George A. Buttrick has written: "He changed its narrowness into wide horizons. The love shown by the old law towards friends is shown in the new law also towards foes, and the loyalty formerly given to one nation is now to be given to all mankind."[6] If we are to understand the vital meaning of the kingdom of God, these new dimensions must be observed in keeping with the real spirit of the law. We cannot hope to win lasting acceptance by our enemies without loving them.

For ethical standards proclaimed by Jesus in this sermon, Matthew 5:23 - 6:8 should be read and prayerfully evaluated in the light of the preceding comments. The ethics of Jesus deal with anger and killing, belittling and slandering, and ill will which require reconciliation before a gift at the altar is acceptable. Great wisdom in dealing with an adversary is required. One may commit adultery in his heart by lust. A person may not put away his wife except for fornication and "whosoever shall marry her who is [thus divorced] committeth adultery."

In regard to oaths, communication shall be forthright "yes" or "no" according to that which is the truth. Do not resist those who do evil against you but be liberally willing to go the second mile. Love your enemies and strive for perfection even as God is perfect. Do not do deeds of charity for show, for if you do there is no reward in the act. Be humble and penitent as you pray, even doing so in secret, not using vain repetitions. This is not to say we should refrain from prayer in public. In the prayer Jesus taught his disciples, he stresses forgiveness that we may be forgiven. How may we expect to be forgiven or derive any benefit from it if we are unwilling to forgive? Fasting is not to be ostentatious. We must be undivided in our loyalties. We cannot serve God and the world at the same time (Matt. 6:24). The remainder of chapter six delineates thought patterns and priorities, placing the establishment of the kingdom of God first in our service to God and to humanity. In chapter seven Jesus condemns hypocrisy and makes a plea for repentance and righteous living. He forewarns against false prophets, implying that we need not be deceived, for every tree is known by its fruit whether it be good or bad. The sermon ends in triumph and describes the astonishment of the people at his doctrine.

Jesus explained many facets of the kingdom of God in parables. Dr. George A. Buttrick has written, "Jesus taught in parables because a parable disarms and wins, when an argument might alienate; and because a story lingers in the mind like music, . . . and because a story is a seed plot ever yielding new and deeper truth."[7]

A man, whose identity I did not recognize for the moment, said to me, "I know you; I still remember a sermon you preached fifteen years ago." What he remembered was a little incident I had told of a butterfly trying to escape through a large plate glass window, until it grew tired and alighted on the windowsill to rest. Whereupon, I gently took it by the tips of its wings and released it outside a less conspicuous open door, right beside the window. It gleefully flew away to the freedom it sought in the outdoors.

I had asked how many of us, like the butterfly, are attracted to the more conspicuous glamour of the world as we miss the open door to the kingdom of God. That simple little story had remained with my friend long after I had forgotten about it.

Jesus was unrivaled in the use of parables. Yet he never used a parable to win an argument, for he knew that human nature resents being outwitted in a dispute. He used ordinary occurrences with which his hearers were familiar to clarify issues for them. Therefore, it is not surprising that he should use parables to teach simple yet profound truths in regard to the kingdom of God.

Jesus had commanded his disciples not to seek the things of this world, but to "Seek first to build up the kingdom of God" (Matt. 6:38 I.V.). Yet by parables he indicated that there were those who would be seeking earnestly to find that kingdom. He told of a treasure hidden in a field, and of the merchant who searched for goodly pearls and found one of great value (Matt. 13:44-45). In both instances the men were willing to dispose of all their other properties in order to purchase that which was of the greatest value. In like manner we must be willing to sacrifice things of lesser worth in order to be able to pay the price required to possess that which the kingdom of God has to offer. There is nothing to be found anywhere that is equal to the riches of eternal living in the kingdom of God.

The shepherd left the ninety-nine sheep which were safely in the fold and went out in search of the one that had wandered away from the flock (Luke 15:3-7). The woman who had lost a coin searched diligently until she had found it (Luke 15:8-10). Both the shepherd and the woman experienced great joy in finding that which was lost. So there is and ever shall be joy both in heaven and on earth when even one sinner repents. Moreover, the father forgave his son and exhibited illustrious rejoicing upon the return of that wayward son, who had wickedly squandered his inheritance in a distant land (Luke 15:11-24).

Surely a person who turns back after he has wandered from the kingdom will be received joyously. This prodigal son had learned the lesson that even the hired servant is better off than a son who wastes his life in the pleasures of the world. When the prodigal son's money was all gone, those he thought were his friends forsook him: "No man gave unto him." The best he could do was to get a job feeding swine, which would be most humiliating to a Jew. This caused a shift to straight thinking. "He came to himself" (Luke 15:17) which led to his decision to clean up his life and return home on the simplest terms. The father received him back as his own, not as a hired servant which the repentant son proposed.

The parables of the sowers (Matt. 13:3-30 I.V.) indicate that there are obstructors and adversaries of the kingdom of God. These range all the way from acts of human weakness to the craftiness of Satan. Some out of weakness permit Satan to snatch away the good seed of the kingdom before it has opportunity to take root. Others have not the depth necessary to maintain a substantial growth. Still others are encumbered by the deceitfulness of riches. Finally, there are those who understand the word in depth. They produce the fruits of the kingdom in various amounts of abundance.

In the second parable, the man sowed good seed in his

field, but while he slept the enemy came and sowed tares. When informed of this, he instructed his servants to let the weeds and the good grain grow together, lest in pulling up the tares they destroy the tender roots of the good young plants. At the harvest the tares will be gathered in bundles and burned, while the wheat is preserved. God is not going to destroy the potential of the righteous in order to eliminate the wicked.

In this same chapter the parable of the grain of mustard seed and that of the leaven placed in three measures of meal go together. They illustrate the powers of growth where the kingdom has a favorable opportunity. Evidently the three measures of meal are not to be interpreted as separate entities but represent the larger amount in which the leaven was placed. "Till the whole was leavened" seems to join the three measures into one amount.

William Barclay has implied that in order to be in the kingdom of God we must accept God's sovereignty over all things past, present, and future, everywhere. It is infinitely more than earthly kingship over a limited territory.[8]

Chief among the sayings of Jesus to support this position is his reply to Pilate when Pilate asked him, "Art thou the king of the Jews?" "My kingdom is not of this world; if my kingdom were of this world then would my servants fight, that I should not be delivered to the Jews: but now is my kingdom not from hence" (John 18:33-36). Jesus taught peace, not violence. The fact that he rode into Jerusalem on a donkey was a symbol of peace. If his kingship were of this world, he would have entered Jerusalem as a conqueror, clothed in armor,

227

carrying a sword or spear and riding on a beautiful horse. But he chose to make his entry in humility. In this regard, his followers may have done him a disservice by laying their clothing and branches of trees along the way in front of him.

At no time did Jesus permit himself to be tricked into a worldly kingship or into saying he was a king, as the Jews accused him of doing. Did Pilate, who seems to have been reluctant to have Jesus crucified, recognize the universally spiritual kingship of Jesus when he refused to change the inscription he had placed on the cross from "Jesus of Nazareth, the King of the Jews," to "He said, 'I am the king of the Jews'"? (John 9:19-20). Pilate was not willing to concede that Jesus was guilty of treason against Rome.

Jesus further emphasized that peace and humility are inseparable when his disciples asked him, "Who is greatest in the kingdom of heaven?" Jesus took a little child, placed him in the midst of them and said, "Verily I say unto you, Except ye be converted, and become as little children, ye shall not enter into the kingdom of heaven. Whosoever therefore shall humble himself as this little child, the same is greatest in the kingdom of heaven" (Matt. 18:1-3). Is not something of the same insight implied when Jesus said to Nicodemus, "Except a man be born again, he cannot see the kingdom of God" (John 3:3)?

A little child is not far removed from the time of his birth. The spiritual rebirth makes one a new creature so that his entire perception of life is modified by love and humility, making it possible for him to envision the kingdom of God. When Nicodemus failed to understand

228

what Jesus meant by being born again, the Master said, "Except a man be born of water and the Spirit, he cannot enter into the kingdom of God" (John 3:5). A man must be humble, full of love, and obedient to the commandments of God to enter the new life of the kingdom.

Nicodemus was thinking in terms of earthly events while Jesus spoke of heavenly, spiritual things. He said: "The wind bloweth where it listeth and thou hearest the sound thereof, but canst not tell whence it cometh and whither it goeth; so is everyone that is born of the Spirit" (John 3:8). He who is born of the Spirit must have that mysterious invisible power working within his soul, motivating him to righteous actions.

According to the teaching of Jesus, the coming of the kingdom of heaven is not an observable event of pomp and show. Being asked of the Pharisees when the kingdom of God should come, he answered them, "The kingdom of God is not coming with signs to be observed; nor will they say, 'Lo, here it is!' or 'There!' for behold, the kingdom of God is in the midst of you" (Luke 17:20 R.S.V.). The Inspired Version renders it "the kingdom of God has already come unto you."

All the righteousness of the kingdom of God was manifested in Jesus, but the people did not discern it. Some years ago I stood for over two hours on a street corner in Honolulu on Kamehameha Day watching the parade in celebration of the achievements of this great Hawaiian king. The pageantry and coloring were indescribably wonderful, yet the kingdom of God does not come in that manner. True it involves the worship of God and the preaching of the gospel in all nations.

However, most important is that unostentatious inner working of the divine Spirit leading men and women to repentance and obedience to God, accompanied by works of righteousness.

Paul's Views of the Kingdom of God

Why single out Paul from the rest of the apostles in order to examine his viewpoint on a question of theology? This is a legitimate question. The answer is simple. Paul, truly an apostle, was not among the first twelve who were taught personally by the Lord. Jesus himself left no written word. Matthew and John who were among the first apostles, along with Mark and Luke who were disciples of Jesus but not numbered among the Twelve, wrote as they perceived what he taught and preached concerning the kingdom of God. Hence there are two possible sources from which Paul may have received his concepts of the kingdom. He could have been taught by those who were directly under Jesus' ministry, or he could have been inspired by the Holy Spirit. As a matter of fact, Paul contends for the latter. Although the ensuing statement (I Cor. 11:23) relates to abuses in regard to the communion services, nevertheless it is characteristic of his contention for the source of his teachings. He wrote, "For I have received of the Lord that which also I delivered unto you. . . ." And also to the Galatians he wrote:

I marvel that ye are so soon removed from him that called you into the grace of Christ unto another gospel; which is not another; but there be some that trouble you, and would pervert the gospel of Christ.

But though we, or an angel from heaven, preach any other gospel unto you than that which we have preached unto you, let him be accursed.

As we said before, so say I now again, If any man preach any other gospel unto you than that ye have received, let him be accursed. For do I now please men, or God? or do I seek to please men? for if I yet pleased men, I should not be the servant of Christ. But I certify you, brethren, that the gospel which was preached of me is not after man. For I neither received it of man, neither was I taught it, but by the revelation of Jesus Christ.—Gal. 1:6-12 I.V.

Paul had three major problems around which most of that which he said and wrote gravitated: (1) Persecution from non-Christian Jews; (2) Christian Jews who endeavored to enforce the Old Testament law on gentile Christians; (3) Apostasy and inequity in gentile churches which he had been instrumental in establishing. That which he left on record in regard to the kingdom of God was written largely as instruction relating to inequity, apostasy, and misunderstandings. At Ephesus he found certain disciples who had not even heard of the Holy Ghost. He taught these properly, rebaptized them, and laid hands upon them so as to entitle them to the gift of the Holy Ghost.

Then Paul went into the synagogue for the space of three months "disputing and persuading concerning the kingdom of God" (Acts 19:1-8). He and Barnabas exhorted disciples at Lystra, Iconium, and Antioch (in Pisidia) "that we must through much tribulation, enter into the kingdom of God." Acts 28 relates Paul's preaching the kingdom of God at Rome, largely to Jews who dwelt there.

We must not overlook the fact that in counteracting

231

sin, misunderstanding, and opposition, Paul's ministry was not primarily a defensive operation or that of condemnation. It contained wholesome elements of missionary outreach and kingdom-building righteousness. A good example of this is found in Romans 14:17: "For the kingdom of God is not meat and drink; but righteousness and peace, and joy in the Holy Ghost." Again in I Corinthians 4:20, he states: "For the kingdom of God is not in word, but in power." In a later chapter, endeavoring to straighten out the Corinthian church on the doctrine of the resurrection, Paul exhorted them:

Then cometh the end, when he shall have delivered up the kingdom to God, even the Father; when he shall have put down all rule and all authority and power. For he must reign, till he hath put all enemies under his feet. The last enemy that shall be destroyed is death.—I Cor. 15:24-26.

Colossians 1:13 affirms that God has translated us into the kingdom of his dear Son. "Lives are delivered from the power of darkness to be made partakers of the inheritance of the saints in light." This truth portrayed in Colossians is confirmed in I Thessalonians 2:11-13 and in II Thessalonians 1:4-5.

A typical example of warning against evildoers being excluded from the kingdom is found in I Corinthians 6:9-10:

Know ye not that the unrighteous shall not inherit the kingdom of God? Be not deceived; neither fornicators, nor idolators, nor adulterers, nor effeminate, nor abusers of themselves with mankind, nor thieves, nor covetous, nor drunkards, nor revilers, nor extortioners, shall inherit the kingdom of God.

Paul's understanding of the kingdom of God included

the strife from the lusts of the flesh against the leadings of the Spirit. His plea is to "walk in the Spirit" and thereby avoid yielding to the lusts of the flesh. He enumerates many lusts of the flesh and states that they who yield to the viciousness of these lusts shall not inherit the kingdom of God. How much more beautiful are the fruits of the Spirit which are enumerated here also (see Galatians 6:14-26). The kingdom of God is composed of those who "live in the Spirit and produce the fruits thereof."

There is nothing in any of Paul's references to the kingdom of God which is out of harmony with the teachings of Jesus as they have been reported by the other apostles and disciples. He also, like Jesus, avoids seeking to give an encapsulated definition of the kingdom. His references are simply affirmations that the kingdom of God is a present reality as well as a future hope. He is unusually emphatic in the need of kingdom of God qualities of living and in denunciation of evildoers who can have no part in that kingdom unless they repent and put away their evil practices.

Paul's teachings were based squarely on his miraculous conversion and his succeeding experiences confirming his unyielding conviction that Jesus is truly the Son of God.

---

1. *The Kingdom of God*, p. 163.
2. *Oxford Dictionary of the Christian Church*, p. 854.
3. *Interpreter's Dictionary of the Bible*, Vol. 3, p. 267 f.
4. Other versions of the Bible make the apostles and prophets the foundation, whereas the N.E.B. represents them as laying the foundation, with Jesus Christ as the foundation stone.

5. *The Interpreter's Bible*, Vol. 7, p. 656.
6. *Ibid.*, Vol. 7, p. 292, Exposition.
7. *Ibid.*, Vol. 7, p. 408, Exposition.
8. William Barclay, *The Mind of Jesus*, Harper and Row, New York and Evanston, p. 47 f.

THE CAUSE **14** OF ZION

THE CAUSE OF ZION

A great and marvelous work is about to come forth unto the children of men: behold, I am God, and give heed unto my word, which is quick and powerful, sharper than a two-edged sword, to the dividing asunder of both joints and marrow: therefore, give heed unto my words.

Behold, the field is white already to harvest, therefore, whoso desireth to reap, let him thrust in his sickle with his might, and reap while the day lasts, that he may treasure up for his soul everlasting salvation in the kingdom of God; yea, whosoever will thrust in his sickle and reap, the same is called of God; therefore, if you will ask of me you shall receive, if you will knock it shall be opened unto you.

Now, as you have asked, behold, I say unto you, Keep my commandments, and seek to bring forth and establish the cause of Zion: seek not for riches but for wisdom; and, behold, the mysteries of God shall be unfolded unto you, and then shall you be made rich. Behold, he that hath eternal life is rich.[1]

Restoration

Two words have come to have a very great meaning to Latter Day Saints: Restoration and Zion.

Restoration is depicted in the words "a great and

marvelous work is about to come forth unto the children of men." God has always been engaged in *restoring* his work (and word) when his children have forsaken it, or torn it down or have departed from the Lord. The whole plan of redemption, including the love of God, atonement, preaching the gospel, repentance, forgiveness, and seeking to build the kingdom of God is incorporated in the work of the Restoration. Restoration is an ongoing process. Those things vital to its achievement were not fully accomplished in the visits of the Lord and angels to Joseph Smith or in the advent of the Book of Mormon, nor even in the organizing of the church on April 6, 1830. These were essential initiatory events, but the "great and marvelous work" is still in progress. God continues to do his part as he awaits our response to his commandments and blessings.

Reformers Look Forward to Our Day

Latter Day Saints are not the only ones who share, or who have shared, in the hope of God's mighty work in the last days. The following quotation is but one illustration:

The supposed extraordinary claims of Joseph Smith seem to harmonize with the spirit and feelings of some of the Reformers who preceded him. The claim that one should come in the spirit and power of Elias, as a "restorer," now seems strange and new; yet Martin Luther said:—

"I cannot tell what to say of myself. Perhaps I am Philip's (Melancthon's) forerunner. I am preparing the way for him, like Elias, in spirit and in power."[2]

The point here to be observed is that the great

reformer, Martin Luther, lived in the expectancy of a greater-than-himself who, as Joseph Smith was told, should appear in the spirit and power (or strength) of Elias.[3] We who believe in the latter-day Restoration, though we may point out obvious errors, should never derogate the work of the Reformers. As D'Aubigne also states:

The history of the Reformation is not synonymous with the history of Protestantism. When we consider the former subject, everything bears the impression of a regenerated state and a social and religious transformation emanating from the power of God. But in contemplating the latter, we too often find a palpable degeneration from first principles, the schism of parties, the spirit of sects and the ideas of petty peculiarities. . . . The history of the Reformation, on the other hand, is calculated to engage the thoughts of every Christian or rather of every member of the human race.[4]

God Has Many Powers at Work

Indeed the Reformation and also segments of Protestantism, in many respects, have built a foundation for the Restoration, and many such now are continuing to help in the accomplishments of God's marvelous work, even though they may not fully agree with nor understand the Restoration and its purpose. During my own years of ministry I have talked with a number of ministers of other denominations who have fully agreed with us on our theology of revelation, our concepts of tithing and stewardship as are divinely initiated, and the fact that Joseph Smith had genuine spiritual experience. Some have maligned and even persecuted the Latter Day Saints, making it necessary for them to utilize defensive tactics. But our calling is not to tear down other structures in attempts to build our own. We must be affirmative in testimony of the Lord Jesus, preaching, teaching, and living by his good message, at the same time firmly believing that God is moving mightily in the world, among his people, to accomplish his designs.

The following message given by a former president and presiding patriarch, Elbert A. Smith, has been accepted in faith by all Reorganized Latter Day Saints:

The Spirit has opened my vision to an extent and indicates to me that two forces are at work in the world. The one is the spirit of hate. That is the spirit which entered into Cain when he slew his brother. And many men today desire to slay their fellow men.

This spirit of hate increases as it is gratified. The more it is glutted with vengeance the greater become its inordinate desires for vengeance.

The other force is the spirit of love. It too increases as it is gratified and becomes bigger and better upon deeds of kindness and mercy. The Apostle John most fully entered upon this spirit. And standing in the midst of the people he uttered these words: "See to it, little children, that ye love one another."

The Spirit of God, which bridges time, and to whom yesterday is as today, brings that injunction also to us, and it is laid upon this people. Yea, saith the Lord, I desire many evangelists of love to preach the gospel of love, not only in word but also in deed. If there is any man here who has not been baptized with the spirit of love, he has not been baptized of me, saith the Lord.

Again, at this time, you are admonished that you be not unduly concerned because you are few in number as compared with the world. That is not your concern, but be concerned only that your righteousness shall be very great. For a few righteous men can accomplish very much, and a little leaven leaveneth a great lump.

I have many forces at work in the world, saith the Lord, I have many spiritual forces at work that you know not of. You see but the smaller part of my work, and the world perceives it not at all.

Therefore be not concerned because you are few in number, but let each one look to himself, and to the condition of his own heart and life. Be humble and righteous and full of love, casting out the spirit of hatred, that you may stand in holy places and receive the blessings of the Lord.[5]

This eloquent message expressed truth that is meaningful for all and speaks for itself. We must look for those forces which God is using, acknowledging and working with them as we observe them.

God Is Concerned About Our Time

Adverting once more to a great latter-day work expected by some of the Reformers, may we consider the preaching of John Wesley?

The times which we have reason to believe are at hand, (if they are not already begun) are what many pious men have termed, the time of "the latter-day glory";—meaning, the time wherein God would gloriously display his power and love, in the fulfillment of his gracious promise that "the knowledge of the Lord shall cover the earth, as the waters cover the sea."

Again, he says:—

What could God have done which he hath not done, to convince you that the day is coming, that the time is at hand, when he will fulfill his glorious promises; when he will arise to maintain his own cause, and to set up his kingdom over all the earth?[6]

This is very similar to the prophetic message of Joseph

Smith quoted at the beginning of this chapter, "A great and marvelous work is about to come forth unto the children of men."

Charles Wesley was the greatest hymn writer England ever produced. He wrote over 5,500 hymns.[7] Consider this prophetic prayer hymn:

Almighty God of love, set up the attracting sign,
And summon whom thou dost approve for messengers divine.

From favored Abraham's seed the new apostles choose,
In isles and continents to spread the soul-reviving news.

O send thy servants forth to call the Hebrews home!
From East and West, and South and North, let all the
   wanderers come.

With Israel's myriads sealed, let all the nations meet,
And show the mystery fulfilled—the family complete. Amen.[8]

This hymn promulgates a restoration theology even to that of the promises of the Hebrew prophets that Israel would be restored to her promised homeland (see Isaiah 11:11-13). This promise is even now in the process of fulfillment. Yet the Latter Day Saint Church had no part in the international arrangement which has made this possible. It is our responsibility to take the restored gospel in its purity to this new nation.

The Restoration in no way suggests that God has changed his plans or that he is acting in any different manner than he has always done. Rather it demonstrates that he is as much concerned about us and our times as he has been about any time in history. The salvation of souls is God's primary objective. Therefore, every act he performs, every promise he makes, every precept he reveals is directed toward that end. "Joy shall be in heaven over one sinner that repenteth, more than over ninety and nine just persons, who need no repentance" (Luke 15:7). God's love for his children motivates his every act.

The Zionic Tradition

Although the etymology of the word *Zion* is very difficult to trace to its origin, it is used extensively (either as Zion or Mount Zion) in the Old Testament and a few times (spelled "Sion") in the New Testament. Zion in the Old Testament and the kingdom of God in the New Testament are closely related if not synonymous. The first mention of Zion in all versions except the Inspired Version is in II Samuel 5:6-9. This refers to David taking "the stronghold of Zion" from the Jebusites, one of the Canaanite tribes still remaining in possession of the city after the Joshua invasion.

This was a very important victory for David and the future of Israel. David at once dwelt in the stronghold of Zion, giving it also the name of the City of David. He moved his seat of government from Hebron, where he had reigned for seven and a half years, to this stronghold. With help supplied by Hiram, king of Tyre, he built his royal palace and extended the city outward from that point. Later he purchased the threshing floor of Araunah, a Jebusite, upon which to build an altar and offer sacrifices to the Lord (II Chronicles 24:24). On this spot Solomon built the temple. David also moved the Ark of the Covenant to his new capital.

An interesting incident is described in II Samuel 5:8:

"And David said on that day, Whoever would smite the Jebusites, let him get up the water shaft" (R.S.V.). Archaeologist Charles Warren (1867) discovered that the early inhabitants of Jerusalem had made water available from the Gihon Spring, east across the Kidron Valley, by a rock-cut passage which enabled the water to flow into a cave inside the walls of the fortress. Extending above this cave a perpendicular shaft forty feet in height had been cut, with a ramp and platform at the top. In case of siege, vessels could be lowered through this shaft to obtain water without going outside the walls of the fortress.[9] It has also been demonstrated that a man may climb up through this shaft, which is alluded to in the King James Version as "getting up to the gutter." This evidently is the means by which David's troops gained access to the fortress. According to I Chronicles 11:6, Joab was the first to make the ascent. If unobserved by the Jebusites, he could have opened the gate of the fortress to let David's army in. A new water course was later made during the reign of Hezekiah 715-686 B.C. to form the pool of Siloam in a more accessible part of the then much larger city. Hezekiah evidently had the new tunnel made to provide water in view of the Assyrian attack on the city by Sennacherib.

The preceding references definitely locate Zion at Jerusalem which city was built originally on two spurs, eastern and western, with the Tyropheen Valley separating them. Mount Zion, where the water shaft and channel from Gihon were found, was on the eastern spur. Jerusalem and Salem, the ancient city where Melchizedek was king and priest of the Most High God, are well defined as being the same city, having the same location.[10] This fact is important as one studies the many references to each in the Old Testament, since these names are often used interchangeably.

Genesis 14 relates a meeting of Abraham with Melchizedek. Melchizedek blessed Abraham and Abraham paid tithes to him at Salem. Salem means "peace."[11] Melchizedek is actually two words, the latter "zedek" meaning king and the former "Melchi" meaning righteousness. Combining the three words—Salem, Melchi, Zedek—we have a profound meaning: "king of righteousness" and "city of peace." But Melchizedek was also priest of the Most High God, which makes of him a very great and important man.[12]

The Psalmist wrote concerning the Messiah:

The Lord said unto my Lord, Sit thou at my right hand, until I make thine enemies thy footstool. The Lord shall send the rod of thy strength out of Zion; rule thou in the midst of thine enemies. Thy people shall be willing in the day of thy power, in the beauties of holiness from the womb of the morning; thou hast the dew of thy youth. The Lord hath sworn, and will not repent, Thou art a priest for ever after the order of Melchizedek.—Psalm 110:1-4.

Excerpts from Hebrews, chapters 5 and 6, give a good idea as to how great this man Melchizedek must have been, especially since the higher priesthood held by Christ was named after him (see Hebrews 5:1-6; 7:1-7). In Melchizedek's Zion there was righteousness and peace which Christ, called of God to this higher priesthood, came into the world to establish. His covenant cannot be broken and Zion must be redeemed to fulfill this new covenant (see Jeremiah 31:31 and Hebrews 8:7-12).

243

David chose Zadok as one of his priests (II Samuel 20:25). It has been suggested that Zadok may have been a Jebusite priest whom David chose to continue the Melchizedek line of priesthood in the Israelite community. Until about the eighth century, there were no vowel points in Hebrew writings. Strike the vowel points from Zadok and Zedek and you have the same consonant words, which indicates that Zadok must have been a Jebusite, likely of Melchizedek lineage.[13]

Mount Zion of ancient times then was located upon the eastern spur where the city of Jerusalem had its beginning, but Jerusalem later expanded to include the western spur also. Zion and Mount Zion were used synonymously with Jerusalem and were so regarded by the Israelite kings and prophets in their writings. David wrote many psalms expressing Zion's beauty and purpose. "Out of Zion, the perfection of beauty, God shines forth" (Psalm 50:2 R.S.V.). The prophets also wrote of Zion with expressive eloquence.

And I will restore thy judges as at the first, and thy counselors as at the beginning; afterward thou shalt be called, The city of righteousness, the faithful city. Zion shall be redeemed with judgment, and her converts with righteousness.—Isaiah 1:26-27.

Zion Is a Cause

The Inspired Version of the Holy Scriptures gives a record of Zion, the city which Enoch built. Two points serve our purpose here preeminently. The first is the covenant God made with Enoch:

And the Lord said unto Enoch, As I live, even so will I come in

the last days, in the days of wickedness and vengeance, to fulfill the oath which I made unto you concerning the children of Noah. And the day shall come that the earth shall rest. But before that day the heavens shall be darkened, and a veil of darkness shall cover the earth; and the heavens shall shake, and also the earth. And great tribulations shall be among the children of men, but my people will I preserve; and righteousness will I send down out of heaven, and truth will I send forth out of the earth to bear testimony of mine Only Begotten; his resurrection from the dead; yea, and also the resurrection of all men. And righteousness and truth will I cause to sweep the earth as with a flood, to gather out mine own elect from the four quarers of the earth, unto a place which I shall prepare; an holy city, that my people may gird up their loins, and be looking forth for the time of my coming; for there shall be my tabernacle, and it shall be called Zion; a New Jerusalem.

And the Lord said unto Enoch, Then shalt thou and all thy city meet them there; and we will receive them into our bosom; and they shall see us, and we will fall upon their necks, and they shall fall upon our necks, and we will kiss each other; and there shall be mine abode, and it shall be Zion, which shall come forth out of all the creations which I have made; and for the space of a thousand years shall the earth rest.—Genesis 7:67-72 I.V.

This reminds us of that which was revealed to John in Revelation 14:1-4:

And I looked, and, lo, a Lamb stood on the mount Sion, and with him a hundred forty and four thousand, having his Father's name written in their foreheads. And I heard a voice from heaven, as the voice of many waters, and as the voice of a great thunder; and I heard the voice of harpers harping with their harps; and they sung as it were a new song before the throne, and before the four beasts, and the elders; and no man could learn that song but the hundred and forty and four thousand, which were redeemed from the earth. These are

they which were not defiled with women; for they are virgins. These are they which follow the Lamb whithersoever he goeth. These were redeemed from among man, being the firstfruits unto God and to the Lamb.

The second point has to do with the quality of life in Zion. "And the Lord called his people Zion, because they were of one heart and one mind, and dwelt in righteousness; and there were no poor among them" (Gen. 7:23 I.V.).

Zion is a new dimension of living for the world in all ages. Isaiah (5:20) wrote, "Woe unto them that call evil good, and good evil; that put darkness for light, and light for darkness; that put bitter for sweet, and sweet for bitter." This is happening in our society today as laws are sought and some are passed to legalize various kinds of evil such as gambling, some types of drug traffic, sex perversion, and other abuses. Many live together without marriage. Communism calls Christianity a hindrance to the ideal society.

Paul described these conditions as a conflict between the flesh and the spirit.

For the flesh lusteth against the Spirit, and the Spirit against the flesh; and these are contrary the one to the other: so that ye cannot do the things that ye would. . . . Now the works of the flesh are manifest, which are these; Adultery, fornication, uncleanness, lasciviousness, idolatry, witchcraft, hatred, variance, emulations, wrath, strife, seditions, heresies, envyings, murders, drunkenness, revellings, and such like; . . . they which do such things shall not inherit the kingdom of God. But the fruit of the Spirit is love, joy, peace, longsuffering, gentleness, goodness, faith, meekness, temperance; against such there is no law. And they that are Christ's have crucified the flesh with the affections and lusts.—Galatians 5:17-24.

246

With keen insight Paul enumerated here, on the one hand, abuses and perversions of God-given endowments that corrupt the social order, bringing woe, frustration, and tribulation. On the other hand, he listed the fruits of the Spirit which follow Christlike living and yield a joyful and peaceful society.

I have made considerable effort to locate Zion of the ancients, but Zion is more than a geographic location. A righteous people must be gathered or developed in order to establish a new and different life-style than that of the world. Albeit, as long as Zion must remain in the world, the Saints cannot escape contact and intercommunication with the world; yet while in the world they must not be of it.[14]

To Latter Day Saints the center place of Zionic living has been designated as Independence, Missouri.[15] Many now feel that Zionic communities may be established elsewhere. We do, however, need to observe the commandment to build up the center place.[16]

The cause of Zion is God's cause; it has always been so. Zion will remain his cause until his total purpose has been achieved. In this sense, as Zion was the hope of Israel, it is our hope and will remain the hope of all future peoples. It is the only hope for our social, economic, and spiritual redemption; social, political, and economic redemption can come only through the observance and action of spiritual forces. Not only must the soul be redeemed but the society in which the soul is environed must be redeemed from the sins of the world. Isaiah said, "The city of righteousness, the faithful city, Zion shall be redeemed with judgment and her converts with righteousness."

Three points are mentioned as commendable qualities of those who lived in Zion of old: (1) They were of one heart and one mind. This is a condition similar to that which prevailed among the disciples of Christ who met on the day of Pentecost: "They were all of one accord" (Acts 2:1). (2) They dwelt in righteousness; (3) There were no poor among them (Gen. 7:23, I.V.).

It is to be admitted that very little is *recorded* in regard to Enoch in other versions of the Bible. The first reference is in Genesis 5:18-24. This reference concludes, "And Enoch walked with God; and he was not; for God took him." The second reference is in Hebrews 11:5, "By faith Enoch was translated that he should not see death." The Inspired Version maintains that the whole city of Zion "in process of time was taken up into heaven" (Genesis 7:27, I.V.).

This miraculous event is easily understood when considered in its total context along with the statement in the RLDS Doctrine and Covenants: "Zion can not be built up unless it is by the principles of the law of the celestial kingdom."[17] The world was not yet ready for that celestial law and kingdom, nor is it now. The third reference to Enoch is in Jude, verse 14. Jude quotes a prophecy of Enoch concerning the Lord's coming in judgment on the wicked, with ten thousand of his saints. The prophecy Jude quotes is generally conceded to be from apocryphal literature. Jude himself evinces no doubt of its authenticity.

Like the people of Enoch's Zion, these New Testament saints gave close adherence to the teachings of Jesus and were motivated by the knowledge of his resurrection. Peter bore testimony to all who had gathered that day "that God hath made that same Jesus whom ye have crucified, both Lord and Christ" (Acts 2:36). About three thousand souls were added to the church that day. "And all that believed were together, and had all things common; and sold their possessions and goods, and parted them to all men as they had need" (Acts 2:44-45).

It will require the same spiritual forces to move us forward today in the full observance of God's law, so that this Zionic economic standard may prevail. We are few in number as compared with the billions in the world, yet God has enjoined upon us the charge of seeking "to bring forth and establish the cause of Zion." This he has done, not for our sakes alone but for the salvation of the whole world.

Such a time and condition was envisioned by Isaiah who called Zion the perfect city:

And it shall come to pass in the last days, when the mountain of the Lord's house shall be established in the top of the mountains, and shall be exalted above the hills, and all nations shall flow unto it; and many people shall go and say, Come ye, and let us go up to the mountain of the Lord, to the house of the God of Jacob; and he will teach us of his ways, and we will walk in his paths; for out of Zion shall go forth the law, and the word of the Lord from Jerusalem; and he shall judge among the nations, and shall rebuke many people; and they shall beat their swords into ploughshares, and their spears into pruning-hooks; nation shall not lift up sword against nation, neither shall they learn war any more.—Isaiah 2:2-4, I.V.

As the law goes forth in the manner described, people will finally realize the futility of war and devote their efforts to the arts of peace, for the welfare of all nations. Isaiah followed by making a plea to the house of Jacob (all Israel) to walk in the light of the Lord.

God called Abraham out of pagan Mesopotamia for Zion's sake. Otherwise, his purpose might have perished from the earth. God made a covenant with Abraham that in him shall all the families of the earth be blessed (Genesis 12:1-2). In Hebrews (11:8-10) we are told that even though Abraham didn't know where he was going, by faith he obeyed because "he looked for a city which hath foundations, whose builder and maker is God."

It is interesting that the Reformers and Protestantism largely missed this concept. Their efforts were evangelistic in bringing people to Christ, but little or no emphasis was placed by them on building a new world society on celestial principles. While such a society may be communal in nature as indicated in Acts 2 and 4, it is by no means communistic. The former protects the freedom of the will and of the soul, so that no one is in bondage except to Christ, while the latter is despotic and makes one a slave to the state.

According to the Book of Mormon, a Zionic condition prevailed here in America after the visit of Christ. The results of the righteousness of the people is thus described:

And it came to pass that there was no contention in the land because of the love of God which dwelt in the hearts of the people. And there were no envyings, nor strifes, nor tumults, nor whoredoms, nor lyings, nor murders, nor any manner of lasciviousness. And surely there could not be a happier people among all the people who had been created by the hand of God. There were no robbers, nor murderers, neither were there Lamanites, nor any manner of "ites"; but they were in one, the children of Christ, and heirs to the kingdom of God. And how blessed were they, for the Lord blessed them in all their doings; even they were blessed and prospered until a hundred and ten years had passed away; and the first generation from Christ had passed away, and there was no contention in all the land.[18]

Note that it was the love of God dwelling in the hearts of the people which brought about this utopian manner of living. What a magnificent change would be brought about in our world today if these righteous principles and acts were adopted by everyone in the whole world.

1. Doctrine and Covenants 6:1-3.
2 . Church History, Vol. 1, p. 1-2; this quotation is found also in *The History of the Reformation* by Merle D'Aubigne, D.D., in the author's latest French edition, published by Ward, Lock & Co., London. It reads slightly different but the meaning remains the same: "I do not know what to say of myself....Perhaps I am the forerunner to Philip (Melancthon). I prepare for him in imitation of Elias, the way in spirit and strength" (p. 348).
3. Church History, Vol. 1, p. 13.
4. Merle D'Aubigne, *The History of the Reformation*, Preface, p. 1.
5. Given at Lamoni, Iowa, Nov. 4, 1917. Published in the *Saints' Herald* Nov. 14, 1917.
6. *Wesley's Sermons*, Vol. 2, Sermon 71. Copied from Church History.
7. See the *Oxford Dictionary of the Christian Church*, p. 1445.
8. *The Hymnal*, Herald Publishing House, Independence, Missouri, Hymn 285; written by Charles Wesley, music by Charles Lockhart.
9. See Jack Finnegan, *Light from the Ancient Past*, p. 178.
10. *Interpreter's Dictionary of the Bible*, Vol. 3, p. 343.
11. *Ibid.*
12. *Ibid.*
13. *Interpreting the Old Testament*, pp. 44 and 421. See also *Interpreter's Dictionary of the Bible*, Vol. 4, p. 928.
14. Doctrine and Covenants 128:8.
15. *Ibid.*, 57:1.
16. *Ibid.*, 98:4-10.
17. *Ibid.*, 102:2.
18. Book of Mormon, IV Nephi 1:17-21.

SECTION III

THE NEW DISPENSATION OF HOPE

A LOOK INTO 15 THE FUTURE

Seeking Understanding

We know altogether too little of the Great Beyond so that it is very easy to give way to imaginative thinking and speculation. At all costs, this must be avoided for the reason that personal deductions, curiosity, desires, and even prejudices may develop into our guidelines. The faith of many can be damaged by putting trust in the resulting theories and fantasies of human conjectures.

Nevertheless, it would be sheer folly to think only in terms of the past and the present. We also should give due recognition to and seek to understand the future, which holds the final key to the last things. The prophets and apostles sought to do this as the Holy Spirit unfolded many mysteries to them. E. Y. Mullins indicates that the doctrine of last things completes the cycle of biblical thought, which is obviously true.[1] Nevertheless, there still remains the problem of correctly interpreting that which the prophets and apostles envisioned and wrote. It is best to make sure that we are on solid footing in whatever conclusions we may reach.

As we look to the future we must become aware of the truth of a further statement by Dr. Mullins which attests that in the gospel message revelation and salvation are conjoined.[2] Salvation in process is revelation. Thus, without revelation there could be no salvation; mankind neither possesses the ingenuity to devise the plan or the power to execute it in seeking to save himself. We are utterly dependent upon an intelligence and a power beyond our own for our salvation. In fact, were it not for such revealed intelligence and power we could never understand the source of our being. Neither science nor philosophy has given us the answer with any certainty.

Divine intelligence and power are infinite and eternal—that is, without beginning or end. For us who are finite and circumscribed by time limitations, this is difficult to grasp. This again stresses the importance of looking to that future in which these limitations do not exist. Then it shall be as Paul wrote, "For now we see through a glass darkly; but then face to face; now I know in part; but then shall I know even as also I am known" (I Cor. 13:12). We cannot begin to imagine what such a future will really be like, but we can rely on the mercy, justice, and goodness of God.

God Is Illimitably Good

Since God has acted so majestically in creation and in history, it is inconceivable that he should do so without plan or purpose or allow his creation to pass into oblivion in some cataclysmic catastrophe. Worlds may come and worlds may go, but the work of God continues without end. Nothing can frustrate or defeat the power of God.

How could the work of God be otherwise since he

himself is eternal and is the Author of the Melchizedek priesthood, which priesthood has "neither beginning of days nor end of life" (Heb. 7:3, I.V.). God declared this principle, which is a quality of the priesthood, as applying to himself. "And God spake unto Moses, saying, Behold, I am the Lord God Almighty, and Endless is my name, for I am without beginning of days or end of years; and is not this endless?"[3]

In the creation process God declared each phase of his creation to be good. Creation began thus, so it must be consummated. We learn two things from God's mighty acts and from his revelation. First, he is without beginning or end, eternal. Second, all things he does are prompted by the goodness of his nature. Surely in this knowledge alone there is hope. J. G. Whittier has expressed this truth so meaningfully:

> Yet, in the maddening maze of things,
> And tossed by storm and flood,
> To one fixed trust my spirit clings;
> I know that God is good![4]

Jesus said, "Why callest thou me good? There is no one good but one, that is God" (Matt. 19:17). All good emanates from God; even Jesus relied on him for his own goodness.

We do not mean to say that God ignores and does not deal with evil even when it is embodied in human actions. It is clear, however, that his intent is that of perfect goodness, both for himself and his creation.

Satan is the author of evil and we are its victims. God constantly strives against evil and seeks to guide our lives in the ways of righteousness because of his love for us. It was to this end that he sent his only Begotten Son into the world, who declared, "God sent not his Son into the world to condemn the world; but that the world through him might be saved" (John 3:17). The importance of experiencing the loving grace of God exercised toward our redemption cannot be overemphasized. As we repent, he forgives and we must accept that forgiveness in forgiving ourselves and in forgiving others. Too many stumble at this point and not only continue to condemn themselves but fail to forgive others. Thereby they cannot know the joys of freedom from sin, nor experience the full love of God in their lives.

Time Versus Eternity

Beginning and end in relation to creation and history are linked to time; they apply to this world and at least in part to the cosmos. "Time only is measured unto man."[5] Time is a finite computation of a fractional portion of eternity.

And the Lord God spake unto Moses, saying, The heavens, they are many and they can not be numbered unto man, but they are numbered unto me, for they are mine; and as one earth shall pass away, and the heavens thereof, even so shall another come.[6]

Now the key to the total design of God is succinctly portrayed in the same message: "And there is no end to my works, neither to my words; for this is my work and my glory, to bring to pass the immortality, and eternal life of man."[7] We are created in the image and likeness of God and of his Only Begotten Son (Gen. 1:29, I.V.).

Either in this world or the next we will have the opportunity of growing "unto the measure of the stature of the fullness of Christ." This by the grace of God is the perfect person (Eph. 4:13). But either in this life or the next one, we must know and abide by Christ's gospel before we can reach the fullness of his stature.

As population has increased upon the earth, not all have had this glorious privilege. The burden is laid upon us, by whatever gifts and means we may have, to help in proclaiming the gospel to every person throughout the whole world.

We have been told that "the hastening time is upon us, . . . [but] it is yet day when all can work. The night will come when for many of my people opportunity to assist will have passed."[8] Time is drawing to a rapid close when it will be merged into eternity. Many things will happen as this merger takes place: the second coming of Christ, the resurrection of the just, perhaps the thousand years reign, the second resurrection, judgment, and the triumph of the kingdom of God. How long the process of this merger will take no one knows. Some events are wisely held within the confines of the divine will until he sees fit to make them known.

For instance, many have attempted to compute or set dates for the coming of Christ. Jesus warned against this very thing. "But of that day and hour knoweth no man, no, not the angels of heaven, but my Father only" (Matt. 24:36). This is an eternal secret which only he who dwells in eternity can know. Christ will act at the Father's bidding. The emphasis Jesus gave in regard to his future coming was that of making ready. "Therefore be ye also ready; for in such an hour as ye think not, the

Son of Man cometh" (Matt. 24:44). Jesus was speaking to his disciples in answer to questions they had raised: "Tell us, when shall these things [the things he had prophesied against Jerusalem] be?" (see Matt. 23:27-24:2), and "what shall be the sign of thy coming, and of the end of the world?" (Matt. 24:3). Many have contended that Jesus thought his return was imminent in their day. But this would contradict his statement that no man, not even the angels, knew the time of his coming. Therefore, we should take heed and be ready lest he might come to us unexpectedly, as the thief comes in the night.

For us who are conditioned by time measurements and its limitations, that which has neither beginning nor end is beyond our finite comprehension. God, being without beginning or end, has always been at work and always will be working for good involving the eternal.

Special Experiences

Extreme caution should characterize any speculation about the future and last things. My intent is by no means to discredit the special experiences some have been granted in timeless realities. The Spirit of God has power to liberate us in this life, temporarily and in part, from our finite consciousness and to enable us to perceive that which is infinite, as God wills. Such experiences are a part of the revelatory process. It is important that these experiences be regarded as sacred and that sound interpretations be made. Never should they be spoken of boastfully as though the recipient has priority with God. Better that such a one be guided by

259

wisdom as Paul expresses:

I knew a man in Christ above fourteen years ago, (whether in the body, I cannot tell; or whether out of the body, I cannot tell; God knoweth;) such a one caught up to the third heaven. And I knew such a man, (whether in the body, or out of the body, I cannot tell; God knoweth;) how that he was caught up into paradise, and heard unspeakable words, which it is not lawful for a man to utter.—II Corinthians 12:2-4.

Floyd N. Filson has given quite a comprehensive treatise on these verses. In this he wrote:

Paul expresses with a word play that he heard "unutterable utterances." This need not mean that he could not understand them; he does not tell them because they are too sacred—they cannot be told. They were a personal blessing and assurance to him, but were not to be told to others.[9]

Those who have a like experience should regard it as a personal blessing. If told to others, this should be done humbly and only when one is specially impressed to do so. When used in this manner, they may become strengthening to another's faith, bring comfort to the bereaved, or bring other thoroughly justifiable ministry. Perhaps more often the divine intent is for the comfort, enlightenment, and guidance of the one receiving the experience, as in the following which was shared with me by letter.[10]

My father was a very good man in all ways but he was not a member of any church. As a youth he had attended the Baptist church. He was a good Bible student and in fact, a student of many subjects.

After his death at age 76, I was concerned about what might be happening to him. I was not worried or emotionally upset about this, but just concerned. I believe that whatever system God has worked out for the afterlife must be the best system.

Then I had a dream (or maybe a vision). I was at the longer side of a rectangular room and looking into it as one would look at a stage. At the right end of the room was a place for a speaker or teacher. There was a slightly elevated platform and a podium or desk. The room was full of student chairs with desks attached to the side like those we use today. They were all facing the right end of the room. But the outstanding thing was the wall of the room opposite me. It appeared to be of polished wood. There was a soft light coming directly through this wood. This seemed to be the only way that light came into the room. It was a warm, soft light but gave ample light for the schoolroom.

Then men came into the room from the left side. There was friendly conversation among them and all was orderly. They were about thirty or so in age. I was annoyed because I didn't want to sit and watch other people have the joy of studying and learning in this room without having that joy myself.

When I looked back at the men who had taken their seats, I saw my father sitting close by and looking directly at me. He smiled and said to me, "Hi, Hemmer." (My mother's father was from England and often called my grandmother Emma by the name of Hemmer. Father in life had called me that. I was named for grandmother.)

My reaction was, "It can't be you. You are dead." Then all was gone.

Many have enjoyed similar experiences which no doubt are for enlightenment and comfort. One can see in this experience an answer to the sister's concern for her father. Some wonder and ask, "Why can't I have such an experience relating to my loved one who has gone on? I would give anything to see my mother, father, sister, or brother." We may ask God for such comforting assurance, but we must trust his wisdom knowing that he is loving, merciful, and just and will answer our prayers in the way that will be best for us.

We may, with profit, examine the scriptures for such light as they afford us, where God's eternal design carries over into the life beyond.

1. E. Y. Mullins, *The Christian Religion in Its Doctrinal Expression*, p. 439.
2. *Ibid.*
3. Doctrine and Covenants 22:2.
4. From "The Eternal Goodness," *Masterpieces of Religious Verse*, p. 69.
5. Book of Mormon, Alma 19:38.
6. Doctrine and Covenants 22:23a.
7. *Ibid.*, 22:23b.
8. *Ibid.*, 141:5 and 142:5b.
9. *Interpreter's Bible*, Vol. 10, p. 406.
10. Shared by Emma (Mrs. Nephi) Phillips.

IMMORTALITY 16 AND ETERNAL LIFE

Creation and Immortality

This is a tremendous subject exhibiting the greatest of challenges. First, definitions of a few words relating to our discussion are in order: (1) That which is *eternal* has neither beginning nor end. (2) *Endless* and eternal are not in complete apposition. *Endless* means without end but does not denote that there was no beginning. (3) *Mortal* signifies subject to death, or relates to that part of our being which is perishable. (4) Therefore, *immortality* pertains to that which is not subject to death.[1]

The apostle Paul wrote: "For this corruptible must put on incorruption, and this mortal must put on immortality" (I Cor. 15:53). You may very well ask: "What part of me is corruptible or mortal that in the resurrection, for which Paul was contending, must be changed from that which now is perishable to become immortal?" The Bible states, "And the Lord God formed man of the dust of the ground, and breathed into his nostrils the breath of life; and man became a living soul" (Gen. 2:7). The substance out of which our bodies are formed is perishable. Death proves that, but as Longfellow wrote:

Life is real! Life is earnest!
    And the grave is not its goal;
Dust thou art, to dust returnest,
    Was not spoken of the soul.[2]

It was the breath of God which gave life to the lifeless form which God had created. Surely that part of God which he has invested in us, the breath of life, conforms to his nature which is eternal and imperishable. Hence, the soul of man already is immortal. The resurrected body, which in order to be immortal and incorruptible must be changed fully into the likeness of its Maker, one of whose attributes is immortality. "Man was also in the beginning with God. Intelligence, or the light of truth, was not created or made, neither indeed can be."[3] Intelligence which was already with God accompanied this spiritual creation or the making of man into a living soul. "The glory of God is intelligence."[4] Immortality, while it applied to God, is not fully adequate in that sense. Creation had a beginning. That which is immortal may have a beginning such as is the case with mankind, but it is without end. Eternal is the more appropriate word. It is "without beginning or end" as applied to God.

Eternal Life

Eternal life is a quality of living that must have certain attributes to endure eternally. Eternal life is everlasting because it has the qualities to endure beyond time. It is, therefore, more than just living forevermore. Eternal life is living the life of God, disclosed in the life of the Lord Jesus.

The apostle John had a clear perception of that life revealed in Jesus which not only dealt with salvation but also with creation.

In the beginning was the gospel preached through the Son. And the gospel was the word, and the word was with the Son, and the Son was with God, and the Son was of God. . . . All things were made by him; and without him was not anything made which was made. In him was the gospel, and the gospel was the life, and the life was the light of men.—John 1:1-4, I.V.

This seems to amplify another text from John's writings: "I am come that they might have life, and that they might have it more abundantly" (John 10:10).

God and Christ work in our behalf unceasingly. Nothing will be left undone that can be done for our salvation, both in this life and in the next. These attributes of eternal life must be achieved by us as far as possible in this life, for no doubt we will start in over there where we leave off here.

Jesus said in his prayer at Gethsemane, "And this is life eternal, that they might know thee, the only true God, and Jesus Christ, whom thou hast sent" (John 17:3). Such knowledge comes by revelation, not necessarily in seeing him with the natural eye. Many have seen Christ thus and have not discerned him. No one can look upon the face of God in this life and live except that person is gifted with a special endowment of his power, as was Moses upon the mountain. The inner presence of his Spirit witnesses of him. We are told how this may be obtained: "He that keepeth his commandments, receiveth truth and light, until he is glorified in truth, and knoweth all things."[5] Knowledge of God and Christ can come only as we "keep his commandments" with purity of heart. The pure in heart shall see God (Matt. 5:8).

The Worth of Souls

Jesus placed inestimable worth upon the human soul. "For what shall it profit a man, if he shall gain the whole world, and lose his own soul? Or what shall a man give in exchange for his soul?" (Mark 8:36-37). It has been stated that "The elements are eternal, and spirit and element, inseparably connected receiveth a fullness of joy."[6] This defines the final means by which man receives immortality and eternal life, and by which he escapes the worst that can happen to him; that of losing his soul, which includes also separation from God and Christ.

The soul must be equipped in righteousness to dwell in an immortalized spiritual body.

The first man Adam was made a living soul; the last Adam was made a quickening spirit. Howbeit, that which is natural first, and not that which is spiritual; but afterwards, that which is spiritual; the first man is of the earth, earthy; the second man is the Lord from heaven.... And as is the heavenly, such are they also that are heavenly. And as we have borne the image of the earthy, we shall also bear the image of the heavenly.— I Corinthians 15:45-49, I.V.

This was written of the resurrection which will be discussed more fully later.

The soul belongs to God because it came from him when he breathed the breath of life into the body. J. Paterson Smythe* says the soul is the conscious per-

---

*Episcopalian Rector of St. George's Montreal; late Professor of Pastoral Theology, University of Dublin.

sonality within us, that which we speak of as "I."[7] Smythe asks a further question, which we should grasp and never let go: Is not this "I" looking out from behind your eyes this moment the real man, of whom the body that you see is only the outer covering of whom the brain is only the outward telegraphic instrument? Should not we adapt our thoughts to that tremendous fact? Instead of thinking I have a soul, should we not rather think I am a soul?[8]

While Dr. Smythe has expressed a profound truth here, we ought not to depreciate the marvels of the human body. What enables that eye to see other than the light of truth? What but the power of God gives us the four other senses? Could "I" have the powers of understanding, intelligence in this life, without a brain? It is true, however, that no one of these senses can function by itself. You are a living soul, which is your total real self, body and spirit.

Does anyone reach the height of his ideals in this life? Our ideals are always so far ahead of us that death seems to sweep in upon us, leaving vast incompletion. The seemingly unfinished life that we know here is ended before we have achieved within ourselves the goal of our ambitions. Immanuel Kant based his argument for immortality on this premise.[9]

God's love for the souls of people is infinite. He could never eternally deny us the opportunity of becoming that perfect person, even as he is perfect. This does not mean that we may become what he is. We cannot become God, nor do we need to in order to attain perfect happiness and fulfill his purpose in our existence. There is no plurality of Gods. "Joy shall be in heaven over one sinner that repenteth, more than over ninety and nine just persons, who need no repentance" (Luke 15:7). Happiness comes to us on earth in a similar manner.

Remember the worth of souls is great in the sight of God; for, behold, the Lord your Redeemer suffered death in the flesh; wherefore he suffered the pain of all men, that all men might repent and come unto him. And he hath risen again from the dead, that he might bring all men unto him on conditions of repentance. And how great is his joy in the soul that repenteth. Wherefore you are called to cry repentance unto this people. And if it so be that you should labor all your days,...and bring save it be one soul unto me, how great shall be your joy with him in the kingdom of my Father.[10]

The eternal design is focused on saving souls, because we are all more precious than we can fully realize to him who gave us life and upon whom we must depend for salvation. This is ultimately living eternally in his kingdom, prepared from the foundation of the world.

Sin and Death

Sin, in any form, is the transgression of divine law. Our sinning may be allegorized in the Garden of Eden story. We are not concerned here as to whether the tree of the knowledge of good and evil was a literal tree and its fruit literal. The important fact is that Adam and Eve were beguiled by satanic devices and disobeyed God, even though they were forewarned by God of the consequences. By Adamic disobedience, sin enveloped the whole human race. Thus Paul wrote: "For as by one man's disobedience many were made sinners, so by the obedience of one shall many be made righteous"

(Romans 5:19). And, "For as in Adam all die, even so in Christ shall all be made alive" (I Cor. 15:22). This does not mean that we may lay the blame for our sins on our original parents. When the Jews in captivity in Babylon complained because of what they felt was divine injustice, the prophet Ezekiel (18:20) spoke the word of the Lord unto them.

The soul that sinneth, it shall die. The son shall not bear the iniquity of the father, neither shall the father bear the iniquity of the son; the righteousness of the righteous shall be upon him, and the wickedness of the wicked shall be upon him.

This whole chapter is a plea for them to recognize the love and justice of God. A wicked person reaps the consequences of his wickedness. The righteous joyfully receive the fruits of their labors.

We are all finite mortals, exposed to the weaknesses and lusts of the flesh. The apostle Paul declared, "For we have all sinned and come short of the glory of God" (Rom. 3:23). Each person is accountable for his own sins, and not those of another, unless he has in some manner caused another to sin, which in itself is a sin for which he will be accountable. Let us be aware, therefore, that many others may be affected adversely by our wrongdoing.

Some may ask, "What would have happened if Adam and Eve had not transgressed God's commandment?" This is actually beside the point. We must face reality rather than conjecture on what might have been. Wickedness spread from Adam and Eve throughout the succeeding generations. Sin is rampant in the world today. "The wages of sin is death; but the gift of God is eternal life through Jesus Christ our Lord" (Romans

6:23). Sin demands forgiveness and death requires resurrection. Finite man is not competent to forgive himself, nor to bring to pass his resurrection from death. God knew that people would sin, and that they would be in need of redemption. Consequently he designed to deal with both situations as they developed. God is never taken unaware.

There are two kinds of evil: moral and natural. Many are troubled because of natural evil. Moral evil stems from our wrongdoing. Natural evil is that which besets humanity in various forms, coming from powers which are beyond our control such as earthquakes, flood, tornadoes, volcanic eruptions, epidemics, and the like. For instance, about the beginning of this century, in Alberta, Canada, without warning, a mountain literally split in two. One-half toppled over the valley, covering a village of several hundred people. No one escaped this disaster. War is a moral evil brought upon us ultimately by evil, designing men. The catastrophes of natural evil cannot be explained so easily. Why does a good God permit such calamities?

While no satisfactory answer as yet has been found, the problem cannot be ignored. Philosophy is not likely to find a satisfactory answer, since the philosophic search is pitting the finite consciousness against the infinite consciousness of God. Theistic faith may ease tensions caused by the problems of natural evil, but faith does not explain their existence.

H. E. Fosdick concluded that, "The mystery of evil is very great upon the basis of a good God, but the mystery of goodness is impossible on the basis of no God."[11] John Hicks offers an objection to this view on the ground that the atheist is not obligated to explain the universe at all. "He can simply accept it at its face value as an enormously complex natural fact."[12] William Temple asserts that "moral good cannot be subordinated to any form of evil."[13] He goes on to say that good cannot add to evil and that good cannot in any sense become evil.

A text from Isaiah has seemed to some to contradict the nature of God, if he is a perfect Being and sovereign Lord of the universe. "I form the light, and create darkness; I make peace, and create evil; I the Lord do all these things" (Isaiah 45:7). The least and perhaps the best which may be said on this is that God has created that in which natural evil exists and also man who is subject to moral evil. James wrote,

Let no man say when he is tempted, I am tempted of God; for God cannot be tempted with evil, neither tempteth he any man; but every man is tempted, when he is drawn away of his own lust, and enticed.—James 1:13-14.

This text affirms two things; (1) God is good because he cannot be tempted with evil. He will not tempt anyone. (2) Temptation comes to us because of the potential within us to be tempted and to commit sin.

It has been stated, "For it must needs be that there is an opposition in all things."[14] Evil is the opposite to righteousness and good the opposite to bad. Without these opposites, free will and agency would have no meaning. Could there be intelligence or any use for it without the right of choice? Without intelligence there would be no ground for our being. The principle of opposition is in all things throughout nature. In some instances, and conditions, this is beneficial. In others, it is harmful.

The resistance that the filament in an electric light bulb offers to the passing of the electric current through it produces incandescent light. But a shock from that same electricity may kill. Heat and cold are opposites but people have perished in extremes of either. God blessed and gave dominion to Adam and Eve and said to them, "Be fruitful and multiply, and fill the earth and *subdue* it" (Gen. 1:28, R.S.V.). "All things have been done in the wisdom of him who knoweth all things."[15] Opposition to righteousness and well-being must be overcome in order to subdue the forces of natural evils and also moral evils.

The Fear of Death

Generally people fear death. This fear in various degrees affects both the dying and the loved ones who are left behind. The factor which possibly contributes most to that fear is the uncertainty of that which lies beyond. Another fear is, "Am I ready for death when it comes?" Sometimes this fear of death beforehand is worse than the experience itself. Still another cause of fear is the separation from loved ones. First, to overcome this fear, we need to understand what death really is. In order to get at this question successfully, we need to ask, "What is life?" This is explained in the Genesis account of creation which we have already dealt with. God formed man—that is, his body—from the dust of the ground. Then he breathed life into that body, making of the two a living soul. Man and woman then are dual creatures composed of spirit and body. The warning was given that they were not to eat of the fruit of the tree of the knowledge of good and evil or they would surely die. Death came by disobedience.

The moral body reaches a state, whether by age, disease, or calamity, when it can no longer retain the spirit or breath of life. Death, accordingly, is the separation of spirit and body. But does the spirit die with the body? The writer of Ecclesiastes states, "Then shall the dust return to the earth as it was; and the spirit shall return to God who gave it" (Eccl. 12:7). Jesus, as he was dying on the cross, said, "Father, into thy hands I commend my spirit: and having thus said, he gave up the ghost" (Luke 23:46). These two texts indicate that in death the body returns to the earth and the spirit returns to God—each to its original source.

Understanding the nature of death does not necessarily relieve the sorrow which accompanies the loss of a loved one. The fact that the spirit returns to God should give assurance that it does not pass into oblivion. We have already learned that God is eternal and the spirit is immortal. Death then opens the door of eternity for the immortal spirit. Hence we are able to say with the apostle Paul, "O death, where is thy sting? O grave, where is thy victory?" Or with James Whitcomb Riley in his poem, "Away":

> I cannot say, and I will not say
> That he is dead. He is just away.
>
> With a cheery smile, and a wave of the hand,
> He has wandered into an unknown land.
>
> And left us dreaming how very fair
> It needs must be since he lingers there.

And you—O you, who the wildest yearn
For the old-time step and the glad return—

Think of him faring on, as dear
In the love of there as the love of here;

Think of him still as the same, I say;
He is not dead—he is just away![16]

In order to have our understanding further illuminated, we will need to take into consideration that which lies beyond death. We may do this by carefully examining what the scriptures have to say about the hereafter.

1. These abbreviated definitions comply with *Webster's New Twentieth Century Dictionary*.
2. From "The Psalm of Life," *Masterpieces of Religious Verse*, p. 304.
3. Doctrine and Covenants 90:5a.
4. *Ibid.*, 90:6a.
5. *Ibid.*, 90:4e.
6. *Ibid.*, 90:5e.
7. J. Paterson Smythe, *The Gospel of the Hereafter*, Hodder and Stoughton, London, New York, Toronto, p. 15.
8. *Ibid.*, p. 19.
9. S. E. Frost, Jr., *The Basic Teachings of the Great Philosophers*, New Home Library, New York, p. 187 f.
10. Doctrine and Covenants 16:3c-f.
11. H. E. Fosdick, *Living Under Tension*, Harper and Row, New York, 1941, pp. 214-215.
12. John Hicks, *Evil and the God of Love*, Harper and Row, New York, p. 11.
13. William Temple, *Nature, Man and God*, Macmillan and Company, London, 1951, p. 358.
14. Book of Mormon, II Nephi 1:81.
15. *Ibid.*, II Nephi 1:114.
16. *Masterpieces of Religious Verse*, p. 585.

RESURRECTION 17 AND JUDGMENT

In the Old Testament

There is a considerable divergence of opinions among biblical scholars and theologians as to whether a doctrine of the resurrection can be substantiated from Old Testament teachings. Most maintain that such a conception was not developed until the latter years of Judaism. However, death came as a result of Adam and Eve's partaking of the fruit of the tree of the knowledge of good and evil; and there is certainly some symbolic significance to the presence of the tree of life in the Garden of Eden. God kept them from eating of its fruit lest they should live forever. Surely, while resurrection is not mentioned, this points to a belief in its equivalent—everlasting life—from the very beginning (see Genesis 2:16-17; 3:22-24).

Some have maintained that the only positive reference to such a resurrection occurs in the apocalyptic book of Daniel.

And many of them that sleep in the dust of the earth shall awake, some to everlasting life, and some to shame and everlasting contempt. And they that be wise shall shine as the brightness of the firmament; and they that turn many to righteousness as the stars forever and ever.—Dan. 12:2-3.

It has been claimed that this is the first clear mention that both the righteous and the wicked shall be resurrected. Other passages in the latter prophets which speak of a restitution have reference to a national, not an individual restitution. Therefore, they cannot be considered as evidence of belief in the resurrection of the dead. Biblical scholars generally maintain that the book of Daniel was not written by that great prophet in Babylon during the exile, but was written later during the reign of the Seleucid (Greek ruler at Damascus) Antiochus IV or Epiphanes as he was frequently called (175-168 B.C.).[1]

It must be admitted that little or no reference has been made directly to the resurrection of the dead in the Pentateuch and other early books in the Bible. Yet, as H. H. Rowley points out, necromancy was both practiced and condemned therein. He also cites the instance where King Saul, though he ruled against witchcraft, asked the witch of Endor to call up Samuel from the abode of the dead. He had received no word through any other medium and wanted to consult him regarding the battle against the Philistines (in which he and his son, Jonathan, were killed). Saul conversed with Samuel (I Samuel 28:3). This is clear evidence of belief in the dead living on in the hereafter, at least as early as ca. 1000 B.C.[2]

A notable passage of scripture which is considered to be very doubtful as applying to the resurrection is found in the book of Job:

Oh that my words were now written! Oh that they were printed in a book! That they were graven with an iron pen and lead in the rocks forever! For I know that my Redeemer liveth,

and that he shall stand at the latter day upon the earth; and though after my skin worms destroy this body, yet in my flesh shall I see God, whom I shall see for myself, and mine eyes shall behold, and not another; though my reigns be consumed within me.—Job 19:23-27.

H. H. Rowley expressed the principle, "We must always be careful not to use a verse for a purpose for which it was not designed, and to examine it carefully in the light of its context."[3] It is true, in this case, that Job is in deep distress and is defending himself before supposed friends who have attributed his suffering to some sinfulness upon his part. They have remonstrated with him to confess and repent. Job reached out from the depths of his sorrow for comfort and yearned for his vindicator or Redeemer to exonerate him. The question is, was Job suddenly inspired to speak the truth relating to that which should happen after his fleshly body was completely destroyed? His desire to have that which follows so permanently recorded evinces the seriousness of his mood at the time. Therefore, Job would naturally speak with integrity concerning that which was of the gravest importance to himself and to others.

Adam Clarke raises the question as to which would be of greater importance to Job—the general resurrection and redemption by Christ or Job's restoration to health, happiness, and prosperity. Clarke maintains that Job was under "especial inspiration and spoke prophetically." He reasons that resurrection and redemption by Christ to eternal life are of infinitely great importance.[4] This would be more significant to Job and also to all humanity. However, we must not become like the Corinthians against whom Paul made his famous defense and exposition of the resurrection, based on Christ's resurrection (I Cor. 15).

Isaiah wrote, "Thy dead men shall live, together with my dead body shall they arise. Awake and sing, ye that dwell in dust, for thy dew is as the dew of herbs, and the earth shall cast out the dead" (Isaiah 26:19). Does this refer to the resurrection of those who had suffered and died in the time of Israel's devastation by her enemies or does it refer to the restoration of all Israel after her days of trouble had passed? The divergence of opinions is not so sharply drawn in regard to this text. It seems clear that the prophet had been inspired by the knowledge that God's eternal victory in the resurrection of the dead shall mitigate all suffering. This was the case in the joy that Christ's disciples experienced in the knowledge of his resurrection. Israel was not totally lost nor cast off forever.[5] The earth shall not hold her dead forever.

The preceding verse often is compared with Ezekiel's vision and prophecy of the valley of dry bones:

The hand of the Lord was upon me, and carried me out in the Spirit of the Lord, and set me down in the midst of the valley which was full of bones, and caused me to pass by them round about; and, behold, there were very many in the open valley; and, lo, they were very dry. And he said unto me, Son of man, can these bones live? And I answered, O Lord God, thou knowest. Again he said unto me, Prophesy upon these bones, and say unto them, O ye dry bones, hear the word of the Lord. Thus saith the Lord God unto these bones; Behold, I will cause breath to enter into you, and ye shall live; And I will lay sinews upon you, and will bring up flesh upon you, and cover you with skin, and put breath in you, and ye shall live; and ye shall know that I am the Lord.

So I prophesied as I was commanded; and as I prophesied, there was a noise, and behold a shaking, and the bones came

together, bone to his bone. And when I beheld, lo, the sinews and the flesh came up upon them, and the skin covered them above, but there was no breath in them. Then said he unto me, Prophesy unto the wind, prophesy, son of man, and say to the wind, Thus saith the Lord God; Come from the four winds, O breath, and breathe upon these slain, that they may live. So I prophesied as he commanded me, and the breath came into them, and they lived, and stood up upon their feet, an exceeding great army.

Then he said unto me, Son of man, these bones are the whole house of Israel; behold, they say, Our bones are dried, and our hope is lost; we are cut off for our parts. Therefore prophesy and say unto them, Thus saith the Lord God; Behold, O my people, I will open your graves, and cause you to come up out of your graves, and bring you into the land of Israel. And ye shall know that I am the Lord, when I have opened your graves, O my people, and brought you up out of your graves. And shall put my Spirit in you, and ye shall live, and I shall place you in your own land; then shall ye know that I the Lord have spoken it, and performed it, saith the Lord.—Ezekiel 37:1-14.

This vision and the accompanying prophecy were given to Ezekiel when Israel was in the most hopeless period of her history (except for the dispersion by the Romans in A.D. 70 forward). The Northern Kingdom had been taken into Assyrian captivity and never returned. After the fall of her capital city Samaria in 721 B.C., Judah, the Southern Kingdom, had been conquered by the Babylonians in 586 B.C. Jerusalem and the temple were completely destroyed and most of the Jews were carried off to Babylon. Undoubtedly, the purpose of the vision and prophecy was to revive the hopes of the Jews while they were in Babylonian exile. Verses 12 and 14 hold the promise that God would bring them again "into the land of Israel . . . and shall place you in your own land."

279

Verse 11 indicates that the vision applied to the whole house of Israel which includes both kingdoms or all the tribes of Israel.

This promise of return was based symbolically on the opening of the graves, in the resurrection of the dry bones to full fleshly bodies in which God placed his Spirit to give them life. There seems to be no reason to deny the validity of either aspect of the import of the vision and its prophecy—that is, the restoration of the house of Israel to their homeland, and their belief in the resurrection. As Adam Clarke writes, "'I will open your graves.' Here is a pointed allusion to the general resurrection; a doctrine properly accredited and understood by the Jews."[6] To what else than a resurrection could these terms refer: "open your graves," "lay sinews upon you," "bring up flesh upon you," "cover you with skin," "put breath in you, and ye shall live"?

Giving due credit to biblical criticism and its benefits, one need not be judged narrow-minded or radically conservative in reaching the conclusion that there is a chain of evidence of belief in the immortality of the soul, life hereafter, and the resurrection throughout the Old Testament. This was carried over into the apocryphal writings of the intertestamental period and into the New Testament itself. Paralleling this are the judgments of God written into Israel's history.

The principle of judgment began with the warning given to Adam and Eve that they must pay the price of disobedience, if they should choose to use their agency in this manner. Judgment involves reward for good and penalty for evil. Cain was warned beforehand:

If thou doest well thou shalt be accepted, and if thou doest not

well, sin lieth at the door; and Satan desireth to have thee, and except thou shalt hearken unto my commandments, I will deliver thee up,. . . for from this time forth thou shalt be the father of his lies.—Gen. 5:9, I.V.

God warns of the consequences of sin in advance of the act and gives the opportunity of repentance after the deed, which cannot always eradicate the effects but can invoke forgiveness. Thus the prophets of Israel such as Amos, Hosea, Isaiah, and Micah forewarned the wicked to repent or they would perish. The Old Testament type of judgment, therefore, is to live righteously or accept the consequences of and penalty for evil deeds. This definition does not exclude the final judgment when "the Day of the Lord" comes.

Between the Testaments

It has been conceded appropriately that there were no prophets among the Jews from the time of Malachi to John the Baptist, a period of about four hundred years. This is confirmed in the Apocrypha (I Maccabees 14:41): "And the Jews and their priests decided that Simon should be their leader and high priest for ever, until a trustworthy prophet should arise." Nevertheless, there was much purported inspirational literature produced during that time, among which were the books of the Apocrypha.[7] These have provoked various opinions and uses as well as rejections from the first centuries of Christianity forward.

The Jews excluded these books from their canon at the Council of Jamnia, ca. A.D. 90. But the Apocrypha already had been included in the Septuagint (Greek translation) fully three hundred years earlier. St. Jerome's Latin Vulgate translation was made from the Greek. Therefore, it included the Apocrypha. This is true of all other Roman Catholic Bibles. The Reformers followed the Jewish tradition and rejected the canonicity of the Apocrypha.

This situation presented a serious problem for the young latter-day prophet, Joseph Smith, as he worked on the Inspired Version of the scriptures. In harmony with his accustomed practice, he sought divine direction and received the following revelation:

> **Verily, thus saith the Lord unto you, concerning the Apocrypha, There are many things contained therein that are true, and it is mostly translated correctly; there are many things contained therein that are not true, which are interpolations by the hands of men. Verily I say unto you, that it is not needful that the Apocrypha should be translated. Therefore, whoso readeth it let him understand, for the Spirit manifesteth truth; and whoso is enlightened by the Spirit shall obtain benefit therefrom; and whoso receiveth not by the Spirit, can not be benefited; therefore, it is not needful that it should be translated. Amen.[8]**

In the absence of prophetic ministry, it is natural that interpolations should occur. However, this revelation is in accord with the viewpoint of the larger part of biblical scholarship and of theologians both past and present. Many recognize and use the Apocrypha and other noncanonical materials for what value they have, but these are not considered to have equal merit, especially in Jewish and Protestant circles, with canonized scripture.

First and Second Maccabees give historical accounts of the Maccabean revolt against Antiochus IV or

Epiphanes, the Greek Selucid ruler of most of Asia, who desecrated the Jerusalem temple and sought to force the Jews to make altars to and worship Zeus. The Jews eventually, under Maccabean leadership, gained independence in 142 B.C. This lasted until 63 B.C. when the Romans displaced the Selucids in Asia.[9]

Not a great deal is depicted in the Apocrypha in regard to the resurrection. However, a positive assurance is contained in II Maccabees 7:9 ff. Those who are being tortured to death give testimony that the King of the universe will restore them to life, but judgment will be the lot of their persecutors. Other non-canonical literature of this period contains much material relating to resurrection, judgment, and eschatological topics in general. It will not be profitable to discuss this in further detail here, especially in view of the time and space which would be consumed.[10]

In the New Testament

Many in discussing resurrection and judgment divide the New Testament teachings into those of Jesus, Paul, and John, especially the latter's writings in the Apocalypse. This method will not serve our purpose here. Rather we will attempt to associate the various writings on these doctrines as they relate to the topic, regardless of who may be the expositor. Paul, who was not of the original twelve, stated, "For I received of the Lord that which also I delivered unto you" (I Cor. 11:23). His writings, therefore, should be regarded as equal in authenticity to any of the other gospel writers.

We recall that the three main tenets of Christian

doctrine are incarnation, atonement, and resurrection. These three are inseparable and are manifested in the life and ministry of Jesus.

Resurrection is rooted in the incarnation. In other words, incarnation is an essential component of resurrection. The resurrection is possible only by the exhibition of divine power and not by any human action. Therefore, God must become incarnate and die in the flesh in order to validate his power to raise the dead to life again. Jesus, in whom God dwelt in the flesh, said to Martha as she grieved over the death of her brother, Lazarus, "I am the resurrection, and the life; he that believeth in me, though he were dead, yet shall he live" (John 11:25). Jesus also said, "I have power to lay it [his life] down, and I have power to take it again" (John 10:18). Not only was the principle of the resurrection taught by Jesus but he possessed the power over life and death within himself.

Paul attested to this truth when he wrote:

But if there be no resurrection of the dead, then is Christ not risen; and if Christ be not risen, then is our preaching vain, and your faith is also vain.... Then they also which are fallen asleep in Christ are perished.—I Corinthians 15:13-14, 18.

Without the resurrection of Jesus there can be no resurrection of anyone because he, the incarnate Son of God, is the only one who possessed this power while in the flesh.

Resurrection is a principle, the central meaning of which is new life. Thus Jesus said to Nicodemus, "Except a man be born again, he cannot see the kingdom of God" (John 3:3). When Nicodemus indicated that he did not understand, Jesus explained,

"Except a man be born of water and of the Spirit, he cannot enter into the kingdom of God" (John 3:5). Here the emphasis is on baptism in water, followed by the baptism of the Holy Spirit.

Paul evinced that he understood this spiritual aspect of water baptism as associated with Christlike living. After giving a dissertation on grace and atonement in Romans 5, Paul continued in the next chapter to write about baptism as it symbolizes our death to sin and resurrection to new life. He said:

Know ye not, that so many of us as were baptized into Jesus Christ were baptized into his death? Therefore we are buried with him by baptism into death; that like as Christ was raised up from the dead by the glory of the Father, even so we also should walk in the newness of life. For if we have been planted together in the likeness of his death, we shall be also in the likeness of his resurrection; knowing this, that our old man is crucified with him, that the body of sin might be destroyed, that henceforth we should not serve sin.—Romans 6:3-6.

The nature of the resurrection is exemplified in the change to the new way of life of the Christian rebirth. To be born again is to be spiritually revitalized. It is the beginning of the return to Edenic living. Indeed, this is the starting point of the ultimate resurrection of the righteous after passing from this earthly life to the Great Beyond.

Jesus spoke of two resurrections, one of the just, the other of the unjust:

Verily, verily, I say unto you, The hour is coming, and now is, when the dead shall hear the voice of the Son of God; and they who hear shall live. For as the Father hath life in himself, so hath he given to the Son to have life in himself; and hath

285

given him authority to execute judgment also, because he is the Son of man. Marvel not at this; for the hour is coming, in the which all who are in their graves shall hear his voice, and shall come forth; they who have done good, in the resurrection of the just; and they who have done evil, in the resurrection of the unjust. And shall all be judged of the Son of man. For as I hear, I judge, and my judgment is just.—John 5:25-30, I.V.

These comments confirm the power over life and death which Jesus possessed within himself. John indicates that these resurrections are one thousand years apart (see Revelation 20:4-6). Judgment accompanied both the first and second resurrection (see also Revelation 20:11-15). Those who come forth in the first resurrection live and reign with Christ for a thousand years. This is usually spoken of as the millennial reign. On them the second death has no power. Then comes the second resurrection when all stand before God to be judged according to that which is written in the books, according to their works.

Only one of these books is named—the book of life. Are the other books those which contain the word of God? Are the dead judged according to their works contained in the book of life, as they may or may not conform to that which God has declared in his word relating to the conduct of our lives? This view harmonizes with Jesus' portrayal of the judgment in Matthew 25:31-46.

When the Son of man shall come in his glory, and all the holy angels with him, then shall he sit upon the throne of his glory; and before him shall be gathered all nations; and he shall separate them one from another, as a shepherd divideth his sheep from the goats.—Matthew 25:31-32.

286

Those on the right hand, because of their righteous deeds, shall inherit God's kingdom prepared "from the foundation of the world." Those on the left hand must depart from him because they failed to avail themselves of their opportunities to do good. Judgment is an eternal principle. The injunction of Hebrews 6:1, I.V., states, "Therefore *not* leaving the principles of the doctrine of Christ, let us go on unto perfection," that we may be judged worthy to merit God's intended place for· us in his kingdom.

1. *Interpreter's Bible*, Vol. 6, p. 542. Also see *Interpreter's Dictionary of the Bible*, Vol. 4, p. 39e.
2. H. H. Rowley, *The Faith of Israel*, Westminster Press, p. 156.
3. *Ibid.*, p. 160.
4. Adam Clarke, *Clarke's Commentary*, Abingdon-Cokesbury Press, Vol. 3, pp. 90-91.
5. *Interpreter's Bible*, Vol. 5, p. 309 f.
6. *Clarke's Commentary*, Vol. 4, p. 524.
7. *Interpreter's Dictionary of the Bible*, Vol. 1, pp. 162-168.
8. Doctrine and Covenants 88.
9. For more extended studies, see the *Interpreter's Dictionary of the Bible*, Vol. 1, pp. 161-168, and Vol. 3, pp. 197-215; also see Vol. 2, pp. 529-535. Hasmoneans is a word equivalent to Maccabeans.
10. For a discussion and listing of these books, see *ibid.*, Vol. 3, "Pseudepigrapha," p. 960 f.

ETERNAL **18** DESTINY

Life Goes On

The spirit of life is immortal, and at death that spirit returns to God who gave it. The spirit has entered the eternal world. The body returns to the earth from whence it came. Our endeavors would be incomplete without exploring what happens after the spirit is separated from its human abode prior to the resurrection and judgment.

In order to make such an exploration, we need to know all that is possible for us to know about the nature of God. We really can know God only as we experience his self-disclosure in our own lives. We may experience God as we worship him. But when we say he is infinite and eternal, to a great degree we have clouded our conceptions, since the human mind is limited by its earthly dwelling. If it were possible to see God face-to-face, would we really know him? Sight is only one of the five senses. Knowing God and Christ is a progressive experience of growing into their likeness (Hebrews 6:1-2, I.V.) and to do this we need to use all the faculties with which he has endowed us.

Will the soul of the righteous, through death, lose any of that which has been acquired in this life? Or will the unrighteous soul be any more righteous, or wicked, because of death? Paul's solution may cover both questions: "Now we see through a glass darkly; but then face to face: now I know in part; but then shall I know even as also I am known" (I Cor. 13:12). We shall know God as he knows us. For the righteous this shall be a blessed experience, but for the wicked it shall not be so. They will see God when they come into his presence, as he sees them. What they thus see in themselves will not be very commendable. Those who had the·opportunity in this life to obey God and learn of him and did not take advantage of their opportunity will be condemned by the judgment of seeing themselves as they really have been and are without God. Instead of joy, there must be remorse and heaviness of sorrow. Jesus said, "The children of the wicked one shall be cast into outer darkness; there shall be weeping and gnashing of teeth" (Matt. 8:12 I.V.).

Nevertheless, God is a God of love, as well as of justice. God, speaking through Ezekiel, said, "Have I any pleasure at all that the wicked should die?. . .and not that he should turn from his ways, and live?. . .For I have no pleasure in the death of him that dieth. . .; wherefore turn ye and live" (Ezk. 18:23, 32). There is a physical death, but there is also a spiritual death. This text is a beautiful, patient plea to the captives in Babylon to avoid spiritual death. Spiritual death does not mean that the spirit actually passes into oblivion, but persistent sinning kills its potential for righteousness. Repentance and obedience will renew that potential.

The wicked will not meet a different kind of God after

death. He has assured us that he does not change; therefore, it appears certain that he will not change his plea for repentance. Thus, sinners will have the opportunity over there to turn to him and live. The opportunity will not be denied just because they have gone into his presence in the eternal world. We are, of course, not dealing with rewards at this point but rather with opportunities. Life will go on in the Great Beyond, with the fleshly limitations removed.

The Unpardonable Sin

Jesus said, "Whosoever speaketh a word against the Son of man, it shall be forgiven him; but whosoever speaketh against the Holy Ghost, it shall not be forgiven him, neither in the world, neither in the world to come" (Matthew 12:32). The Lord does not act without a cause or a purpose. Therefore, there must be a reason underlying this unforgivable sin. It is unforgivable because it is of such a character that it cannot be forgiven. No one can be forgiven who refuses to repent. The one who refuses to repent, or who turns entirely away after having tasted of the goodness of God through the Holy Ghost, places himself beyond the reach of salvation ministry. He does this by denying— blaspheming against—the Holy Spirit. One must be born again, in order even to see the kingdom of God (John 3:3-5).

The writer of the Hebrew epistle elaborates on this sin and helps clarify it for our understanding.

For he hath made it impossible for those who were once enlightened, and have tasted of the heavenly gift, and were

made partakers of the Holy Ghost, and have tasted the good word of God, and the powers of the world to come, if they shall fall away, to be renewed again unto repentance; seeing they crucify unto themselves the Son of God afresh, and put him to an open shame.—Hebrew 6:4-6.

An equivalent to the sin against the Holy Spirit is for one who has received the covenant of the holy priesthood to turn altogether away from it.

Therefore, all that my Father hath shall be given unto him; and this is according to the oath which belongeth to the priesthood. Therefore, all those who receive the priesthood receive this oath and covenant of my Father, which he can not break, neither can it be moved; but whoso breaketh this covenant, after he hath received it, and altogether turneth therefrom, shall not have forgiveness of sins in this world nor in the world to come.[1]

The tragedy in each instance is that those alluded to have rejected the Holy Spirit which leads souls to repentance and to Christ. Cleansing from sin can be brought about only by the power of the Spirit of God. By persistent rejection of it, these souls have placed themselves beyond the reach of Christ and their heavenly Father. God has only one alternative: "He that is unjust, let him be unjust still; and he that is filthy, let him be filthy still" (Rev. 22:11). The same verse goes on to say: "And he that is righteous, let him be righteous still; and he that is holy, let him be holy still."

The Revelator described previously that which leads to the second death: "But the fearful and unbelieving, and the abominable, and murderers, and whoremongers, and sorcerers, and idolaters, and all liars, shall have their part in the lake of fire and brimstone; which is the second death" (Rev. 28:8). Likewise, we are told in

Revelation 20:14-15 that after the judgment, "death and hell were cast into the lake of fire. This is the second death. And whosoever was not found written in the book of life was cast into the lake of fire."

Now the questions arise: What is the state of and of what duration is the state of those who partake of the second death? Jesus declared, "Then shall he say also unto them on the left hand, Depart from me, ye cursed, into everlasting fire, prepared for the devil and his angels" (Matt. 25:41). These are they who have given themselves completely over to Satan. They are cast out to dwell with him. In order to get the full picture, one should read Jesus' description of the final judgment (Matt. 25:31-46). This indicates that at the last judgment, which also is described in Revelation 20:11-15, the wicked shall go away into everlasting fire prepared for the devil and his angels. By putting these statements together, we know they are condemned to hell, to dwell in everlasting fire of some sort, which was prepared originally not for them but for the devil and his angels.

This seems to be a harsh punishment when viewed by today's definition of "damnation" (John 5:29), "hell," and "everlasting fire." It would appear to be entirely outside the act of a loving and just God. I suffered as a small boy after listening to a preacher who, in making his plea for souls to give their hearts and lives to God right then, said if we died with one sin unforgiven, we would go to hell to be tortured forever and ever in literal fire. An illustration was used to describe what "forever" meant: If a sparrow were to empty the Pacific Ocean into the Atlantic, carrying one drop each trip, by the time it had finished this impossible task it would merely be sunrise in hell. We may very well ponder the question, can fire touch or damage the immortal soul?

Where the words *damnation*, *damnable*, and *damned*, etc., appear in the King James version, revised versions of the Bible have changed the translation to the less severe words *condemnation* and *judgment*.[2] In the Inspired Version in several places, where the words *damnation* and *damnable* are used in the King James version, they are translated with a much less grave connotation. For instance, where Jesus spoke of the resurrection of "those who have done evil" as coming forth in the resurrection of damnation (King James version) the Inspired Version uses the word "unjust" (John 5:29). In II Peter 2:1, the King James version uses the phrase "damnable heresies"; the Inspired Version reads "abominable heresies"; and the Revised Standard Version translates this phrase "destructive heresies." J. Paterson Smythe gives evidence that when the King James version of the Bible was translated, the words derived from "to damn" meant to "condemn."[3]

The same author gives extensive attention to getting at the root meaning of hell, as it appears in the Bible. *Hell* comes from the Greek word *Hades* which simply means the abode of the dead. It also is derived from the Hebrew *Gehenna* which was the name of the valley just outside Jerusalem where the refuse of the city was thrown to be burned. This valley also was called Hinnom. Dr Smythe points out that in the Jewish Talmud, "The ungodly will be judged in Gehenna against the day of judgment. The ungodly shall be judged in Gehenna, until the righteous shall say of them,

We have seen enough. There is no everlasting damnation in the Talmud."[4] As he proceeds, Dr. Smythe contends strongly against the use of "everlasting," stating that the revisers have substituted *eternal* for *everlasting.*[5]

It is significant, in light of the preceding that the Doctrine and Covenants portrays the following in regard to those who have been guilty of the unpardonable sin.

Thus saith the Lord concerning all those who have known my power, and have been made partakers thereof, and suffered themselves, through the power of the Devil, to be overcome, and to deny the truth, and defy my power; they are they who are the sons of perdition, of whom I say it would have been better for them never to have been born; for they are vessels of wrath, doomed to suffer the wrath of God, with the Devil and his angels, in eternity, concerning whom I have said there is no forgiveness in this world nor in the world to come; having denied the Holy Spirit, after having received it, and having denied the only begotten Son of the Father; having crucified him unto themselves, and put him to an open shame. . . . Wherefore he saves all except them; they shall go away into everlasting punishment, which is endless punishment, which is eternal punishment, to reign with the Devil and his angels in eternity, where their worm dieth not and the fire is not quenched, which is their torment, and the end thereof, neither the place thereof, nor their torment, no man knows; neither was it revealed, neither is, neither will be revealed unto man, except to them who are made partakers thereof.[6]

In spite of the fact that "the fire is not quenched," which is their torment, immediately following this it is stated that "the end thereof, . . . no man knows," which implies that while the punishment is in eternity, there is an end which no man knows except those who are partakers of it.

294

The ensuing quotation gives a plausible explanation to the whole matter of judgment and punishment:

And surely every man must repent or suffer, for I God am endless; wherefore, I revoke not the judgments which I shall pass, but woes shall go forth, weeping, wailing, and gnashing of teeth; yea; to those who are found on my left hand; nevertheless, it is not written that there shall be no end to this torment; but it is written endless torment. Again, it is written eternal damnation; wherefore it is more express than other scriptures, that it might work upon the hearts of the children of men, altogether for my name's glory.... For, behold, I am endless, and the punishment which is given from my hand is endless punishment, for Endless is my name; wherefore— Eternal punishment is God's punishment. Endless punishment is God's punishment.[7]

The general trend in the preceding is in agreement with Dr. Smythe's views. We cannot give any further description of the nature of the punishment of those who harden their hearts beyond the point of repentance than that their punishment is God's punishment. It is under his control whose nature is eternal love and justice. His "works and designs" cannot be frustrated. The words of Jesus may be quite apropos in regard to those who suffer the condemnation of the unforgiven sinner. He said:

Agree with thine adversary quickly, while thou art in the way with him; lest at any time thine adversary deliver thee to the judge, and the judge deliver thee to the officer, and thou be cast into prison. Verily I say unto thee, Thou shalt by no means come out thence, until thou hast paid the uttermost farthing.— Matthew 5:27-28, I.V.

Sin brings the unrighteous to judgment, but God in his wisdom administers the penalty. Concerning that which is "unrevealed," no further comment is advisable.

Consciousness and Recognition

God is an intelligent Being, knowing all things. We are created in his image and have the gift of intelligence, but we are limited by our finite consciousness. Death opens the door to eternity for us, and separates the spirit of life from the human body; but death does not reduce our inner conscious selfhood. The body is the instrument through which our finite consciousness reaches its earthly expression. But the body without the spirit is neither conscious nor intelligent. Therefore, since the spirit of life is essential to intelligence here and since it returns to God who gave it (Eccl. 12:7) that entity should not, and in fact does not, lose any of its powers of consciousness in the transition. We are the same persons in the hereafter that we were here on earth. This is not to say that, in all respects, the two existences are parallel.

The rich man ignored the suffering and needs of Lazarus, the destitute man "who was full of sores" and was left at the rich man's gate to beg for the crumbs which fell from the rich man's table. Each died. Lazarus was carried by angels into Abraham's bosom. The rich man in Hades saw Abraham afar off with Lazarus in his bosom. All three (Abraham, Lazarus, and the rich man) were conscious. They recognized each other and the rich man and Abraham conversed. Lazarus was comforted, which could not be unless he had the faculty of cognition for he no longer was in his earthly body. The rich man remembered his five brothers still on earth. Therefore, he was not only conscious in Hades but he remembered those he had left behind when he died

(Luke 16:19-31). While conscious recognition was not the main point of Jesus' parable, he does not use that which is unreal to illustrate realities. Therefore, the preceding conclusions may be legitimately drawn from the parable.

Many other supportive illustrations could be drawn from the scriptures such as Paul's testimony of being caught up into paradise, which he identified with the third heaven, where he heard "unspeakable words which it is not lawful for a man to utter" (II Cor. 12:2-4). Then there was the great experience on the Mount of Transfiguration. In this Moses and Elias appeared and conversed with Christ (Matt. 17:1-9). Marvelous things transpire in the eternal world. Here are two great prophets, living on earth perhaps five hundred years apart, who appeared together to Jesus, Peter, James and John and talked with Jesus some eight hundred or more years after the latter of the two had lived on earth. According to the best computations, the Exodus of which Moses was the leader began in the early part of the thirteenth century B.C.[8] Elijah lived during the time of King Ahab of North Israel who reigned from 874 to 833 B.C.[9] Little wonder Peter said, "It is good for us to be here." We can only conjecture on how much these three apostles learned about the Great Beyond in that experience. Certainly the opening of some wonderful insights must have occurred.

God shall comfort the sorrowing and the distressed.

And God shall wipe away all tears from their eyes; and there shall be no more death, neither sorrow, nor crying, neither shall there be any more pain; for the former things are passed away.—Revelation 21:4.

One glimpse into that eternal world will assuage for all the suffering we may have had to endure here. Paul wrote to the Philippians:

For me to live, is to do the will of Christ; and to die is my gain. For I am in a strait betwixt two, having a desire to depart, and to be with Christ; which is far better. Nevertheless, to abide in the flesh is more needful for you.—Philippians 1:22-24.

Paul must have been greatly impressed by that journey into paradise, when he was caught up to the third heaven. His great desire was to return there and be with the Lord, yet he realized that it was better for the church that he remain here for a time.

Paradise

Try to visualize three crosses on a desolate hill outside the walls of Jerusalem. On either side of the center cross hung two thieves. Jesus Christ the Son of God, suffering agony that we cannot know, hung on the center cross. One of the thieves railed at him, saying, "If thou be the Christ, save thyself and us." The other malefactor remonstrated with the rebellious thief, saying, "We suffer justly for our deeds, but this man hath done nothing amiss." Then like the penitent prodigal, he turned to Jesus and said, "Lord, remember me when thou comest into thy kingdom." Jesus answered him, "Verily I say unto thee, Today shalt thou be with me in paradise" (Luke 23:40-44). Jesus was well aware of where he was going when he died. This statement together with Paul's testimony of having been caught up to the third heaven, which he equated with paradise, tends toward the conclusion that paradise is the interim abode of the righteous after death.

However, the root of the word *paradise* comes from the Hebrew and Aramaic through the Greek to the Persian. The meaning in each is "garden" or "park." In the Hebrew, it was often used to parallel the Garden of Eden, which harmonizes with Revelation 2:7, "To him that overcometh I will give to eat of the tree of life, which is in the midst of the paradise of God." The tree of life was in the Garden of Eden. God drove Adam and Eve out of the garden so that they could not partake of the fruit of the tree and live forever (see Genesis 2:22-24). However, the general Jewish idea seems to have developed that Gehenna was the abode of the wicked and paradise that of the righteous after death.[10] Perhaps one of the best illustrations of this general idea is to be found in the Apocrypha: "The furnace of Gehenna shall be made manifest and over against it the paradise of delight."[11]

There is a question regarding whether or not both Judaism and Christianity embraced the thought that all went to Sheol first, and there the separation took place between the righteous and the wicked, either before or after the resurrection.[12] This, however, is not consistent with Jesus' promise to the thief on the cross, when he said: "Today shalt thou be with me in paradise." We could associate this with I Peter 3:18-20 which relates to Jesus going to preach to disobedient spirits in prison, and assume that Jesus took the unfortunate criminal with him. This does not seem like a reasonable assumption.

The Book of Mormon is clear on this point and speaks forthrightly:

Behold, it has been made known unto me, by an angel, that the spirits of all men, as soon as they are departed from this mortal body; yea, the spirits of all men, whether they be good or evil, are taken home to that God who gave them life.

And then shall it come to pass that the spirits of those who are righteous, are received into a state of happiness, which is called paradise; a state of rest; a state of peace, where they shall rest from all their troubles, and from all care, and sorrow, etc. And then shall it come to pass, that the spirits of the wicked, yea, who are evil; for behold, they have no part nor portion of the Spirit of the Lord: for behold they choose evil works, rather than good: therefore the spirit of the devil did enter into them, and take possession of their house; And these shall be cast out into outer darkness; there shall be weeping, and wailing and gnashing of teeth; and this because of their own iniquity; being led captive by the will of the devil. Now this is the state of the souls of the wicked; yea, in darkness, and a state of awful, fearful, looking for, of the fiery indignation of the wrath of God upon them; thus they remain in this state, as well as the righteous in paradise, until the time of their resurrection.[13]

Three other statements in the Book of Mormon regarding paradise are in accord with this one. The righteous when meeting God at death are assigned at once to paradise where they remain, still doing his service as is required of them, following the pattern as given by our Lord. The wicked are assigned to Hades to await the resurrection of the unjust.[14]

Beyond Hades and Paradise

J. Paterson Smythe writes of three stages of personal existence: (1) our present existence upon the earth, which is very important because this is a probationary state in which to make preparation for the life hereafter;

(2) the near hereafter, or the intermediate existence between death and the resurrection, in which the righteous dwell in paradise and the unrighteous are confined to Hades; and (3) the far hereafter which occurs after the Millennium, the final resurrection and judgment.[15]

There are at least three groups who commit sin against the Holy Ghost: (1) those who deny the Holy Ghost and its powers after having received it; (2) those who persistently harden their hearts and minds so that the Spirit of God cannot lead them to repentance; and (3) those who after having received the priesthood and the powers of its ministry turn altogether away and knowingly deny that power. Each commits a comparable sin but differs in the manner of sinning. At the last judgment these go away into everlasting fire prepared for the devil and his angels.

One time a minister of another denomination wrote me, "Why don't you come out and tell the people what you know to be true, that you are not an apostle." I replied by letter stating, "I do not think you know what you are asking me to do. You are asking me to deny my Lord; for before my call to that ministry, the Holy Spirit manifested to me with undeniable testimony that this is where he designed I should serve. His Spirit has continuously accompanied my ministry as an apostle, enabling me to witness with power and assurance that Jesus is Christ. How can you consistently, then, ask me to sin against Jesus and the Holy Spirit?"

Those who persist in falsifying that which they have known to be true will find themselves after the final judgment in that lake of fire, where the devil and his angels are (Revelation 20:15 and Matthew 25:41). Their condition and its end are not known.

Nevertheless, there are many other categories of sin, some lesser and others more serious, as they vary in degrees of wrongdoing. What about those who with honest intent are deceived? What about those who are proud and prejudiced who fail to accept and/or obey Christ? How will God deal with those who have never known Christ, such as the pagans who have not heard the gospel preached?

The basic means of salvation is divine grace. There is no other gospel than that of the grace of Christ (see Galatians 1:6-9). But grace does not exclude nor take the place of works of righteousness (Eph. 2:8-10). Salvation is an act of God which we cannot perform, but judgment is predicated upon man's response to God's act of salvation. Everyone is rewarded according to his works (Rev. 22:12). This means that the Judge will take all things into consideration. Does it not appear just that there should be grades of glory into which each may enter according to how he has made use of his opportunities to perform good works in harmony with the laws of righteousness? Yet the performance of good works in no way substitutes for divine grace; for without God's grace manifested in the atonement for sins, works would not be adequate to salvation.

The apostle Paul compares these grades with three degrees of light and power in the cosmos—those of the sun, moon, and stars (see I Corinthians 15:35-44). These constitute three classifications of glory in which rewards are received and in which three levels of eternal life are enjoyed. But Paul does not explain the nature of each of these glories, nor does he classify the qualities of the lives of those who enter each.

More light on this is portrayed in contemporary revelation. The requirements and blessings of each are set forth as follows:

1) *The glory of the sun or celestial glory* is the highest of the three. Those who receive celestial glory come forth in the resurrection of the just. They have received the testimony of Jesus and believe on his name. They were baptized in water, and have received the baptism of the Holy Spirit by the laying on of hands. They have overcome by faith and are sealed by the Holy Spirit of promise. They are just and true and of the church of the firstborn. Among these are priests and (so called) kings after the Order of Melchizedek. They are the sons of God and all things are theirs. They shall dwell in the presence of God and Christ forever. Christ will bring these with him when he comes in the clouds of heaven to reign over the earth. They will come to Mount Zion, the city of the living God. They become an innumerable company of angels to the general assembly of the church of the Firstborn. They are just persons made perfect through Jesus the Mediator of the new covenant. Their bodies are celestial and their glory is that of the sun, even the glory of God. No wonder Paul quoted Isaiah saying: "Eye hath not seen, nor ear heard, neither have entered unto the heart of man the things which God hath prepared for them that love him."

2) *The terrestrial glory* differs from that of the celestial as the moon is different from the sun. Those who inhabit this glory have died without law. They are also the spirits of persons whom the Son visited in prison

and to whom he preached the gospel. They did not receive the testimony of Jesus in the flesh. They are the honorable men of the earth who were deceived by the craftiness of men. They receive the presence of the Son but not the fullness of the Father. They are those who were not valiant in the testimony of Jesus.

3) *The telestial glory* differs from that of the terrestrial as the stars differ from the moon. (It may be well to remember that each star differs from the others and Paul wrote: "for one star differeth from another star in glory. So also is the resurrection of the dead" (I Cor. 15:41-42). These received not the gospel of Christ, neither the testimony of Jesus, but they did not deny the Holy Spirit. They, at death, are sent to Hades rather than to Paradise. These come forth in the last resurrection and are not redeemed from the devil until Christ shall have finished his work. They are ministered to by those of the terrestrial glory, while those of the terrestrial glory are ministered to by celestial angels. Even this, the least of the glories, surpasses all understanding.

As one star differs from another so is the reward of those who receive the telestial glory. Among them are those referred to by Paul who quoted them as saying, "I am of Paul; and of Apollos; and of Cephas" (I Cor. 1:12). They will not be caught up to the church of the Firstborn. Among these also are those who were liars, sorcerers, adulterers, and whoremongers. They suffer the wrath of God until the fullness of the times when Christ shall have subdued all enemies and shall deliver up the kingdom to the Father. They shall be judged and, having been punished for their sins, receive their reward according to their works.[16] Revelation, chapters 20 and 21, are also apropos. After all the preceding has taken place in the final judgment, John states:

And I saw a new heaven and a new earth; for the first heaven and the first earth were passed away; and there was no more sea. And I John saw the holy city, new Jerusalem, coming down from God out of heaven, prepared as a bride adorned for her husband. And I heard a great voice out of heaven saying, Behold, the tabernacle of God is with men, and he will dwell with them, and they shall be his people, and God himself shall be with them, and be their God. And God shall wipe away all tears from their eyes; and there shall be no more death, neither sorrow, nor crying, neither shall there be any more pain; for the former things are passed away. And he that sat upon the throne said, Behold, I make all things new. And he said unto me, Write; for these words are true and faithful. And he said unto me, It is done. I am Alpha and Omega, the beginning and the end. I will give unto him that is athirst of the fountain of the water of life freely.—Revelation 21:1-6.

No doubt the marvelous works of God are beyond our fondest imaginations. No one can adequately put into words that which is yet ahead of us as God accomplishes his "great and marvelous work."

Peter gives additional light on what may happen on behalf of those who die with their sins unforgiven:

For Christ also once suffered for sins, the just for the unjust, being put to death in the flesh, but quickened by the Spirit, that he might bring us to God. For which cause also, he went and preached unto the spirits in prison; some of whom were disobedient in the days of Noah, while the long-suffering of God waited, while the ark was preparing, wherein few, that is, eight souls were saved by water.—I Peter 3:18-20, I.V.

Because of this, is the gospel preached to them who are dead, that they might be judged according to men in the flesh, but

live in the spirit according to the will of God.—I Peter 4:6, I.V.

After Christ died for the sins of the world, his power was not limited to the world. It is evident Peter understood that Jesus, quickened by the Spirit, preached the gospel to those who were confined in Hades, among them were the disobedient in the days of Noah. Preaching the gospel means a call to repentance. This assures that those to whom it was preached might still have the opportunity to come forth to "be judged as men in the flesh, and live according to the will of God in the Spirit." This could not be until they recognized Jesus as Lord and repentantly turned to God for his forgiveness. This may well have been the initiation of a continuous ministry, until Christ shall have put "all enemies under his feet" and finally delivers "up the kingdom to God, even the Father" as Paul writes in I Corinthians 15:24-25.

This is not to suggest universal salvation. The scriptures indicate that there are unforgivable sins and persons unworthy of any glory at all in the final judgment. They shall become inhabitants with the devil and his angels. The nature and duration of their punishment is not known. They must pay the utmost "farthing" (Matt. 25:26).

It is in this life, however, that the burden is laid upon us to be valiant in the testimony of Jesus. We are called to preach the gospel that the gospel may be in all the world to bring souls to Christ. Speculation about matters which are beyond our knowledge are unprofitable and are better left in the province of God. Our ministry must be such that it will win souls to Jesus Christ. We also are called to assist persons to become worthy of the highest recompense, which is celestial glory. Instruction and encouragement have more recently been given to remind us of our stewardship in this regard:

Let my word be preached to the bruised and the brokenhearted as well as those who are enmeshed in sin, longing to repent and follow me. Let the truths of my gospel be proclaimed as widely and as far as the dedication of the Saints, especially through the exercise of their temporal stewardship, will allow. My Spirit is reaching out to numerous souls even now and there are many who will respond if you, my people, will bear affirmative testimony of my love and my desire for all to come unto me. Be steadfast and trust in the instructions which have been given for your guidance. I will be with you and strengthen you for the tasks that lie ahead if you will continue to be faithful and commit yourselves without reservation to the building of my kingdom.[17]

Transcendent Expectations

The scriptures are resplendent with promises of the triumph of God's kingdom against all opposing satanic powers, philosophies, and evil actions. At the risk of being accused of using quotations out of context, a few examples should add final assurances as we near the termination of this enterprise. Without burdening the reader with that which precedes and follows each reference and also with its historical setting, he or she should be able to see that these form an unbroken chain of evidence relating to the expectations and hopes of God's people throughout the centuries of time.

Isaiah envisioned this triumph and analogically described that which is yet to happen.

And righteousness shall be the girdle of his loins, and

faithfulness the girdle of his reins. The wolf also shall dwell with the lamb, and the leopard shall lie down with the kid; and the calf and the young lion and the fatling together; and a little child shall lead them. And the cow and the bear shall feed; their young ones shall lie down together; and the lion shall eat straw like the ox. And the sucking child shall play on the hole of the asp, and the weaned child shall put his hand on the cockatrice' den. They shall not hurt nor destroy in all my holy mountain; for the earth shall be full of the knowledge of the Lord, as the waters cover the sea.—Isaiah 11:5-9.

Isaiah went on to tell of marvelous things which are now happening and will yet happen to all of Israel. Yet his promises are not confined to Israel. He represents the work of the Lord to be universal.

Daniel sought to uphold the faith of the persecuted and oppressed Jews. (Whether Daniel wrote in the time of the Babylonian captivity or during the time of the desecration of the Jerusalem temple when Epiphanes sought to enforce upon the Jews the worship of Zeus—as many Bible scholars claim—makes no difference to our purpose here.) He declared:

And the kingdom and dominion, and the greatness of the kingdom under the whole heaven, shall be given to the people of the saints of the Most High, whose kingdom is an everlasting kingdom, and all dominions shall serve and obey him.—Daniel 7:27.

Thus, Daniel described the wonders of God's kingdom and foretold its universality and triumph.

Jesus sought to restore the confidence of his disciples when he had spoken of his death and departure from them.

Let not your heart be troubled; ye believe in God, believe also in me. In my Father's house are many mansions; if it were not

308

so, I would have told you. I go to prepare a place for you. And if I go and prepare a place for you, I will come again and receive you unto myself; that where I am, there ye may be also.—John 14:1-3.

Jesus began his ministry by preaching the gospel of the kingdom of God, saying that it was at hand (Mark 1:14-15). Wherever Jesus is, there the kingdom of God is manifested. There is little doubt that he was pointing to a step in its final culmination.

Paul described the final victory of Christ in the consummation of the kingdom.

Having made known unto us the mystery of his will, according to his good pleasure which he hath purposed in himself: That in the dispensation of the fullness of times, he might gather together in one all things in Christ, both which are in heaven, and which are on the earth; even in him.—Ephesians 1:9-10.

Here Paul expressed the intent of God's eternal design, that kingdom unity might be established eternally in Christ. Then in another letter Paul portrayed the everlasting victory achieved by Christ. He stated:

Then cometh the end when he shall have delivered up the kingdom to God, even the Father; when he shall have put down all rule and all authority and power. For he must reign till he hath put all enemies under his feet. The last enemy that shall be destroyed is death.—I Corinthians 15:24-26.

The writer of the Epistle to the Hebrews tells of the call of God to Abraham and the faith of Abraham in responding thereto.

By faith Abraham, when he was called to go out into a place which he should after receive for an inheritance, obeyed; and he went out, not knowing whither he went. . . . For he looked

309

for a city which hath foundations, whose builder and maker is God.—Hebrews 11:8, 10.

This was in response to God's promise to Abraham: "In thee shall all the families of the earth be blessed" (Gen. 12:3).

The sublime statement of our Lord stands the test of time and eternity: "This is my work and my glory, to bring to pass the immortality, and eternal life of man."[18]

Upon giving emphasis to the necessity of faith in God's unceasing efforts to entice his people to trust him and engage in the work of establishing his kingdom on earth, John Bright made these comments.

Nor will he who walks the path of faith walk in darkness. True, he can never see the ineffable glory of the rule of God triumphant on the earth, nor can all his efforts usher it in. But because he has in faith said yes to the calling of Christ, he will understand the New Testament mystery that "the Kingdom of God is at hand"; the future victory has become to him a present fact.... The future he will leave with God, who is Lord of the issues of history.

The path of the future is indeed dark, and the end of it may not be seen. But because it has been granted to us to hear the summons of the Kingdom of God which comes to us here and now, we will face it without fear and with the prayer of all Christendom on our lips: "Thy Kingdom come; thy will be done. For thine is the Kingdom, the power and the glory forever."[19]

Many mysteries of God's kingdom are beyond our finite understanding, but let us lift our eyes, our hearts, and souls in everlasting gratitude and praise to God for his wondrous justice, mercy, and love, based upon the glory of his intelligence, as he continues his self-disclosure in the mighty works of his eternal design.

1. Doctrine and Covenants 83:6f-h.
2. See *Cruden's Complete Concordance*, p. 122.
3. *The Gospel of the Hereafter*, pp. 175-6.
4. *Ibid.*, p. 178 f.
5. *Ibid.*, pp. 182-3.
6. Doctrine and Covenants 76:4a-e, i-j.
7. *Ibid.*, 18:1d-2e.
8. *Interpreter's Dictionary of the Bible*, Vol. 2, p. 191.
9. *Mysterious Numbers of the Hebrew Kings*, p. 205.
10. See *Interpreter's Dictionary of the Bible*, Vol. 3, p. 655.
11. *Apocrypha*, II Esdras 7:36. Regarding the RLDS position on the *Apocrypha*, see Doctrine and Covenants 88.
12. *Interpreter's Dictionary of the Bible*, Vol. 3, pp. 655-656.
13. Book of Mormon, Alma 19:43-47. See also II Nephi 6:31, IV Nephi 1:15, Moroni 10:31.
14. *Ibid.*, II Nephi 6:31, IV Nephi 1:15, Moroni 10:31.
15. *The Gospel of the Hereafter*, p. 24 ff.
16. Doctrine and Covenants 76:5-7.
17. *Ibid.*, 153:9.
18. *Ibid.*, 22:23b.
19. *The Kingdom of God*, pp. 273-274.

BIBLIOGRAPHY

Anderson, Bernard W. *Understanding the Old Testament.* Prentice Hall, Inc., Englewood Cliffs, New Jersey.

Albright, William F. *From the Stone Age to Christianity.* Doubleday Anchor Books, Garden City, New York.

Apocrypha, 14 books excluded from the Jewish Canon and Protestant Bibles. (Found as an appendix in the Oxford Annotated Edition of the Revised Standard Version.)

Aulen, Gustaf. *Christus Victor.* The Macmillan Company, New York.

_____. *The Faith of the Christian Church.* Fortress Press, Philadelphia.

Barclay, William. *The Bible and History.* Abingdon Press, Nashville and New York.

_____. *The Mind of Jesus.* Harper and Row, New York, and Evanston.

Barrett, C. K. *The New Testament Background Selected Documents.* Harper and Row, New York and Evanston.

Bartlett, John. *Familiar Quotations.* Blue Ribbon Books, New York City.

Becker, Carl L. *The Heavenly City of the Eighteenth-Century Philosophers.* Yale University Press, New Haven and London.

Bible, K.J.V., I.V., R.S.V., N.E.B.

Bright, John. *A History of Israel.* The Westminster Press, Philadelphia.

_____. *The Kingdom of God.* Abingdon Press, New York and Nashville.

Brunner, Emil. *Eternal Hope.* The Westminster Press, Philadelphia.

Bultmann, Rudolf. *Jesus Christ and Mythology.* Charles Scribner's Sons, New York, 1958.

Buttrick, George A. *Christ and History.* Abingdon Press, New York, and Nashville.

_____. Commentary Editor, *The Interpreter's Bible*, 12 volumes. Abingdon Press, New York and Nashville.

_____. Dictionary Editor, *The Interpreter's Dictionary of the Bible*, 4 vols. Abingdon Press, New York and Nashville.

Clarke, Adam. *Clarke's Commentary*, 6 volumes. Abingdon-Cokesbury Press, New York and Nashville.

Cross, F. L. Editor, *The Oxford Dictionary of the Christian Church*. Oxford University Press, London, New York, Toronto.

Cruden, Alexander. *Cruden's Complete Concordance of the Old and New Testaments*. The John C. Winston Company, Philadelphia, Toronto.

D'Aubigne, Merle. *History of the Reformation of the Sixteenth Century*. Ward, Lock and Company, London.

Dimont, Max I. *Jews, God and History*. A Signet Book, New American Library, New York.

Doctrine and Covenants, Reorganized Church of Jesus Christ of Latter Day Saints, Herald Publishing House, Independence, Missouri.

Durant, William. *The Story of Philosophy*, Simon and Schuster, New York, 1952.

Eaton, Ralph M. *Descartes Selections*. Charles Scribner's Sons, New York.

Edge, Findley B. *A Quest for Vitality in Religion*. Broadman Press, Nashville.

Edwards, F. Henry. *The Joy in Creation and Judgment*. Herald Publishing House, Independence, Missouri.

Finegan, Jack. *Light From the Ancient Past*. Princeton University Press, Princeton, New Jersey.

Fisher, George P. *History of the Christian Church*. Charles Scribner's Sons, New York, 1976.

Fosdick, H. E. *Living Under Tension*. Harper and Row, New York.

Frost, S. E., Jr. *Basic Teachings of the Great Philosophers*. New Home Library, New York.

Garer, Joseph. *How the Great Religions Began.* A Signet Book, New American Library, New York.

Halverson, Marvin, and Cohen, Arthur A. *A Handbook of Christian Theology.* World Publishing Company, Cleveland and New York.

Harrelson, Walter. *Interpreting the Old Testament.* Holt, Rinehart, and Winston, New York, Chicago, Toronto, London.

Harvey, Van A. *A Handbook of Theological Terms.* Macmillan Company, New York.

Heschel, Abraham J. *The Prophets.* Harper and Row, New York and Evanston.

Hester, H. I. *The Heart of the Hebrew History.* Quality Press, Liberty, Missouri.

Hicks, John. *Evil and the God of Love.* Harper and Row, New York and Evanston.

Jones, E. Stanley. *Is the Kingdom of God Realism.* Abingdon-Cokesbury Press, New York, Nashville, 1940.

Josephus, Flavius. *Antiquities of the Jews.* D. Lathrop and Company, Boston.

Kramer, Samuel Noah. *History Begins at Sumer.* Doubleday Anchor Books, New York.

Luther, Martin. *The Bondage of the Will.* Fleming H. Revell Company, Westwood, New Jersey.

Morrison, James Dalton (Ed.). *Masterpieces of Religious Verse,* Harper Brothers, New York.

Moltmann, Jurgen. *Theology of Hope.* Harper and Row, New York and Evanston.

Mullins, E. Y. *The Christian Religion in Its Doctrinal Expression.* Broadman Press, Nashville.

North, Christopher R. *The Suffering Servant of Deutero Isaiah.* Oxford University Press.

Oakman, Arthur A. *Resurrection and Eternal Life.* Herald Publishing House, Independence, Missouri.

Oates, Whitney J. (Ed.). *The Basic Writings of Saint Augustine,* 2 volumes. Random House, New York and Toronto.

Petry, Ray C. *Christian Eschatology and Social Thought.* Abingdon Press, New York and Nashville.

Rashdall, Hastings. *The Idea of Atonement in Christian Theology.* Macmillan and Company Limited, London, 1920.

Rowley, H. H. *The Faith of Israel.* Westminster Press, Philadelphia

Rules and Resolutions, Reorganized Church of Jesus Christ of Latter Day Saints, Independence, Missouri.

Sanford, Elias B. *Cyclopedia of Religious Knowledge.* S. S. Scranton Company, Hartford, Connecticut, 1910.

Sartre, Jean Paul. *Existentialism and Human Emotions.* Philosophical Library, New York.

Schwartz, Leo W. (Ed.). *Great Ages and Ideas of the Jewish People.* Random House, New York.

Schweitzer, Dr. Albert. *The Quest of the Historical Jesus.* Macmillan Company, New York.

Smith, Joseph, Jr., Translator. Book of Mormon, Herald Publishing House, Independence, Missouri.

_____. The Holy Scriptures, Inspired Version. Herald Publishing House, Independence, Missouri.

Smith, W. Wallace. Sermon: "Of Hope and Salvation," *World Conference Bulletin,* April 18, 1966. Herald Publishing House, Independence, Missouri.

Smith, Joseph III; Smith, Heman C.; Edwards, F. H. *The History of the Reorganized Church of Jesus Christ of Latter Day Saints,* 8 volumes, Herald Publishing House, Independence, Missouri.

Smythe, J. Paterson. *The Gospel of the Hereafter.* Hodder and Stoughton, London, New York, Toronto.

Streeter, Burnett Hillman. *The God Who Speaks.* The Macmillan Company, New York.

Summers, Ray. *The Life Beyond.* Broadman Press, Nashville.

Taylor, Vincent. *The Atonement in New Testament Teaching.* Epworth Press, London.

Temple, William. *Nature, Man and God.* Macmillan and Company, London, 1951.

Thielie, Edwin R. *The Mysterious Numbers of the Hebrew Kings.* Eardmans, Grand Rapids, Michigan.

Tillich, Paul. *Systematic Theology*, 3 volumes. Harper and Row, New York and Evanston.

Tullidge, Edward W. *The Life of Joseph the Prophet.* Board of Publication, Reorganized Church of Jesus Christ of Latter Day Saints, Plano, Illinois, 1880.

Wesley, John. *Wesley's Sermons*, Vol. 2, Sermon 71.

Wright, George Earnest. *Biblical Archaeology.* Westminster Press, Philadelphia, 1957.

_____. and Filson, Vivan (Ed.). *The Westminster Historical Atlas of the Bible*, Revised Edition. The Westminster Press, Philadelphia.